DOSTOEVSKY

Also by Louis Breger

Clinical-Cognitive Psychology
(EDITOR), 1969

The Effect of Stress on Dreams
(WITH I. HUNTER AND R. W. LANE), 1971

From Instinct to Identity:
The Development of Personality, 1974

Freud's Unfinished Journey: Conventional and Critical
Perspectives in Psychoanalytic Theory, 1981

DOSTOEVSKY

The Author as Psychoanalyst

Louis Breger

NEW YORK UNIVERSITY PRESS
New York and London

Library of Congress Cataloging-in-Publication Data
Breger, Louis, 1935–
Dostoevsky: the author as psychoanalyst/Louis Breger.
p. cm.
Bibliography: p.
Includes index.
ISBN 0-8147-1112-x (alk. paper)
1. Dostoyevsky, Fyodor, 1821–1881 — Biography — Psychology.
2. Dostoyevsky, Fyodor, 1821–1881 — Criticism and interpretation.
3. Novelists, Russian — 19th century — Biography. 4. Psychoanalysis
and literature. I. Title.
PG3328.B74 1989
891.73'3 — dc20
[B]   89-12339
CIP

New York University Press books are printed on acid-free paper,
and their binding materials are chosen for strength and durability.

Book design by Ken Venezio

For Barbara

All human beings, driven as they are at different speeds by the same Furies, are at close range equally extraordinary.

ANTHONY POWELL

Contents

ix

Contents

Contents

Acknowledgments

I must begin by expressing my gratitude to all those Dostoevsky scholars, translators, and Slavists who have made the novels, and much related material, available in English. I owe a special thanks to Sidney Monas; his excellent translation of *Crime and Punishment* is a model for how a text can be transformed across language and time while retaining its essential spirit. Professor Monas has been good enough to answer my questions on Russian language and culture, to share his own work in progress, and to give his reactions to portions of the manuscript.

A number of friends and colleagues gave generously of their time and help as the book was being written. The analysis of *Crime and Punishment* took shape in courses that I taught with Stuart Ende. Valuable critical reactions to earlier drafts were offered by Barbara Gale, Victoria Hamilton, N. Katherine Hayles, Albert Hutter, Jay Martin, George Pigman, Robert Rosenstone, Randy Splitter, and Judith Viorst. Useful reference material was suggested by Robert Frysinger and Richard J. Rosenthal.

Acknowledgement is made to the following for permission to reprint previously published material:

Liveright Publishing Corporation for permission to reprint from *Dostoevsky: Reminiscences,* by Anna Dostoevsky, translated and edited by Beatrice Stillman. Translation copyright © 1975 by Beatrice Stillman.

Acknowledgments

Editorial apparatus copyright © 1975 by Liveright Publishing Corporation.

Penguin Books Ltd for permission to reprint from *Dostoevsky: Notes from Underground, The Double,* by Fyodor Dostoevsky, translated by Jessie Coulson (Baltimore: Penguin Classics, 1972), copyright © Jessie Coulson, 1972. Reproduced by permission of Penguin Books Ltd.

New American Library for permission to reprint from *Crime and Punishment,* by Fyodor Dostoevsky. Copyright © 1968 by Sidney Monas. Reprinted by arrangement with New American Library, a division of Penguin Books USA Inc.

The University of Chicago Press for permission to reprint from *The Gambler,* by Fyodor Dostoevsky, edited by Edward Wasiolek, translated by Victor Terras. Copyright © 1972 by The University of Chicago.

Princeton University Press for permission to reprint from *Dostoevsky: The Seeds of Revolt, 1821–1849,* by Joseph Frank. Copyright © 1976 by Princeton University Press.

DOSTOEVSKY

The Horse, the Courier

My first personal insult,
The horse, the courier.

Raskolnikov, hero of Dostoevsky's novel *Crime and Punishment,* conceives a plan to murder an old pawnbroker to whom he is indebted. Just prior to committing the murder he has a dream; he sees himself as an innocent young boy, watching with horror as a drunken peasant beats an old horse to death. The dream contains an orgy of violence, along with sympathy for the victimized mare and a pervading sense of helplessness. Raskolnikov awakens and immediately recognizes the connection between the dream and his plan: he has imagined smashing the pawnbroker with an ax in just the way the peasant smashes his horse; in both dream and plan the rage is directed at a worn-out creature, a useless "old nag."

The dream of the suffering horse has become one of the best known in all literature; its rich imagery expresses meaning on many levels. Where, in Dostoevsky's own experience, might some of these images come from? As he constructed his novels, he recorded outlines, associations, ideas, and drafts in notebooks; it is our good fortune that many of these have been preserved. In *The Notebooks for "Crime and Punish-*

ment," amidst material dealing with the pawnbroker and the murder, we find the line, "My first personal insult, the horse, the courier." This is a direct link with the horse-beating dream and refers to an event in Dostoevsky's adolescence that left a powerful and long-lasting impression. He was fifteen and his mother had died a few months earlier, after a protracted siege of tuberculosis. His father was taking him, along with his brother Mikhail, from their Moscow home to the Academy of Military Engineering in Petersburg where, his father had determined, they would train for practical careers. Military engineering was far from the minds of the young brothers, aspiring writers who dreamed of poetry, romantic dramas, and "everything beautiful and lofty." Their romantic preoccupations were rudely interrupted when the carriage was stopped at an inn. They saw a government courier, a large man in an impressive uniform, drive up, rush into the station house for a glass of vodka, and return to a fresh carriage with a new driver, a young peasant. The courier then raised his fist and began beating the driver on the back of the head and he, in turn, lashed the lead horse with his whip. Dostoevsky describes his impressions some forty years later:

Here there was method and not mere irritation—something preconceived and tested by long years of experience—and the dreadful fist soared again and again and struck blows on the back of the head. . . . [The driver who] could hardly keep his balance, incessantly, every second, like a madman, lashed the horses. . . . This disgusting scene has remained in my memory all my life. Never was I able to forget it, or that courier, and many an infamous and cruel thing observed in the Russian people. . . . This little scene appeared to me, so to speak, as an emblem, as something which very graphically demonstrated the link between cause and effect. Here every blow dealt at the animal leaped out of the blow dealt at the man.

In the remainder of the article, Dostoevsky, moving to a metaphorical level, says that "couriers no longer beat the people, but the people beat themselves, having retained the rods in their own court."

Dostoevsky was forty-four when he drew on this memory in writing *Crime and Punishment;* he was fifty-four when he recorded it in *The Diary of a Writer*. Whatever the actual events were at age fifteen, they had no doubt become blended with much that occurred earlier and later in his life. I am suggesting that we think of his account of the horse and courier not as a "memory"—as a literal rendition of fact—but as a story, a creation that weaves together emotions and themes from many different periods. It is like one of the "scenes" in Freud's case studies, like a particularly rich, compressed dream.

The horse-courier scene may be thought of as a nodal point, radiating out in many directions. One connection is with the concurrent events: his mother's death, his father's coercive control of his education. Other paths extend back into childhood and forward to the numerous "personal insults" of his adult life. Of special importance is the way the scene-memory contains, in highly condensed form, many of the themes that will be elaborated in the great novels: the clash of romantic ideals with harsh reality; man's capacity for violence and cruelty, along with feelings of love and sympathy; the effect of tyrannical authority on the oppressed and the victim's identification with their oppressors.

Dostoevsky strongly identified with the scene; it remained vivid in his imagination for many years. This is one illustration of his unique capacity to absorb people and events into himself; he felt himself to be courier, driver, and horse, just as Raskolnikov, in his dream, is peasant, young boy, and old nag. Dostoevsky's gifted use of identification was central to his craft; in the novels, he gives expression to different aspects of himself, and the "others" he has incorporated, through a diversity of fully realized characters.

The image of the horse and courier is not only a fitting emblem for life in tsarist Russia—as Dostoevsky himself noted—it can also serve as an emblem for many of the events and themes in his own life and work.

CHAPTER I

The Author
as Psychoanalyst

The true artist is never but half-conscious of himself when creating. He does not know exactly who he is. He learns to know himself only through his creation, in it, and after it. Dostoevsky never set out to find himself; he gave himself without stint in his works. He lost himself in each of the characters of his books, and, for this reason, it is in them that he can be found again.—ANDRÉ GIDE

Gide's perceptive comments call attention to an important dimension of Dostoevsky's work: its self-exploratory or self-analytic character. Many authors use their writing as a path to self-awareness, but they do so to very different degrees. Much popular literature—not to mention movies and television—is based on fantasies of fairly direct wish fulfillment. Soap operas, romance novels, sadistic thrillers, and family sagas, are vehicles in which an author—and his audience—achieve oversimplified solutions to life's conflicts and difficulties. Good literature also has its beginning in the private world of memory, conflict and obsession but, in turning this material into a public communication, the author moves beyond wish fulfillment and explores the real dimensions of human experience. The novelist Iris Murdoch defines good novels as "therapy which resists the all-too-easy life of consolation and fantasy" while bad novels . . . work out the author's "personal conflicts" with no respect for things as they are rather than as the author might wish them to be.

How does the author of good literature do this? We can approach this question by considering dreams and how they are used, both in psychoanalysis and the creation of literature. Think of a continuum that has the dream as dreamt, but not remembered, at one end, and the dream recalled and subject to a thorough-going interpretation, at the other. The unremembered dream is unconscious fantasy in pure culture, it is an experience that is not shared with others, not even with the dreamer's waking self: it remains unconnected with life, with consciousness. At the other extreme is the dream that is subjected to a thorough analysis. Here, unconscious material is made conscious, defenses are confronted and overcome, and discoveries are integrated into an understanding of oneself and one's life. The writing of literature is clearly more like dreams analyzed than dreams dreamt. The author begins with his private fantasies and turns them into public communications. Bad novels just do not move vary far along the continuum. While the author draws on his imagination—while there is some awareness of dream and fantasy—it is a limited form of consciousness, hedged about with defenses, idealizations, and stereotypes. All good literature does more than this, and, in the works of a Shakespeare or a Dostoevsky, we find access to the widest array of memory, fantasy, and unconscious material, along with a creative working over of this material.[1]

Freud was fond of saying that "the poets" discovered the unconscious before he did. One can find versions of almost all psychoanalytic phenomena in the world's great novels, stories, dramas, and poems. The most profound authors do more than simply display unconscious material; they are engaged in something analogous to the process of psychoanalysis itself. Meredith Skura, in the most sophisticated book yet written on the interaction of psychoanalysis and literature *(The Literary Use of the Psychoanalytic Process)*, argues that the poets not only discovered the unconscious before Freud, they discovered *psychoanalysis* as well. As she puts it:

It is not the mere presence or expression of primitive and unconsciously apprehended elements but the attempt to come to terms with them and to work them into the texture of conscious experience that makes the poets the predecessors of Freud.

Great literature is analogous to dreams interpreted; this is what Skura means when she says the poets discovered *psychoanalysis,* that literature may be likened, not just to the display of unconscious contents, but to the psychoanalytic *process* in which these contents are analyzed and understood.

The attempt to apply psychoanalysis to literature has a long and troubled history. While many have sensed an affinity, ("the poets discovered the unconscious before I did"), in a number of instances the fields have not been brought together in ways that please psychoanalysts, writers, or critics. At its worst, psychoanalytic criticism reduces fiction to symptom and psychosexual category, author to patient. Even the more sophisticated psychoanalytic critics, on the literary side, tend to derive their interpretations from theory rather than a first-hand knowledge of psychoanalytic practice. At the other extreme are critics who are restricted to the categories of consciousness and rational philosophy, who ignore so much of what psychoanalysts know about character and human motivation. What is needed—and what we are beginning to see in the best current work of people with a solid background in both fields —is an approach that does justice to the complexities of literary texts, the creative process and the real lives of authors, on the one hand, and the accumulated wisdom of many years of psychoanalytic observation, on the other.[2]

The key is to take the *psychoanalytic method*—the way psychoanalysis is defined in practice—as our guiding model. Too often, applications to literature have relied on particular psychoanalytic observations —the Oedipus complex, the primal scene,—or some version of theory —orthodox Freudian, Lacanian. But observations and theory can only be guidelines in the application of the method—the particular way of listening, observing, and interpreting that constitutes the living process. Skura shows how the psychoanalytic process can serve as an encompassing model, one that includes many observations and theories, to use in reading literary texts. I would argue that it is also the best model for biographical literary studies, for approaching a great writer such as Dostoevsky. That is, we should think of him not as a "patient" to be analysed, but as a fellow psychoanalyst, someone who, in the creation of his novels, carried out an exploration of himself and his fellow man. His was not just any self-analysis of course; the insights to be found in his novels parallel those in Freud. Dostoevsky as psychoanalyst, the Freud of fiction—this defines an approach that will do justice to his achievements, an approach that will enable us both to understand him in new ways and to learn from him.

What is it about Dostoevsky's work that qualifies him as the greatest of psychological—or psychoanalytic—novelists? While many great authors transform their personal dreams and fantasies in insightful and adaptive ways, he does so with greater scope. His novels contain a wider array of fully realized character types, a broader spectrum of conflicts and themes, drawn from different developmental levels, and more forms of conflict resolution. His uniqueness as a psychological novelist can be highlighted by comparing him with another great master whose fiction is rife with unconscious themes: Franz Kafka. Kafka's work gives public expression to his personal nightmares. He took his almost unbearable emotional states—the residues of his family life—and expressed them in allegories and densely symbolic stories and novels. The process of writing, and the literature itself, allowed him to go on living; indeed, it was only in his fiction that his inner self really did live; to parents, friends, his fiancée, and others, he presented a mask of politeness and compliance (see the biographies by Brod, 1960, and Pawel, 1984). The transformation of his suffering into literature was his most meaningful connection with the world. In his writing he kept depression in check and warded off suicide, though he nurtured his tuberculosis and seemed eventually to welcome the death that it brought him. The fiction itself presents an unrelentingly horrible picture of human relationships; Kafka is the poet of alienated modern life.

When we read Kafka, we are confronted with his raw unconscious, a nightmare world, exposed to public view. There are parts of Dostoevsky's novels that reveal his nightmares: scenes that are Kafkaesque, if I may use an anachronism. But the novels are filled with an abundance of other materials, pointing to a crucial difference between these two writers. Kafka's fiction contains variations on a single theme—brilliantly realized variations, to be sure, but ones that are extremely narrow in scope. In addition, there is no development over time: the themes, relationships, and emotional tone are the same in such early stories as *The*

Judgement and *Metamorphosis* as they are in late works like *The Burrow* and *A Hunger Artist*.

Kafka and Dostoevsky share access to their inner world and the artistic talent to bring this dream landscape to life on the page; in this they are both poets who discovered the unconscious. But Dostoevsky's work is "psychoanalytic" in ways that go beyond Kafka's. Let me elaborate two of these features. First, there is a working-through process that moves across developmental levels. That is, when his novels are read in chronological order, one sees the sort of progress from early to late stages that can be observed in a successful personal analysis. Themes are introduced and experimented with in the early novels and then, in midcareer, taken to a deep level of regression in *Crime and Punishment*. The psychological structure of this novel, written in 1865, is the world of the infant and the needed-depriving mother; it is pervaded by images of oral deprivation, rage, and a splitting of the primary love object. Genital-sexual themes appear in the next work, *The Idiot* of 1868, and there is continued progression until the last novel, *The Brothers Karamazov* of 1880, which is centered on themes of oedipal rivalry. Splitting is more extreme and idealizations more unrealistic in the earlier novels; the treatment of these issues also shows developmental change; the evil figures become less demonic and the saintly types less angelic; in *The Brothers,* everyone is more human, more a mixture of realistic good and bad qualities.

The second feature that qualifies Dostoevsky as specially psychoanalytic is his awareness of the self-exploratory process. In terms more familiar to us, we might say that he is present as an observing ego, even in the midst of the deepest emotional chaos. Indeed, it is his ability both to experience powerful regressed states *and* to transform them into fiction that gives his novels their unique flavor. Dostoevsky's self-awareness is revealed in several ways; one finds it to some degree in his own comments and his correspondence, for example. But, more than this, it is a feature intrinsic to the novels themselves. What is most characteristic of him is the presence of multiple points of view; he is never, as an author, completely identified with one character. Rather, he expresses different aspects of himself through several characters while also remaining—or moving to—a position of observation outside each of them. Again, this is a feature common to all literature to some degree, for however much an author embodies himself in a character, he remains the author, the person outside writing the story. Dostoevsky does more with this feature than almost any other novelist. The Russian literary critic Mikhail Bakhtin sees this as the way in which Dostoevsky has carried the novel to its greatest heights. In Bakhtin's words

Dostoevsky . . . creates not voiceless slaves but *free* people, capable of standing *alongside* their creator, capable of not agreeing with him and even of rebelling against him.

A plurality of independent and unmerged voices and consciousness, a genuine polyphony of fully valid voices is in fact the chief characteristic of Dostoevsky's novels.

Polyphony and dialogue, free from the author's domination—this could serve as a definition of the ideal state of free association during a psychoanalytic session, a state in which one attempts to give free reign to all sides of oneself while keeping an observing ego apart, in alliance with the analyst. Moving to another point of view about oneself is what psychoanalytic insight is, after all, breaking free from the grip of unconsciously driven perceptions and "seeing" oneself in new ways. Bakhtin believes that Dostoevsky's ability to assume multiple points of view is matched only by Shakespeare's.

Dostoevsky's novels reveal unconscious material in the free-ranging manner of an ideal psychoanalytic session. This is the necessary first step in what can be called the writing-as-psychoanalysis process; that is, gaining awareness of the many different sides of oneself, of forbidden desires, unsavory fantasies, whole secret selves. The next step involves the "analysis" of this material, the full exploration of its origins, functions within the personality, and consequences. Dostoevsky carries out the literary version of this analysis by creating characters who embody different sides of his conflicts—who represent his different inner selves —and setting them free to live out their fates. To cite an important example, he harbored a fair amount of rage in his soul and this formed the basis for his attempts, in a number of novels, to create what he called the "Great Sinner" type. These were meant to be men who could live beyond ordinary moral rules, who could murder, rape, and commit every sort of outrage with impunity. Variations on this character type are a stock-in-trade of popular literature, of course: figures of implacable evil and their counterparts, heroes who are equally implacable in their goodness. But every time Dostoevsky sets one of these Great Sinners free on the page—Svidrigailov in *Crime and Punishment*, Rogozhin in *The Idiot*, Stavrogin in *The Possessed*—they simply do not behave in a way to gratify his, or the reader's, fantasies of wanton aggression or revenge. They start out that way but then reveal their human complexities. Their monstrous evil deeds are revealed as petty sexual perversions, they are overtaken by guilt and alienation: both Svidrigailov and Stavrogin end their lives in suicide.

This process, in which the figure of fantasied evil is humanized, is similar to what occurs in psychoanalysis when one acquires insight into destructive fantasies. One exposes them initially in their extreme wishful form, comes to see their childish underside and consequences (if I hate and attack everyone I am left with nothing but guilt and isolation), becomes aware of other motives that the fantasies are shielding—the need for love, in each of Dostoevsky's characters—and, eventually, can arrive at a more tempered, a more realistic position. Dostoevsky worked and reworked this character type in his novels; it was much like the process of psychoanalytic working through of a deeply embedded unconscious conflict. By the end of his life, he had reached a more mature position; in *The Brothers Karamazov* there is no attempt at a figure of idealized evil. The Great Sinner has been decomposed into his human elements: Dmitri has the poorly controlled rage, but is more an unruly adolescent than a demonic being. The rest of the configuration is divided among Ivan, who has the cynicism and alienation, Smerdyakov, who is the actual murderer, and the father, who is much more a selfish child than a figure of evil. In sum, what appears in the earlier novels as a wishful expression of rage, free from guilt, is progressively analyzed, tempered, and understood in terms of its realistic features and consequences.

This discussion of the novelist-as-psychoanalyst may make the creative process seem too conscious, rational, and planned. Dostoevsky had a variety of things in mind when he set out to write a novel, most of them having to do with its surface structure: the plot, characters, and moral-political messages he was concerned with. Both the opening up of unconscious material and its "analysis" occurred during the process of writing and rewriting. An actual psychoanalysis is not so conscious or rational either, of course. As Gide, himself a novelist of some skill, notes in the passage with which I began this chapter, writers acquire insight through the dynamic process of creation. This was certainly the case with Dostoevsky, whose life and writing were closely intertwined. Typically, he would allow himself to fall into an extreme situation which heightened his emotions and intensified his conflicts. For example, he was prone to intense feelings of guilt and hated borrowing, yet his "carelessness" with money, not to mention his compulsive gambling, repeatedly put him in positions of humiliating indebtedness. He would then write his way out of these unpleasant situations with novels that worked through the issue of impulse expression and guilt.

Let me describe this in other terms. Dostoevsky had within him a variety of different selves (what others call "introjects," "internal objects," or, more precisely, self-other schemes or scenarios).[3] These rattled around in a free, if somewhat chaotic manner. His overriding identity was that of writer: this is what held everything together, what prevented complete disorder. He had some awareness of this. Here, he refers to it in a letter written from prison in 1849:

My nervous irritability has notably increased, especially in the evening hours; at night I have long hideous dreams, and latterly I have often felt as if the ground were rocking under me, so that my room seems like the cabin of a steamer. From all this I conclude that my nerves are increasingly shattered. Whenever formerly I had such nervous disturbances, I made use of them for writing; in such a state I could write much more and much better than usual.

Dostoevsky had the unique ability—as a person and a writer—to give himself over to one or another of his self-other scenarios; he would let one of his inner selves play itself out in his life. This is the living version of what Bakhtin, referring to the novels, calls "polyphony" and "dialogue": The creation of "free people, capable of standing *alongside* their creator." He would bring his inner actors on the stage of his life as he fell into one of his extreme situations. Once there, with emotions aroused and the scenario exposed to view, the writer-self could come on the scene and begin to control things by transforming the experience into literature.[4] To make a comparison with the process of psychoanalysis, once again, it is analogous to a patient's experiencing some aspect of himself in an intense form in the transference relationship and then stepping back, with the analyst, and looking at this experience from a different point of view. In a personal analysis, this stepping back is the work of interpretation and insight; for Dostoevsky it was the work of self-exploration via the writing of novels. To quote Gide again, "he learns to know himself only through his creation, in it and after it."

In the next three chapters I will examine Dostoevsky's literature as a form of self-exploration in the creation of what is, for me, the most focused and coherent of his major novels, *Crime and Punishment*.

CHAPTER 2

Crime and Punishment:
The Author's Life

Through a convergence of unhappy circumstances and his own contrivance, Dostoevsky's life had reached a calamitous state by 1864, just before he began *Crime and Punishment*. An examination of the way he turned life into literature will shed light on his unique mode of creativity. In this chapter, I will sketch out the pertinent dimensions of his life; the next will present a detailed analysis of the novel. Let me begin with some early history—a complete picture will be given in later chapters—and then look more thoroughly at the period around 1864.

Dostoevsky was the second of seven children born to a physician and his young wife. As was typical of middle- and upper-class families in the nineteenth century, he was cared for by more than one "mother": a peasant wet nurse, a long-term family servant (Aliona Frolovna) throughout his childhood, and his actual mother, Maria. His father was a terribly insecure man, very jealous of his wife's time and affection. His mother, the main source of security and love in the family, was burdened by their meager financial resources, her difficult and irascible husband, and her many pregnancies and offspring. She succumbed to tuberculosis when Dostoevsky was fifteen. She was, for him, both the idealized love object and the woman he repeatedly lost to rivals, the source of much of his frustration, rage and guilt. Her death was the final loss and he reacted to it by developing a "mysterious throat and chest ailment," which I would see as the symptomatic incorporation of his mother—illness and all—into his own body.

He was sent off to school soon after her death; this was the journey when the horse and courier scene so impressed itself on his memory. Without the support of his wife, the father—living on their country estate—sank into alcoholism and debauchery. He was murdered by his own serfs some two years after Maria's death. Dostoevsky was left to make his own way in the world.

A central feature of the family atmosphere was scarcity and a jealous competition for resources. The psychological center of this was competition for love, but it early became tied to money: the letters between Dostoevsky and his father are filled with guilt-inducing pleas and counterpleas for money. Dostoevsky emerged from his childhood with imaginative talent, a sense of career in literature, many strengths, and a core of intense ambivalence toward his mother (and father). Deprivation of the love and acceptance he so much needed engendered a great deal of frustration and rage. As is often observed with this sort of primitive conflict, splitting of the love object (mother and, later, other women) into good and bad, idealized and hated versions was a prominent adaptive measure. There was, as is also frequently observed, a great deal of guilt tied to the rage.

As early as his years in the engineering academy, Dostoevsky evidenced an unconscious living out of his primary ambivalence with money as the main symbol. He never had enough and was continually pleading and borrowing from friends and relatives. Yet, whatever he got passed through his hands like water: he allowed his servant to steal it and gave it or gambled it away. He was, thus, always in the position of the deprived one, the one in need, while, at the same time, his guilt prevented him from keeping what he received. This pattern persisted throughout a good portion of his life.

Dostoevsky achieved early success as a novelist but was then arrested, convicted of political subversion, subjected to the famous mock execution, and sent to prison in Siberia for four years. He was released in his early thirties and began forced service in the army in a small Siberian town. It was here that he fell into the first great romantic passion of his adult life. The woman was named Maria, she was married to an alcoholic, had a young son, and the beginning signs of the tuberculosis that would kill her some seven years later. These features—her name, her status as wife and mother, and her illness—were all qualities shared with his mother. I am suggesting that his love for her was an unconscious reenactment, an attempt to recapture the early idealized relationship.[1] Like most such reenactments, it contained the seeds of its own destruction. Her husband drank himself to death, Dostoevsky persuaded her to marry him, and their relationship was at once a disaster: the real Maria had little in common with his wishful fantasies. When he returned to Petersburg and picked up the threads of his career in 1860, they mainly lived apart. He carried on several affairs with other women, most prominently Polina Suslova, a spirited and rebellious young writer.

Maria succumbed to her illness in 1864; Dostoevsky stayed with her in the final days, writing *Notes from Underground.* His brother Mikhail, literary collaborator, friend, and confidant since childhood, died unexpectedly a few months later. Another friend and literary colleague, Grigoryev, died a few months after that. Along with these deep personal losses went the collapse of *The Epoch,* the journal that he and Mikhail had worked so hard to establish.

This was Dostoevsky's position in 1864 at the age of forty-three; Maria, the initially idealized woman, had degenerated into a half-mad state and died; he had lost his brother and a good friend. He was left with a mountain of debts and numerous personal obligations: the care and support of his stepson and of his brother's wife and four children. Even Mikhail's mistress petitioned him for help. While many of these tragedies and obligations were visited upon him, he had a hand in bringing about or augmenting others. Maria showed the first signs of tuberculosis when he fell in love with her, in fact, it was probably one of the features that attracted him, and his debts were not simply due to a sense of obligation and generosity; he let himself be exploited by publishers such as Stellovsky, with whom he signed a potentially ruinous contract, and by the many demanding relatives.

Most clearly self-inflicted was the debt brought about by his gambling mania. It was just when things were at their worst that he took the little money he had and fled to Europe, met his former mistress Polina Suslova, and gave way to his urge for roulette, as he had with her two years earlier. He lost all the money he had, and all he could get by pawning, and found himself alone in Germany. The hotel refused him food because the bill was unpaid, Polina had left for Paris, his gambling "system" had failed once again; penniless, he was forced to write letters begging from friends (Wrangel), from the emigré writer Herzen, from Polina—who had just rejected him—and even from his rival novelist, Turgenev, toward whom he was ambivalent, at best. He had contrived to put himself in what was the most humiliating and indebted of positions. And it was precisely from this position that his new novel began to flood forth; although various plans and outlines had been present earlier, the first great burst of work on *Crime and Punishment* was done in his hotel at Wiesbaden, at the nadir of his personal and financial fortunes.

Consciously, he saw the new novel as the solution to his practical difficulties: he could make money, pay off debts, and reestablish his reputation as a writer. This is how he speaks of it in his correspondence. Of greater significance was the meaning that was not conscious, initially, and that is only clear in the finished book itself. Dostoevsky had created in his life, a version of his deepest emotional conflict. He could then draw on this living experience and work the conflict through in his writing. I am suggesting a very different interpretation than that offered by most biographers and commentators. They describe his destitute state and marvel that he was able to write a great novel in spite of it. I think, quite to the contrary, that the conditions in his life were absolutely necessary for the creation of this novel; in fact, he had a large share in bringing them about. In other words, the writing was an exploration of the very issue that he had raised to such a feverish pitch in himself.

What was the issue? Being humiliated and having to beg for money is the first level of a theme that finds its full expression in *Crime and Punishment*. The analysis of the novel that follows will discuss the theme in detail; yet with the facts so far described, it should be obvious that one of the forces driving him was guilt. The pattern of guilt and atonement, following the death of a loved one, is well known. This reaction will be particularly strong when two conditions are met: first, when there is marked ambivalence and, second, when the relationship echoes a similar one from an earlier period. These two conditions fit both the deaths of Mikhail and Maria. Dostoevsky had strong rivalrous feelings with all his "brother" writers and his ambivalence toward Mikhail is clear in their correspondence. In addition, the man Mikhail, the fellow editor and collaborator who died in his mid forties, was that same favored older brother with whom Feodor competed as a child.

Guilt and the need to atone were even more powerful in the case of his wife's death. Dostoevsky's comments in his private journal show, quite directly, the mixture of love and hate that he felt for her. Additional evidence is provided by the reality of the marriage: he mainly lived apart from her and carried on love affairs with other women. What is more, the death of this Maria from tuberculosis evoked the death of the first Maria, his mother, from the same disease. There is never any direct mention of his mother in his letters but, as we will see, the emotional core of *Crime and Punishment* is ambivalence toward mother figures and women. This is the thread that leads to Dostoevsky's earliest emotional conflicts.

By assuming an excessive burden of debt and obligation—by suffering poverty, humiliation, illness, and rejection—he did penance for his anger. All of this fits the general reaction pattern following death and loss. But nothing was ever that simple with Dostoevsky. At the same time that he described his life as torn apart by death and failure, he spoke of the curious feeling that he was about to be reborn. He had a sense that his writing would take him beyond his guilty, self-punishing state. All of his actions up to the final point in Wiesbaden served to exaggerate and intensify the humiliation and guilty indebtedness. As he put it later in a related context:

There is an urge for the extreme, for the fainting sensation of approaching an abyss, and half-leaning over it—to peep into the bottomless pit, and, in some very rare cases, to throw oneself into it head-forward as in a frenzy.

Indebtedness, real enough in its own right, served as the concrete version of personal guilt of a much wider sort. By taking the indebtedness to an extreme, Dostoevsky could experience all the emotions and fantasies associated with this wider guilt, including the most violent, murderous impulses. The conflict was played out in all spheres of his life: with friends and lovers—Polina's diary and his fictionalized version of their relationship in *The Gambler* show how they alternately loved and tormented each other—with brothers and rivals, Mikhail, Herzen, Turgenev; with creditors and dependent children; and on his very body through hunger and epileptic seizures. His fantasies, dreams, and conscious preoccupations were all centered on his frenzied state. Then, with his total being activated in this way, all became focused on the new novel. He took this living material and channeled it into a work that explores the emotions and conflicts that were inside and all over him. In this process, current conflicts are traced to their developmental roots and a variety of paths toward resolution are explored. The final outcome is greater control, organization, awareness, and eventually, changes in his life situation.

How are these goals achieved in *Crime and Punishment?* The novel is not just an expression in fantasy of what could not be carried out in reality; it is not just catharsis, a spilling out of emotion, or a plea for sympathy. While Raskolnikov is enraged at those to whom he is indebted and, in fact, kills two women, it is not a novel in which revenge finds satisfaction. And while there are many poor, unfortunate, and suffering characters, it is not a tearjerker that plays on our feelings for the downtrodden. If Dostoevsky had gone in these directions he might have produced a soap opera rather than a masterpiece. Catharsis or tearjerkers are dreams dreamt, to return to the terminology used earlier; what Dostoevsky does is the equivalent of dreams analyzed or interpreted. This is the central way in which his writing parallels the psychoanalytic process.

Like the author at the time he created him, Raskolnikov is a man caught between fantasies of greatness and humiliating poverty. He indulges his grandiose ideas and commits a crime. It is as if Dostoevsky were carrying out an experiment in the safe space of a fictionalized dream: "What would happen if I were to kill one of those hateful people to whom I am indebted and steal all their valuables?" He then has Raskolnikov do just that and we see the consequences as guilt and the need to confess overtake him. Revenge is expressed and its real consequences explored.

The subplots of the novel may be thought of as additional fantasy solutions to the underlying conflict. In the figure of Svidrigailov, for example, it is as if Dostoevsky were saying, "Wouldn't it be satisfying to do whatever you wanted—to gratify lust and let your aggression run free—without feeling the guilty torment of conscience?" Svidrigailov starts out as one of these conscienceless "Bronze Men" or "Great Sinners" that so preoccupied Dostoevsky but, as he evolves in the novel, he becomes less bronze and more human, shows his need for love and his self-loathing. Again, the wish is first expressed and then explored in its real dimensions.

The novel contains a whole series of relations with women that present Dostoevsky's feelings and inner scenarios in this sphere. Marmeladov's dying tubercular wife, Katherine, is modeled on Dostoevsky's own wife, Maria. Svidrigailov displays an angry—in fact, murderous—need for women in relations with his wife, Raskolnikov's sister, Dunia, and several young girls. And Raskolnikov himself is caught up with pairs of women who represent the two sides of his ambivalence: his landlady and her maid; the old pawnbroker and her innocent half sister, Lizaveta; his actual mother and sister; and Katherine Marmeladov and her stepdaughter Sonia.

Sonia, the prostitute who loves and accepts him, is the one woman in the novel to whom Raskolnikov exposes all of himself: his need for love and his murderous rage. Just as Katherine Marmeladov represents the disastrous marriage to Maria, Sonia had her counterpart in Dostoevsky's real life. As he worked on the final portions of *Crime and Punishment*, he became involved with a healthy young woman, Anna Snitkina, whom he married shortly thereafter. The marriage became an enduring and satisfying one for both parties. I believe Dostoevsky's capacity to enter into and maintain this relationship was in large part due to the changes he had wrought in himself by literary self-analysis. That is, by working issues through in his writing, his life was no longer dominated by this particular form of anger, guilt, and unconscious reenactment.

Before taking up *Crime and Punishment* itself, a few words about the analysis of dreams, since this will provide an important interpretive framework. The term *dream* will be used in several senses. There are actual dreams, to which only the dreamer has access; Dostoevsky was closely in touch with his and drew on them in constructing his novels. Everything we know about him suggests this. It is even the case that he did most of his writing during the night when others were asleep: they dreamt while he wrote dreamlike literature. But, when I speak of dreams analyzed I am not referring to Dostoevsky's actual dreams. I use the term analogically; I am suggesting that we think of the novel as a shared series of dreams. In this scheme, there is a main dream—the central plot involving Raskolnikov, his crime, and what follows from it—and several secondary dreams—the subplots centered around Marmeladov, Svidrigailov, and other minor characters. Thinking of the novel in this way allows us to apply the interpretive schemes for a series of dreams from the same person. When we have a series of dreams in the same psychoanalytic session, or in contiguous sessions, we assume that the dreamer is working and reworking the same underlying issue, trying out different fantasy solutions to a common problem, as it were. Because we have before us the data of these related yet differing versions, it becomes possible to see the issue more clearly. Finally, within the plot and subplots, there are several fictionalized dreams: Raskolnikov's dream in which the horse is beaten to death, Svidrigailov's nightmares, and others. I don't mean to confuse things by overusing the term *dream,* there is a point to it: theory and interpretive rules from clinical work with dreams will prove of great value in understanding this particular novel. (See chap. 1, n. 1 for a more detailed discussion of dream theory.)

CHAPTER 3

Crime and Punishment:
The Novel

First Impressions

There are times when the initial contact with a patient contains, in condensed form, a great deal of what we will later discover about him. Dostoevsky introduces us to Raskolnikov in just this way: we find him ruminating in his closetlike room. In order to leave the room he must pass his landlady's kitchen; already there is deep conflict. He is in debt to the landlady and fears meeting her. As he sneaks past her door he feels "a nauseous, cowardly sensation." He has been lying in the room for at least a month, depressed, talking to himself, eating little, neglecting his appearance, and avoiding people.

As he came out onto the street the terror that had gripped him at the prospect of meeting his landlady struck even him as odd. "Imagine being scared of little things like that, with the job I have in mind!" he thought, smiling strangely.

The "job" is, of course, his plan to murder and rob an old woman, a pawnbroker to whom he is indebted.

Two sides of Raskolnikov emerge with great force from these initial passages. Contact with reality—with the world of people, sights, sounds, and sensations—is oppressive, irritating, even terrifying: it must be avoided.

Outside the heat had grown ferocious. Closeness, crowds, scaffolding, with lime, brick and dust everywhere. . . .The intolerable stench of saloons . . . the melancholy and repulsive tone of what confronted him. An expression of the deepest loathing flashed for a moment across his sensitive face.

He has, for the most part, withdrawn from all this into the world of his thoughts and schemes. And here, "somehow, and even against his will, the 'hideous' dreams had turned into a project, though he did not yet quite believe it." He struggles to see the "project" as an original act, a transgression requiring courage and will, something that can redefine his isolation as greatness rather than inferiority.

From the outset the project—the plan to murder and rob the pawn-broker—forms itself in his mind as a solution to all that has been troubling him. His rage acquires a definite target, someone whom he can hate with justification. And his fear seems less demeaning; he is frightened because he is engaged in a daring and dangerous crime. The project is like the thought structure of an obsession; it is at once a defensive resolution of unconscious conflict and a symbolic statement of that same conflict. Once the crime has been committed, Raskolnikov's fear and guilt will seem to center exclusively on it. But we should remember that the core reactions—the isolation, anger, fear, and guilt—were all present before the murder. The crime is itself a symbolic act, in need of interpretation.[1]

What hypotheses are suggested by these first impressions, by Raskolnikov's emotional state, the relationship with his landlady, and the project he is planning? One is immediately struck by the severity of his disturbance, his isolation from people and withdrawal from reality, the lability of his moods, and the crazed quality of his thoughts. And this includes a distortion of the reality of his own body—his outer self—which he treats as an unimportant shell. Thoughts and fantasies have come to dominate the whole person and they become grandiose.

The manner in which Raskolnikov experiences his room and surroundings, and the relationship with the landlady, suggest a first hypothesis concerning his disturbed emotional state. This is his home and the landlady the source of food, shelter, and comfort; she is his "mother," the woman in his current life responsible for maternal care. And it is clear that, for Raskolnikov, this care is oppressive (the cupboardlike room) and wrought with almost unbearable conflict. Despite his not having eaten for two days, the odors from her kitchen make him nauseous. He is in debt to her and feels such a mixture of anger and need that he is afraid to meet her and must sneak in and out of the building. Intense and pervasive feelings of guilt are bound up with these reactions.

After the crime has been committed, Raskolnikov is summoned to the police station because the landlady has filed a claim for unpaid rent. He, and the reader, at first connect the summons with the murder. This, plus the fact that he is indebted to both pawnbroker and landlady, suggest a link between the feelings of guilt in both relationships.

All of this leads to the hypothesis that the landlady is a maternal figure whose care is bound up with anger, fear, and guilt. Later, we will see that Raskolnikov has made her into such a figure, for we learn that his view is not to be trusted. His friend, Razumikhin, meets her and reports that she is not so unreasonable about the rent, she just needed a little friendly attention. He even finds her an attractive woman, something that one would never have guessed from Raskalnikov's image of her. And we also learn that Raskolnikov's poverty is due to his own refusal to work. He could have earned money doing translations, as Razumikhin has done, but he chose not to. So his lack of money as well as his persecution by the landlady, are matters of his own creation.

He needs to have a "bad," depriving mother outside himself. This tendency to split the primary love object—the source of maternal comfort and care—is completed by the character of Nastasia, the landlady's maid, who feeds Raskolnikov and attends to his needs in a simple and straightforward manner. The relationship with her is singularly lacking in guilt. A brief word about splitting—much more will need to be said later—which will prove so central to an understanding of Raskolnikov: this is a primitive form of defense that occurs when the young child feels strong ambivalence to a needed parent, most frequently love and anger toward the mother. The child, caught in an impossible position and lacking other resources, is forced to deal with his ambivalence by splitting the mother into good and bad versions. Fantasy, repression, projection, and other skills are all brought to bear as the child desperately attempts to preserve the good mother he needs and get rid of the depriving, frustrating, and rage-inducing mother. One sees images of this is children's stories and fairy tales (good fairies and bad witches) and in much adult fiction—and life—as well.

Why must Raskolnikov maintain a split image of the maternal figure? We learn later that a few years prior to the events being described, he was engaged to the landlady's daughter, a sickly girl who died before the marriage could take place. He was drawn to her, as he is to a number of other victims and abused children. Here is how he puts it:

She was quite sick—he lowered his eyes—ailing all the time. She used to love giving to beggars, and she was always dreaming about a nunnery. Once when she started to tell me about it, she wept. Yes, I remember, I remember that very well. Sort of a homely-looking thing. I don't know why I felt so attached to her, to tell you the truth, maybe because she was always sick, if she had been lame or hunchbacked I might have loved her even more.

Raskolnikov's attachment to this girl suggests two dynamics. There is the indirect hostility involved in a relationship with a degraded love object. His speech, quoted above, is directed at his attractive mother— who had opposed the marriage—and his beautiful sister; it carries an implicit rejection of them. The sickly girl serves as Raskolnikov's statement to the world of the inadequacy and uselessness of women. This is one meaning of his attraction to degraded and damaged women, but it is not the main one. He has more direct ways of expressing his hostility. Of greater significance is his identification with victims. His involvement with these poor creatures, and his acts of generosity toward them, express what he wants for himself. In a deep way he feels deprived, sick, and unfairly treated by life; he craves love and care that will restore a sense of well-being, health, and integrity.

If the rage that fuels the murder—along with guilt in relation to women—is one side of Raskolnikov's reaction to maternal figures, identification with victims is the other. It symbolizes the longing to be taken care of, the wish to be dependent, to give in, all of which are associated with a sense of helplessness so powerful that it prefigures death. Another way of stating this is in terms of the sadistic and masochistic components of his dilemma. He can attack the maternal figure or submit to her. He is caught between these two possibilities and, whenever he moves toward one, dangers are felt and he moves toward the other. As we will see, two of the subplots of the novel deal with these two sides, expressed in exaggerated terms: Svidrigailov the sadistic and Marmeladov the masochistic.

The project to murder the pawnbroker emerges from Raskolnikov's initial state as a solution to the conflicting forces that have left him nearly paralyzed. Calling it a "project" is his effort to isolate, depersonalize, and scientize his emotional turmoil. From a state of helplessness, deprivation, and crippling guilt, he imagines himself as powerful—even great—a man whose rage is justified, who will right the wrongs perpetuated on the weak, and acquire treasure to fill up the world's needy ones. The project, like his creation of a bad mother in the landlady, is an attempt to externalize his overwhelming ambivalence so that he can take action in the world.

The Marmeladov "Dream"

Raskolnikov goes to the pawnbroker's a first time, in preparation for the crime. Returning home, he wanders into a saloon where he sits, watches, and listens as if in a dream as Marmeladov tells his story. In psychoanalysis when we hear two dreams together they typically display related aspects of a single underlying theme. The setting and characters may change as the dreamer struggles with his conflicts, yet small elements serve as clues linking the dreams together. One dream may be anxious and the next show the anxiety overcome, or the two may experiment with different solutions to a common problem. Taken together, the pair of dreams contain converging sources of information that we can use in formulating an interpretation. I propose to treat Marmeladov's story as if it were a dream, a second source of information from a common unconscious reservoir.

Marmeladov, a middle-aged clerk, a "titular councillor," sunk in the depths of alcoholism, is one of those characters who regales everyone with his pitiful saga. On the first encounter with Raskolnikov, he calls attention to the connection between them: they are both educated men, men of talent and abilities despite their poor and disheveled appearance. And, as the story unfolds, it is revealed that the destitution they suffer is not due to external misfortune in any simple way; each had a hand in creating his own plight.

The outline of Marmeladov's story is as follows. A widower with a fourteen-year-old daughter, Sonia, he marries Katherine, herself a widow with three young children. He works for a time, supporting the new family but, eventually, through a combination of bad luck and his own weakness, falls into drink and his present state of destitution. Not only is he a drunk but, he confesses, the family's lack of money has driven Sonia into prostitution and, even then, he does not stop: he sells his wife's clothes, steals money from the house, and even takes Sonia's earnings to keep himself in alcohol. All of this is told with an exaggerated sense of self-pity.

When I am destitute no one is quicker to humiliate me than I myself. . . . *Do you dare*—you who gaze on me as I am now—do you dare state definitely that I am not a pig?

Marmeladov is a man who humiliates himself before others, makes himself ridiculous, destroys his integrity and very body, but why? What lies behind all this? The relationship with his wife emerges as a central factor.

Well, then, so be it. I am a swine. But *she* is a lady! I am the shape of a beast, but Katherine Ivanovna, my wife—she is an educated person, she was born the daughter of a staff officer. So be it, so be it. I am a scoundrel, while she is lofty in spirit, and her feelings have been ennobled by education. Ah still, if only she pitied me! My dear sir, why my dear sir, everyone needs a small place somewhere, where he knows he will be pitied!

When his story is examined closely, we see that, mixed in with the attack on himself, is an attack on her. His very praise, exaggerated as it is, has a mocking underside. He rescued her and her children from their impoverished state, yet she throws up the memory of her first husband to him. She is proud, he says again and again, yet he describes her as self-centered. She loves her children, spends all day scrubbing and cleaning, yet she beats them when they cry and is, throughout, useless as a mother. She is cruel to her stepdaughter, Sonia, drives her into prostitution, and then falls at her feet. And she is sick, wasting away with tuberculosis, which aggravates her temper and instability. In all these ways, Marmeladov shows her to have the outer appearance of a fine woman—a good mother and wife—an appearance that is belied by her actions. She lives in the past, in a fantasy of lost social status, and seems little able to give to the real people in her current life: to her stepdaughter, her children, and her husband. Indeed she shows affection for him only when he assumes a respectable position and that is precisely when he throws it all away and sinks into drink. His actions reveal his rage at her failure to accept him.

Marmeladov attacks his wife, both directly and with masochistic aggression. He does the opposite of what she demands of him, losing his job and respectable position. He steals her clothes and sells them to support his drinking, including the woolen shawl she needs to keep warm, thus hastening her death from tuberculosis. He breaks into her chest, just as Raskolnikov will with the pawnbroker, steals the family money, and, having drunk it all up, returns home with Raskolnikov and allows himself to be attacked, accepting his punishment from her:

Suddenly she seized him in a frenzy by the hair and dragged him into the room. Marmeladov made it easier for her by meekly sliding after her on his knees.

"And I tell you I enjoy it! I tell you I feel no pain, but I actually enjoy it, my dear sir!" This he shouted out as he was being shaken by the hair, and once his forehead even struck the floor.

His enjoyment of punishment—a definition of masochism, after all—has more than one side. It alleviates guilt; it is penance for his transgressions; and it is penance that permits him to go out and get drunk once more. And, it serves to locate the aggression in Katherine. By provoking her to attack him, he succeeds in demonstrating to one and all—and these scenes are always played before an audience—that she is the aggressor and he the victim. The masochist attacks by dragging others down, by arousing angry and uncomfortable feelings in them. Marmeladov is continually heaping excrement on himself, but a lot of it splatters on those nearby.[2]

Let us return to the view of the Marmeladov story as a dream that presents an alternative solution to the conflicts Raskolnikov suffers. In other words, think of Marmeladov as the masochistic side of Raskolnikov, a side displayed in extreme form. This dream shows the danger of the masochistic course, for Marmeladov ultimately succeeds in destroying both himself and his wife. Raskolnikov comes upon him after he has been run over by a horse and carriage, drunk and dying in the street. He has him carried home. There he dies, while Katherine berates him and carries on her fight with the neighbors over social position.

Marmeladov's blood, and that which Katherine is already beginning to cough up from the tuberculosis that will kill her, are almost too obvious links with the murders. Blood is one of those dream elements that ties the Marmeladov subplot to the central action. It stands for the guilt associated with aggression leveled at the maternal figure, directly in the case of Raskolnikov's murder of the pawnbroker, and masochistically in the case of Marmeladov and his wife. Another significant element in both dreams is the presence of the idealized, potentially loving and forgiving woman. In the murder scene, it is the innocent Lizaveta; in the Marmeladov family, it is Sonia who, we later learn, was a close friend of Lizaveta's. Raskolnikov first sees Sonia as he leaves Marmeladov's deathbed, himself covered with blood. He has offered money and help to the family, out of his own sense of guilt, and the possibility of a connection with an innocent child-woman arouses hope for a way out of his conflicted and isolated state.

To sum up the connections between Raskolnikov and Marmeladov, we note that both appear poor and disheveled on the outside but feel more valuable within. Both have humiliated themselves by borrowing money, Raskolnikov from the pawnbroker and Marmeladov—as always, in a more ludicrous fashion—from a "high official." Both steal money from the maternal figure, breaking into her treasure chest in similar ways. And both kill the woman—directly and indirectly—feel guilt, and seek punishment. Of course there are important differences: where Marmeladov is garrulous and humiliates himself, Raskolnikov is isolated and proud. Marmeladov exemplifies the masochistic and dependent course—let us not forget that he is an alcoholic, devoted to the escape and gratification of the bottle—while Raskolnikov, when they first encounter each other, is wavering between action and passivity, attack and submission, sadism and masochism.

A Letter from Home, a Dream, and the Murder

The encounter with the Marmeladov family leaves Raskolnikov in a state of uncertainty about his project. He is then propelled into action by two experiences: reading a letter from his mother and a dream, both of which illuminate, in striking fashion, the unconscious forces at work within him. The letter is our first contact with his actual mother: it is a masterpiece at revealing her character. Dostoevsky understood the double bind long before it was discovered by modern students of the schizophrenic family. The letter begins:

My dear Rodia, it is a little over two months now since I've chatted with you by mail, and this has caused me some distress and I've even lain awake nights thinking about it. But you won't blame me for my involuntary silence. You know how much I love you. You are all we have left, Dunia and I, you are our everything, all our wishes and all our hope.

Immediately, the theme of blame is introduced with the implication that someone is causing someone else pain. The mother is in distress, she lies awake at night: why? Because *she* hasn't written to *him*. But he shouldn't blame her—was he about to?—because it was "involuntary" and, besides, she loves him. This communication can be decoded as: "You may be about to blame me but, before you do, I block it, let you know that I love you and am suffering on your account." The very next passage then turns the blame on Raskolnikov: why did he leave the university, why isn't he working? Mother has almost no money, but she will send what little she has. The guilt has been shifted onto his shoulders, but subtly; mother's accusations are indirect and always mixed together with protestations of love and references to her suffering and self-sacrifice. There are a number of additional instances of these double-binding communications, and there is the central theme of the letter; it too places Raskolnikov in an impossibly conflicted position.

Mother describes Dunia's suffering on Raskolnikov's behalf. She was employed as a governess in the Svidrigailov household in order to earn money to support her brother at the university. Svidrigailov conceives a passion for her—we learn more about his later—and asks her to run away with him. His wife, Martha Petrovna, overhears some of this, does not know that Dunia has rejected his advances, and drives her from the house in a shameful manner. Martha then spreads gossip about the town, causing Dunia and her mother much humiliation and pain. Dunia is strong, she bears all this but the mother "takes sick." Martha then learns of Dunia's innocence and goes to great lengths to undo the harm she has caused. Dunia's reputation is cleared and, through Martha's efforts, a suitor is found, Luzhin, a prosperous lawyer and businessman. The mother's description of Luzhin and the proposed marriage is, again, a masterpiece of doublethink. He is "in general quite a solid and reliable man. A bit morose, perhaps and haughty. But this may be merely a first impression," and he is "an extremely worthy man . . . a practical man" but "a little bit vain and enjoys having people listen to him." She adds, "of course, love is not especially involved, either on her side or his."

There is more of the same, making it clear that Luzhin is really a grasping, self-centered prig whom Dunia is only considering because of the family's financial straits. Just in case Raskolnikov hasn't gotten the message, his mother includes the following information: Luzhin says that he wishes to marry

an honorable girl who had no dowry and who knew what it was like to be poor; for, as he explained, a husband should not be obliged to his wife for anything, since it is much better the other way around, if the wife considers the husband her benefactor.

Luzhin is, in other words, a crass version of the type who controls others with obligation and indebtedness; for him this takes the place of love. Mother has just been controlling Raskolnikov with guilt, and we have seen his rage at the landlady and the pawnbroker, to whom he feels indebted. What the mother's letter conveys, in its indirect way, is that she and Dunia are sacrificing themselves for Raskolnikov.

Love her as she loves you; and know that she loves you infinitely more than she loves herself. She is an angel; but you, Rodia, you are all we have—all our desire and all our hope.

As Raskolnikov says later, in reference to his mother and sister's efforts to sacrifice themselves for him:

She's [Dunia's] a proud one! Refuses to admit she wants to play the benefactress! Oh what low characters! They even love as though they were hating, oh how I hate them all!

His mother's letter arouses strong and conflicting feelings: hope for closeness and love, frustration and rage, guilt and unworthiness. Yet it is so mystifying that Raskolnikov cannot consciously focus these reactions; the feelings of oppression and rage are quickly displaced away from her. At first, he cries when reading the letter, then becomes angry; his heart pounds, and his thoughts are confused:

He felt it grow close and stuffy in that little yellow room so much like a chest or cupboard. . . . His mother's letter made him suffer. About the most important point . . . he had no doubt at all. . . . . "As long as I'm alive this marriage will not take place, Mr. Luzhin can go to hell!"

The oppressive feeling her letter creates in him is projected onto his physical surroundings, his room, and the rage that should be directed at her is shifted to Luzhin. He is a suitable candidate, of course, since the mother describes him as someone who controls others by keeping them obligated and in debt. Throughout is the theme of exploiter and victim. Those without are controlled and victimized by those who have, Dunia by the Svidrigailovs and, if the marriage takes place, by Luzhin, the mother herself by her creditors, and Raskolnikov by all those to whom he is indebted. The rage engendered by this is about to explode, and first does so in a dream of extreme violence.

Raskolnikov dreams he is a small boy walking with his father in the country. They pass a tavern overflowing with drunken, rowdy peasants, led by Mikolka, owner of a large wagon that is hitched to an aged, skinny mare. At Mikolka's urging a group piles in the wagon, and he begins to beat the horse, though it is obvious she cannot move the heavily loaded wagon from its tracks. The more he beats her, the less able she is to pull and the more enraged he becomes until he smashes her to death in a violent frenzy. To the protests of onlookers he yells "my property"; his ownership of the horse entitles him to kill her, and she is old and useless anyway. The boy Raskolnikov in the dream is horrified, he makes futile efforts to help, flings himself at Mikolka, and embraces the dead mare, kissing her on the eyes and mouth. Raskolnikov wakes from the dream and immediately knows its connection with his project.

"God" he exclaimed. "Will I really? Will I really take the ax, will I really hit her on the head, split open her skull, will I really slip in the sticky warm blood, break open the lock, steal, and shiver and hide, all bloody with the ax, Good Lord, will I really?"

In Raskolnikov's own interpretation he sees himself as Mikolka, the dream portraying his plan to kill the aged and useless old pawnbroker. In the image of Mikolka, the rage is laid bare, stripped of its intellectual justifications. But we can add additional interpretations. Since a dream arises entirely from the mind of the dreamer, its different characters and emotions represent different sides of his personality. Raskolnikov is not only the angry attacker, he is also the innocent young boy who loves the maternal figure and is horrified at the violence visited upon her. And he is, as well, the victim, the beaten old mare. We have seen several other examples of his identification with those treated unjustly. Indeed, it is precisely this sense of the unfairness of life that fuels his rage.

While these different meanings are all present in the dream, Raskolnikov's first reaction recognizes its active, emotional core. He has been impelled along a single road from the outset of the novel: money owed the landlady and the pawnbroker; anger at those who have and to whom he is indebted; the guilt-inducing letter from his mother, with the anger immediately displaced; the dream in which the anger explodes at a useless old nag; and now, he is ready to put his project into action.

The dream has revealed his own motives to him. At first, he tries to convince himself that he won't go through with it, but he has become superstitious; that is, he allows external events to move him along the path of his own unconscious intentions. He overhears some students discussing the pawnbroker and her sister, and also hears that Lizaveta will be out of the apartment at a specific time, and this tips the balance, he will carry out his project.

He sneaks out of his room, hides an ax under his coat, enters the pawnbroker's apartment with a phony item to pawn and, while she examines it, brings the ax down on her head. He strikes her twice more and, as her blood gushes out, takes her keys and goes searching for her money and pledges. As he is stuffing his pockets he hears someone enter the apartment, runs back, and finds Lizaveta staring at her murdered sister. She backs away from him, hardly raising her arms or protesting as he splits her head with the ax. The two women make sharply different impressions on him. The pawnbroker is hostile and suspicious and only grudgingly lets him into her apartment; as he hits her she appears physically repulsive, with greasy hair in a "rat's-tail plait." Lizveta is all innocence; she barely protests as he moves to kill her; her posture is almost receptive.

Having killed the second woman, panic and disgust overtake him. He cannot go back for the rest of the money or jewelry, his thoughts are confused, he becomes obsessed with washing the blood off the ax, his hands, and his clothes, and he thinks of escape. He was only marginally in control of himself to begin with and this second, unexpected, murder has shifted the precarious inner balance toward fear and guilt. Two men approach the apartment, and he hides inside the door as they bang and shout for the old lady. They leave, he makes his escape and returns to his room in a terrible state. Even before the crime, on his way to the pawnbroker's, the thought had flashed through his mind that he was being led to his own execution. Now, the crime has been committed, and the punishment begins.

Guilt, the First Phase

Having killed the two women, Raskolnikov returns to his room and collapses in a feverish delirium. For the next few days he is powerfully torn in two opposing directions. There is the wish to confess, get it over with, give in, and not have to bear his guilt and isolation. And there is the impulse to mock authority, his rage, and pride at having gotten away with it. The impulse to confess appears as both a conscious wish and as a variety of unconscious acts that betray him. Dostoevsky was aware of how a person can unconsciously seek punishment for his crime. Like Edgar Allen Poe, he anticipated what Freud later called "criminality from a sense of guilt."

Both sides of Raskolnikov's state are revealed by some incidents at the police station. He is summoned because of the money he owes the landlady and he both argues with the officials and courts their favor. Then, hearing them discuss the murders, he faints, drawing suspicion to himself. Yet, later, he swings to the other extreme.

"Damn it all!" he thought suddenly in a fit of boundless rage. . . . "How I lied today, how I humiliated myself! How nastily I fawned and played up to the bastard Ilia Petrovich [the police assistant superintendent] awhile ago. That's dumb, too! To hell with them all, I don't care."

This raging, prideful state causes him initially to reject the concern of his friend Razumikhin. And it finds a suitable target in Luzhin when he visits Raskolnikov in his room. He provokes an argument over Luzhin's theories of "enlightened self-interest."

"What are you worried about?" Raskolnikov unexpectedly broke in.
"All this fits in with your theory!"
"What do you mean it fits in with my theory?"

"If you took what you were preaching a little while ago to its logical conclusion, it would turn out people can be done away with. . . ." Raskolnikov lay there, face pale, breathing hard, upper lip quivering.

He rages on at Luzhin over the latter's wish to control Dunia, to "lord it over her and remind her she's in your debt." Of course it is Raskolnikov who has "done away" with people, and precisely those to whom he is in debt.

His guilt and the wish to confess are as strong as his rage: both drive him along a vacillating course. He meets a police clerk in a tavern and makes a mocking, hostile confession to his face, then pretends it was a joke. He returns to the scene of the murders, rings the bell and talks to the workmen who are repairing the apartment. He even asks them about the blood that was on the floor. As in the police station, he draws suspicion to himself and, as he leaves, seems on the brink of turning himself in. It is then that he comes upon Marmeladov who has been run over by the horse and carriage.

Though some readers may see his encounter with the dying Marmeladov as merely a clumsy device to keep the plot going, it has, I think, a much deeper significance. Marmeladov represents Raskolnikov's masochistic side and his death symbolizes the logical end of this course. It is a reminder to Raskolnikov of the danger of confessing, of giving in to his guilt. He emerges from the Marmeladov family scene with a new will to live, and with hope for rebirth in a relationship with a different kind of woman. But it will take some time for this to happen. His mother and sister make their appearance, and, again, he faints from guilt. Why? Clearly they remind him of whom he has killed—and whom he still feels like killing—though his rage at his mother remains unconscious.

Raskolnikov's vacillation between pride and guilt—between angry isolation and the wish to confess and rejoin humanity—continues for a very long time. Indeed, more than half the novel is taken up with this protracted struggle; it is only at the very end that he makes the decisive move back into life.

In my account so far I have kept to the chronology of the novel. I will depart from this format now and trace Raskolnikov's struggle as it appears in four relationships—with his mother, Porfiry Petrovich, Svidrigailov, and Sonia—each followed to its conclusion. Each of these characters represents a possible solution to Raskolnikov's dilemma. They all come to know of his crime and he seeks something from each: love, forgiveness, a model, a cure, and rebirth. If we again use the analogy of the novel as trial dream solutions, we can view the playing out of these four dramatic lines as the exploration of different approaches to Raskolnikov's plight. Only one, that embodied in Sonia, will succeed.

Mother

The mother has revealed herself in her long letter to Raskolnikov, a letter that "made him suffer" and aroused his rage at Luzhin. She and Dunia arrive in Petersburg, and Raskolnikov comes upon them in his apartment.

He did not know why they had been the last people in the world he had expected, why he had never thought of them, although twice that day he had received news that they were on their way and would be there at any moment.

This is another of Dostoevsky's marvelous psychological touches: Raskolnikov's mother is blotted out of his mind, which is filled, instead, with her symbolic replacements, the landlady, the pawnbroker, Katherine Marmeladov. To see her before him is most threatening. She and Dunia fling themselves on him with joy, "yet he stood there as one dead. A sudden intolerable awareness struck him like a thunderbolt. And he could not even lift his arms to embrace them." He faints and, when he is revived, sends them away. When his mother expresses concern he responds, "Don't torment me. . . . I can't stand it. I can't stand it. . . . Don't torment me! Enough. Go away, I can't stand it!" This is plain enough talk, though everyone is only too eager to attribute it to his "illness." He delays them long enough to express his anger at the Luzhin affair before they leave.

What is it about his mother that Raskolnikov finds so tormenting? What is it that arouses a rage so powerful it leads to murder? As we have seen, she is continually putting him in a guilty position, letting him know of her love and self-sacrifice. This arouses anger that he finds difficult to express directly, especially since she so readily weeps and becomes sick. Her arousal of guilt accounts for part of his anger but is not sufficient to account for the full extent of the rage. Its deeper source is to be found, I believe, in her total inability to see him as himself, to respond to him as the person he is. She has an idealized version of him —he is "their everything, all their wishes, all their hope"; in her eyes he is brilliant, has a great career before him, is beautiful—and she clings to this image with great tenacity. Her idealization is one source of Raskolnikov's own grandiosity, of course, it puffs up his sense of himself. But it is not based on a realistic assessment and therefore must lead to disappointment and frustration.

Here are further examples of the mother's unrealistic idealization. Raskolnikov has driven her and Dunia from his apartment, displayed his wrath over the Luzhin affair, and insulted his sister; he then makes a small gesture of reconciliation to Dunia:

"And how well he brings it off" his mother thought to herself. "What noble impulses he has. How simply and delicately he ended the whole misunderstanding of yesterday. . . . What beautiful eyes he has, and how beautiful his whole face is!

And, later, after he tells her he has given away her money to the Marmeladov family:

"Enough, Rodia. I'm convinced that everything—everything you do—is excellent!" his mother said, over-joyed.
"Don't be too sure;" he answered, twisting his mouth into a smile.

Her idealization of him shows the hollowness of her love. She cannot respond to Raskolnikov, only to her own image, and her continued attempts to define his character as pure, virtuous, and loving is a gross distortion of the reality of his refusal to work, his self-induced poverty and dishevelment, and his obvious anger. The more she persists in this sort of "love," the more frustrated he becomes. His anger—the irritability and outbursts as well as the murders themselves—is an effort to break out of her false and oppressive definition of him. It is a communication to her, to Dunia, and Sonia, to the world: "This is how I really am, filled with rage, a murderer. Can you still love me?" He needs a woman who will see him as he really is, not as a purified image, and the impulse to confess is a search for such an accepting figure.

The mother's lack of empathy and inability to see people as they are, are portrayed in several additional ways. She is naive, trusting and always ready—on the surface—to think well of others. But her naiveté masks a blindness that places her children in destructive situations. She is taken with Luzhin—a man of wealth and respectable appearance—and supports his marriage to Dunia. There is plenty of evidence that reveals Luzhin's unsavory intentions but the mother doesn't want to see this until Dunia, Raskolnikov, and Razumikhin force her too. Her response to Sonia shows another side of this same trend, for Sonia is disreputable on the outside but virtuous within. Sonia functions in the novel as a touchstone of the perceptiveness of the other characters: which of them can see her real worth beneath her degraded appearance? The mother's first reaction to Sonia is hostile: "I have a premonition, Dunia. Believe it or not, as soon as she came in I thought—here we have what's behind it all." As with Luzhin, the mother has great difficulty in seeing the person beneath the social facade.

The destruction brought about by a mother who is fixated on appearance—who cannot see the members of her family as real and complete people—is exemplified by Katherine Marmeladov. All the Marmeladovs are exaggerated versions of the characters and conflicts in the central plot and Katherine serves, in this way, as a commentary on Raskolnikov's mother. Both women are initially taken in by Luzhin and both are ready to turn against Sonia. Katherine's obsession with social standing, and her unrealistic idealization of her father and first husband, are central to her sadomasochistic struggles with Marmeladov. As she becomes sicker and crazier, these qualities become more extreme and her final madness and death display the full tragedy of her inability to see others, and herself, as they are. Her dying words, "Enough! It's time! Goodbye you poor thing [Sonia]. They've finished off the old nag! She's overstrai—overstrained!" tie her to Raskolnikov's dream in which the old mare is beaten to death, to the murders, and back to his mother, who, like Katherine, is destined to go mad and die in a similar fashion.

Raskolnikov goes to see his mother a last time before turning himself over to the police. At this point, his secret is out: he has confessed to Sonia, Svidrigailov has overheard the confession and passed it on to Dunia, and Porfiry has guessed it. He seeks his mother's acceptance and she has enough information to guess what has happened. Yet the possibility of really knowing her son drives her to ever more frantic distortions. She has read his article in which murder is justified for "extraordinary men":

"I may be stupid, Rodia, but I can tell that you will soon be one of the top people in our learned world, maybe the very top. And they dared to think you were mad."

He tries to tell her what is really going on in his life:

"No matter what had happened, Mama dear, no matter what you had heard about me, what people said to you about me—would you still love me as you do now?" He asked this all of a sudden, as if it flowed out of him, as if not thinking about his words or weighing them.

And her reply:

"Rodia, what's wrong with you, Rodia? How can you even ask such questions! Who is going to say anything to me about you? Anyway, whoever came to me, I wouldn't believe anybody—I'd simply chase them away."

She must turn away from reality; she cannot see his anger or his pain. No wonder that, a bit further on, we find him thinking, " 'Enough, Mama dear' Raskolnikov said, regretting deeply that he had decided to come."[3]

The mother must maintain her idealized image of Raskolnikov to the very last and the increased distortion of reality that this requires characterizes her final madness. He has been tried, convicted, and sent to Siberia and Dunia and Razumikhin—aware of the mother's inability to deal with this—attempt to shield her from the truth. She develops a "rather peculiar mental derangement." While there is, by now, abundant evidence—including his unexplained absence and the lack of letters that she always depended on—to suggest that something has gone seriously wrong, she pretends that all is well. She carries on to one and all about her son's many accomplishments, sleeps with a copy of his article under her pillow, and stops strangers in the street to boast of his brilliant future career. Her contact with reality increasingly slips away until she finally becomes convinced of his imminent return:

After an alarming day given to fantasies, happy delusions, and tears, she took sick. . . . Within two weeks she died. In her delirium she uttered words indicating she surmised more about her son's awful fate than they had suspected.

One might say that she died rather than openly face the reality of her son's rage and pain.

Porfiry

Porfiry Petrovich is the court investigator charged with uncovering evidence about the murders. He is very much a psychologist, relying on his understanding of the subtleties of human motivation, his interviews are clever games, mixtures of philosophical discussion, indirect probing, teasing, and confrontation, all of which Raskolnikov finds most unsettling. Porfiry is not a typical official; he is Razumikhin's cousin, hence part family and friend, and there is "something almost maternal" about him. In a final interview, he tells Raskolnikov he knows he is the murderer and could have him arrested, but he shows sympathy and gives helpful advice. Despite these softening qualities, Raskolnikov finds him a mocking, accusing figure. Porfiry arouses fear and anger as he strips secrets and rationalizations bare.

In their long first interview, Porfiry reveals his familiarity with Raskolnikov's article "On Crime." This is where the theory is put forth that "extraordinary" individuals like Napoleon are morally justified in overstepping the law in carrying out their great deeds. Porfiry pushes and prods Raskolnikov as they discuss this theory and even asks whether:

"You thought yourself—well, just a little bit, now, you know—one of those "extraordinary" men, somebody who has a *new word* to say. . . . And if that were so, you might have decided yourself, well, in view of the setbacks and limitations in your day-to-day life, maybe even to hurry mankind progressively along a bit, to transgress an obstacle? Let's say, for example, to murder or to rob?"

In the interview, such probing puts Raskolnikov on guard and arouses his anger. He tries to cover his tracks and fears Porfiry will find him out. There is a deep source for this fear; Porfiry, the student of motivation, concentrates on Raskolnikov's psychological defenses, particularly the extraordinary-man theory, which serves as intellectual justification for the crime. This theory is Raskolnikov's grandiose defense against profound feelings of inferiority, as seen in his preoccupation with whether he is a Napoleon or a louse, whether he is a great man or a worthless, dependent bloodsucker. In justifying the crime he has tried to convince himself that the pawnbroker is a louse and his actions worthy of Napoleon.

In other words, Porfiry upsets Raskolnikov both by guessing that he has committed the crime and by ridiculing his pretensions to greatness. It is the second—the attack on his great-man theory—that is most unsettling, that tips Raskolnikov's inner balance into inferiority. Indeed, the effect of the interview is a breakthrough of terrifying feelings of guilt and helplessness and a profound distortion of reality. We see this shortly after the meeting with Porfiry when Raskolnikov encounters an artisan on the street—we can't tell whether this is a hallucination or not—who calls him, "Murderer!" He returns to his room and falls into one of those states of semidelirious free association; it is here that we see his grandiosity break apart.

"No, such people [like Napoleon] aren't made like that. The real *master* to whom all is permitted. . . . No, it's clear, such people are made of bronze, not flesh and blood. . . . Napoleon, the pyramids, Waterloo—and that vile, skinny clerk's widow, that wizened old bag, the pawnbroker woman with the red trunk under her bed—well, how could even Porfiry Petrovich make a stew of that one! . . . Would Napoleon sneak up to an old bag like that along her bed! Oh, hell! . . . The old bag's rubbish!" he thought heatedly and impetuously. "She may even have been a mistake; anyway, she's beside the point! The old woman was only a disease I wanted to step over as quick as I could. . . . All I could do was kill. Couldn't even do that it would seem. . . . I'm an esthetic louse and nothing more," he added suddenly and laughed like a madman. "Yes, I'm really a louse," he went on. He fastened on the thought, reveling in it, playing and picking at it for comfort. . . . "And so, I am decisively a louse," he added, grinding his teeth, "because I am myself nastier and fouler than the louse that was killed. . . . Oh, not for anything, not for anything, shall I ever forgive that old hag! . . . My mother, my sister, how much I loved them! Why do I hate them now? Yes, I hate them. . . . Oh, how I hate that old hag now! If she came to, I think I'd kill her again! Poor Lizaveta! Why did she have to turn up at that point! Strange though, wonder why I almost don't think of her, as if I hadn't killed her at all? Lizaveta, Sonia! Poor creatures . . . they give everything away, they look out meekly and gently, Sonia, Sonia! Gentle Sonia!"

He passes directly from this state of delirium into a dream in which he returns to the scene of the crime, finds the old hag in a chair, and again smashes her head with the ax. But his blows have no effect; she sits silently laughing at him and the room fills with people, laughing and staring as he is unable to move.

In these remarkable passages Dostoevsky shows us what lies beneath Raskolnikov's grandiosity, beneath his philosophical preoccupations and theories. He has tried to get rid of his own sense of guilt and helplessness by projecting them onto the pawnbroker: she is the louse and he will rid the world of her. His inner rage will be justified, he will be a great man. But, as is inevitable when action is based on projection and splitting, it doesn't work. He still feels a louse, guiltier than ever for having openly expressed his rage. What is more, he has killed an innocent woman— Lizaveta, a loving figure—along with the hated "old hag." His delirious associations even link the murderous rage directly to his mother and sister. Porfiry's attack on his grandiosity brings Raskolnikov's identification with victims—"I am myself nastier and fouler than the louse that was killed"—to the surface. His fantasy of being a great man to whom "everything is permitted" expressed a wish for complete emotional autonomy, but his actual state—having committed the sordid, sloppy murder with blood and dirt everywhere, living in isolation in a filthy cramped room—make him feel anything but great.

The dream that follows the delirium shows that his acted-out plan, with all the hatred unleashed, has not produced any sense of relief: he remains as angry as ever. Killing the split-off hated woman is useless; it intensifies guilt and helplessness, as portrayed by the mocking laughter and his ineffective actions. And there is the additional danger, one kills the innocent loving woman in the process. This is one of the rare times that Raskolnikov even thinks about his murder of Lizaveta. The delirium ends, as have related states, with his hope for a way out: a connection with Sonia, the loving woman who gives freely.

In their later interviews, Porfiry makes it increasingly plain to Raskolnikov that he knows he is the murderer. To Raskolnikov's challenge that he arrest him, Porfiry responds that he prefers to let him run loose and be done in by his own guilt. In any case, there is nowhere to run to:

Not just that he isn't going to get away from me—he has no place to get away to. *Psychologically* he won't get away from me.

Raskolnikov cannot get away with the crime, even if the police cannot prove he did it, because his guilt is within. Porfiry ends their final interview by urging that he confess, take his punishment, and go on living.

Raskolnikov reacts to Porfiry with suspicion, fear, and mounting rage. As he approaches their second meeting, he suddenly felt he was trembling and he seethed with indignation at the thought that he was terrified before the prospect of confronting the odious Porfiry Petrovich. He felt the most terrible thing of all was having to meet this man again. He hated him without measure, infinitely, and even feared he might somehow give himself away through this very hatred.

Why does Porfiry provoke such fear and rage? I think an analogy with psychoanalytic therapy is useful. Porfiry is like a crude psychoanalyst who knows the patient's secret and strips away his defenses so that the unconscious material is revealed. In one sense he is effective; his tactics break Raskolnikov down and the unconscious material, his identification with victims and feelings of inferiority, bursts forth. But it is not "insight" that the patient can use, it is too frightening, too overwhelming, and, most important, the process by which the insight was achieved feels like an attack. While Porfiry is correct in his understanding of Raskolnikov, and while he urges the course that Raskolnikov will utlimately take, Raskolnikov cannot hear or accept what he says because of the nature of the relationship and the form in which it is presented. If Raskolnikov is to confess and rejoin humanity it will be in a context of empathy and acceptance, not one of exposure and forced insight.

The Svidrigailov Dream

Raskolnikov awakens from the frightening dream in which he is trying, ineffectually, to kill the old woman:

Strange, though. The dream seemed still to be going on. His door was wide open, and a man he didn't know at all stood on the threshold and was examining him intensely.

Thus does Svidrigailov emerge out of Raskolnikov's dream, a representation of another side of his personality. Other characters in the novel can be seen as aspects of Raskolnikov—Marmeladov his masochistic side, Porfiry his accusing conscience—but Svidrigailov is the most explicit "double"; he floats into the action as if he were a part of Raskolnikov's mind. There are, of course, a number of explicit connections between them. Svidrigailov was deeply in debt and was bought out of prison by his wife who has a hold of indebtedness on him similar to the pawnbroker's (landlady's, mother's) hold on Raskolnikov. The wife's death is attributed to a beating administered by Svidrigailov and, when Raskolnikov has just dreamed of the woman he beat to death, Svidrigailov tells of being visited by his wife's ghost. Svidrigailov uses the money from his wife's estate to help the needy—he saves the Marmeladov orphans and Sonia—thus actually doing what Raskolnikov intended to do with the pawnbroker's money. They are both aware of their connection; when Svidrigailov tells of being visited by his wife's ghost, Raskolnikov comments

"Why was it I thought something like this was happening to you?" Raskolnikov said this suddenly, astonished that he said it. He was quite excited.
"You don't say? That's what you thought?" Svidrigailov asked in surprise. "Really? Well, didn't I tell you we had a certain something in common, ah?"

When Raskolnikov makes his confession to Sonia, Svidrigailov is conveniently positioned behind a door, listening. On the face of it, this seems a cumbersome plot device but, if we think of Svidrigailov as another side of Raskolnikov, as another self living in his mind, then "overhearing" the confession is less contrived. As Svidrigailov notes later, "When I said we were berries from the same field, wasn't I right?"

Many commentators on the novel have seen Svidrigailov as Raskolnikov's double and this seems to have been Dostoevsky's intention. But what, exactly, does Svidrigailov represent? Here, things become more complex. In *The Notebooks* Dostoevsky says:

Svidrigailov knows mysterious terrors about himself which he doesn't relate to anyone, but which are revealed by the facts: This is a convulsive and bestial need to tear apart and to kill, coldly passionate. Animal. Tiger.

Raskolnikov aspires to be a Bronze Man, a Napoleon whose actions are not constrained by the fears and weaknesses of those made of flesh and blood; Svidrigailov is meant to be such a creature. He is not so much immoral as he is amoral, he has no conscience, feels no guilt, all acts are of equal value—or lack of value—to him. He is rumored to have killed, we see his lust, yet he is charming and altruistic—more effectively so than the "moral" and guilt-ridden Raskolnikov.

In these ways Svidrigailov functions as a representation of impulse unchecked by morality, as a man without God. Svidrigailov's boredom, his inability to find any meaning in life, and his eventual suicide are counterposed with Raskolnikov's guilty struggle and eventual confession. The attraction to Svidrigailov represents an alternative to the confession and reunion with the moral universe that Sonia stands for.

It was either her (Sonia's) way or Svidrigailov's. At the moment especially, he was in no shape to see her. No, it was better to try Svidrigailov, wasn't it? What was he up to? Within himself he could not help realizing that he really had needed Svidrigailov for some reason for a long time.

Just as Marmeladov runs out the possibilities of dependence and masochism to their end, Svidrigailov plays out the drama of amorality and self-indulgence. This is what Dostoevsky intended, it is how many critics have viewed Svidrigailov, and it states part of the truth. Yet, more than any other character in the novel, Svidrigailov takes on a life of his own. While Dostoevsky may have originally meant him to serve only as a symbol of general amorality, he is not characterized by raw and pandemic violence. Indeed, as we learn more about him, it becomes questionable just how violent he has been: his wife may have enjoyed the few switches he gave her. Dunia, who was in the household, reports that he never beat anyone.

What, then, constitutes his immorality? Sexual depravity. As more is revealed about him, it becomes clear that Svidrigailov is a Don Juan, an expert at the seduction of women and that he has a particular sexual perversion: he is drawn to young girls.[4] It is of great interest that, of all the possible forms of criminal, illegal, and immoral activity, this specific crime is revealed at the heart of his character. It is of great interest because it can be explained by—and helps explain, in turn—the dynamics of Raskolnikov.

Svidrigailov's sexual activity expresses another version of Raskolnikov's unconscious conflicts: the need for maternal love, the hatred associated with its frustration, and the taking of revenge on women. Svidrigailov is driven by the same forces as Raskolnikov, and his fate reveals why he, like Marmeladov, is ultimately a false trail; the path he represents cannot be a solution for the underlying conflicts that he and Raskolnikov share.

Svidrigailov is all sexual license and Raskolnikov all sexual repression. Raskolnikov is young and attractive, yet at no point in the novel does he show the least sexual or romantic interest in women. His engagement to the landlady's sickly daughter and his attraction to Sonia are both devoid of sexuality—he seeks a childlike innocence in these victimized women. Such an absence of normal romantic interest—Razumikhin is, again, a healthy contrast—suggests an inhibition with a powerful unconscious source. Raskolnikov is blocked from the direct experience of sexual desire and this inhibition can be traced to the conflict between early need and rage. He is not inhibited because he feels guilty about sex per se—the sort of conflict that would arise from a later or oedipal level of development—he is cut off from sexual feeling in the same way, and for the same reasons, that he is cut off from all life-related emotions.

Svidrigailov, in contrast, seems to have no sexual inhibitions whatsoever. As a double, he expresses what is missing in Raskolnikov. But, again, his sexual depravity is not a general, amoral sinfulness: it takes a specific form. In their last long encounter this form is revealed. Svidrigailov tells of coming to Petersburg in search of women: sex is all that can give a spark of interest to his life. During the years of his marriage, he and his wife had an understanding: he had a free hand with the young servant girls as long as he confessed to her. Dunia, then governess in the house and, like Raskolnikov, "terribly chaste—to an unheard-of-degree . . . perhaps to the point of morbidity" is appalled by Svidrigailov's pursuit of the servants and attempts to reform him. Experienced Don Juan that he is, he lets her try, sensing that her heated sermons and moral passion, may lead to other forms of passion and heat. He almost succeeds in this seduction but his lust is too strong; he gives himself away and she turns on him in anger. Her rejection inflames him all the more; now he must have her.

Lest there be any doubt about his proclivity for young girls, he tells Raskolnikov of his proposed marriage to a girl not yet sixteen:

an unopened bud, and she colors, and blushes like the dawn . . . I don't know how you feel about feminine faces; I think these sixteen-year-olds, with their eyes still child like, their modesty, their sweet little tears of shyness—I think what they have is better than beauty. . . . Whenever I go there I take her on my knee at once and I don't let her down. Well she colors up like the dawn, but I keep kissing her.

To which Raskolnikov, himself drawn to young girls, but only for the most "moral" of purposes, responds, "In brief, this monstrous age difference rouses your lust."

What lies behind Svidrigailov's Don Juanism and the particular need for young girls? From what is known, clinically, about such patterns, and from what we see in the novel, the following hypothesis suggests itself. A man who engages in repeated games of seduction has experienced deprivation, frustration, rejection, or humiliation at the hands of women—most often his mother in childhood—and now turns things around. He seeks to control women sexually as his mother once controlled him emotionally, obtains the pleasure and gratification now that he was denied in the past, and takes his revenge—expresses his anger— by playing with them: by lying, seducing, and using them. But why young girls? They are children, of course, easy to manipulate, less critical, and ready to idolize an older man. But there is more that arises from the two sides of the unconscious conflict. While the seductions serve the purpose of revenge, there is also an identification with the young girls that represents the search for love. Svidrigailov would like to be a sweet and innocent young child who is taken on someone's knee and kissed. Both he and Raskolnikov respond sympathetically to deprived children; they see themselves in these poor victims and their desire to help is both genuine and a wish to provide love for the self they see in the child. Svidrigailov tells Raskolnikov, "But I love children, in general. I am very fond of children," and describes how he befriended a penniless thirteen-year-old girl and rescued her from a situation in which she was almost seduced by an older man. Action based on this identification gives some satisfaction to the need for love, but it is dangerous: when one goes too far in this direction one can feel too much the victim. There are connotations of helplessness and the anger returns. Playing the seducer is a safer course; it is a compromise in which sexual satisfaction—if not other forms of affection—is obtained and anger is expressed. Most important, the seducer remains in control, it is all a game.

But, ultimately, it is an empty game and Svidrigailov has become bored to the point of death. His attraction to Dunia has more behind it than just the urge for another conquest; what began as a game of seduction has drawn him closer to real love and, together with her rejection of him, has disrupted the smooth functioning of his Don Juanism. His confrontation with her represents a crucial turning point in his life. He has lured her into his Petersburg apartment and attempts both to seduce her and declare his love and win her affection. He tells her of

Raskolnikov's crime—now all the hidden immorality is in the open— and begs and pleads for her love:

"I love you, too, I love you incredibly. Let me kiss the hem of your dress—let me, please! I can't bear hearing it rustle. . . . I'll do anything. I'll do the impossible. Don't you know you are killing me."

The childlike side of his need for her is apparent here. Like Raskolnikov, he longs for a woman's love. But this is quickly overtaken by rage: he tries to blackmail Dunia with his knowledge of her brother's crime and then is on the verge of raping her; helpless love has turned to cold, sexual violence. She draws a revolver and fires a shot that grazes his head. He enjoys this: now love and murderous rage are all at play. He asks her to shoot again but she throws the revolver aside. He puts his arm around her, a crisis has been reached:

"Let me go" Dunia said imploringly. . . .
He asked softly . . . "You don't love me?"
Dunia shook her head in the negative.
"And, you could, never?" he whispered in despair.
"Never," Dunia whispered.

A "terrible struggle" takes place within him; he releases her and she leaves the apartment. He takes the revolver, and from that precise moment we know he will use it on himself. He has approached the genuine love of a woman, come as close as he could to breaking free of his Don Juanism. But it was not close enough and Dunia's rejection is the final note. He is condemned never to love or be loved; he has lost hope of finding the idealized woman, the "positive" to which the seduced or tricked woman is the "negative"; he is trapped in the repetitive hell of his perversion.

His final nightmares reveal, with great clarity, both his deepest needs and the failure of his perverted sexuality to satisfy them. He wanders through streets in the rain and finally comes to spend the night in a version of Raskolnikov's room, a "cell so tiny, he could hardly stand up in it," with the familiar shredded yellow wallpaper. The images are of disgust, despair, and loneliness. It is rainy and cold, it feels as if the whole city would be flooded and he dreams of vermin running over his body in the cramped and smelly room. He also dreams of a young girl only fourteen, but her life had been broken and she had destroyed herself, outraged by an offense that had horrified and appalled her childlike sensibility and infused that soul of angelic purity with a sense of undeserved shame, wrenching from her a last despairing cry that went unheard and was brazenly cursed on a dark night in the gloom, in the cold, in the damp thaw, while the wind howled.

This girl, apparently a victim of his lust, is an example of innocent love corrupted and destroyed. Then comes the final and most significant dream. He is walking in the dark corridors of the hotel and finds a girl of five "in a sopping wet dishrag of a dress, weeping and shivering." She babbles at him about her "mommy"; he gathers she is the unloved child of a drunken mother, beaten and abandoned. He picks her up, takes her to his room, removes her wet clothes, and tucks her snuggly in his warm bed. He reproaches himself for having gotten involved, but goes to look at her beneath the covers. She is blissfully asleep. But then her cheeks begin to flush, her lips look hot and burning, and she opens her eyes and looks at him provocatively. As he watches, she undergoes a transformation from an innocent, deprived little girl to a shameless voluptuary:

She was laughing, laughing openly. Something brazen and provocative radiated from that completely childlike face. It was corruption. It was a harlot's face, the brazen face of a venal French whore. . . . There was something infinitely horrible and outrageous in that laughter, in those eyes, in all the lewdness in the child's face. "What? A five-year-old?" Svidrigailov whispered in genuine horror. "Oh, you damned!"

He awakens. It is morning. He takes Dunia's revolver, leaves the room, goes out, and puts a bullet in his head.

How does this final dream help us understand the meaning of Svidrigailov? As in Raskolnikov's dream of the suffering horse, we must keep in mind that the different characters all symbolize aspects of the dreamer. Svidrigailov feels like a deprived and abandoned little child—Dunia's final rejection has confirmed this—and his deepest wish is to receive the sort of love and care that he first gives to his little girl–self in the dream. He rescues this victim from a bad mother and gives her loving maternal attention. Seeing her/himself turn into a whore shows him the other side of himself. He has spent his life seducing young girls and chasing whores, keeping away from his deep desire to receive the love a mother can give to an infant. The dream confronts him with the perverted solution to his deprivation and longing, a confrontation that leaves him disgusted and ashamed. In other words, dreaming of himself as a little girl—whore symbolizes his self-defilement, her mocking laughter represents his own cynical, self-mocking side. Taken together with the failure of his final effort to obtain a woman's love, he is left without hope; only suicide remains.

The possibilities symbolized by Svidrigailov have been played out to their end. The "dream" has run its course and Raskolnikov wanders back on stage:

His clothes were in terrible shape, dirty and shredded and torn from a whole night spent out in the rain. . . . He had spent the whole night alone. God knew where. But at least he had made up his mind.

The path of Svidrigailov has led to death, Raskolnikov is now left with the road that has beckoned him for so long, and which he has been so reluctant to follow: that represented by Sonia.

Sonia: Rebirth

The figure of Sonia, an innocent young woman forced into a life of shame by the troubles in her family, has captured Raskolnikov's attention from very early in the novel. He hears about her before the murders, during his first encounter with Marmeladov. From the beginning, there is something about her childlike nature and position as a victim that draws him; he imagines her as a solution to his terrible dilemma. Though she exists in his consciousness from very early, he circles warily around, repeatedly testing her. Sonia passes all tests, her love and acceptance are steadfast, she is a saint. Indeed, her saintliness makes her quite unreal as a character and has posed a problem for critics. Dostoevsky was clearly capable of creating characters of full-bodied reality, why did he make Sonia one-sided to the point of artificiality? We know from *The Notebooks* that he deliberately modified her in this direction; in earlier drafts there were suggestions of romance and she was capable of anger, he had her quarreling with Dunia, for example. There is none of this in the final version, no hint of romance or sexuality. Sonia's response to all provocations is resignation, sympathy for the other, and understanding.

Sonia is so saintly, so one-sided, because this is precisely what Raskolnikov needs. She offers him a way out of the isolated state in which he is precariously balanced between the need for love and rage. Dostoevsky has created the fantasy of a perfect therapist for a person like Raskolnikov. Sonia is a mirror for him, he sees his victimized child-self in her. But she is a mirror that reflects the possibility of a different self, a way other than the angry-guilty path he is on. In the end, Raskolnikov goes over to Sonia's way, he accepts the suffering he has endured and moves past his prideful rage. Having accepted it, he is capable of love, a love not fouled with indebtedness, anger, and guilt.

We must remember that Raskolnikov's reactions to women are dominated by splitting, he feels them to be all bad or all good, all withholding or all giving, all hateful or all loving. He sees Sonia, initially, as the idealized female figure. She "gives everything away," her love is free, and, contrasted to such "bad mothers" as the pawnbroker, Katherine Marmeladov, and his actual mother, she never responds in a way that makes him feel guilty. He tests her again and again on this issue, most importantly by confessing to the murder of Lizaveta; he must be absolutely certain that she won't make him feel the rageful indebtedness that has pervaded his relations with the other women in his life.

Raskolnikov's first sustained contact with Sonia occurs when she comes to invite him to her father's funeral. His mother and Dunia are there and the whole Luzhin affair has just been aired, with all its machinations and deviousness. Sonia appears as a stark contrast:

He saw a modestly, rather shabbily dressed girl, quite young, still childlike, modest and attractive in manner, with a bright but somewhat cowed face. . . . He suddenly realized that this downtrodden creature was downtrodden to such a degree that he felt sorry for her. She made a frightened move to run away, and something inside him seemed to heave.

Immediately, we see his visceral identification with her fear and downtrodden position. Her childlike innocence also strikes him: "Although she was eighteen, she still seemed like a little girl much younger than her years, almost a child."

She has only come to deliver a message, but Raskolnikov insists on seating her—a prostitute—next to his respectable mother and sister, an incident that Luzhin later tries to use against him. Throughout this meeting, the contrast between Sonia on the one hand and his mother,

Dunia, and Luzhin on the other is apparent. Sonia is the "criminal," the shameful and degraded one, yet her shame seems like humility. She is modest and possesses the innocence of childhood. The others, outwardly respectable, are scheming, exploitative, and dishonest. Raskolnikov is drawn to Sonia for this reason, as well as by his identification with her pain and unhappiness.

They meet next when Raskolnikov goes to her room. He has chosen her as the one to hear his confession but, during this visit, he must first test her reactions. Her room, like his, is small, poor, and dirty with the same shabby yellow wallpaper. He begins by interrogating her about Katherine, her stepmother. Didn't she beat you, he asks? expecting her to feel anger as he would in her situation. Sonia says no, she loves Katherine, feels sympathy for her, and understands why this unfortunate woman has mistreated her.

"A kind of *insatiable* compassion, if one may put it that way, suddenly etched itself into all the lines of her face." Though they are in the same position vis-à-vis their mothers, Sonia's reaction is the opposite of his. He can find no anger in her.

He next attempts to try her faith: Katherine will die, Sonia cannot make enough money as a prostitute, the younger children will be forced on the streets. "God will not permit such a horror!" she cries. "He permits others. . . . Maybe there's no God at all," Raskolnikov counters. She holds firm and he backs away from his attack: he falls to the floor, kisses her foot, says he is bowing down to "all of suffering humanity" and calls her a "holy fool." His mood shifts again, he berates her for accepting her shame and degradation and asks why she hasn't killed herself. It is clear in all this that he sees himself in Sonia; the struggle he projects onto her is his own. While upset by his attack, her faith does not waver.

Raskolnikov then picks up a Bible—it is Lizaveta's significantly— and asks Sonia to read the story of Lazarus. The symbolism here is obvious, he is asking her to lead him out of his dead existence; he will be reborn, as Lazarus was, in her love and faith. He tells her he has abandoned his family, that she is all he has, that they must be together; he becomes carried away in his identification with her.

"Haven't you done the same? You, too, have transgressed, you found within yourself you were able to transgress. You laid hands on yourself, you took a life, *your own*—what's the difference! . . . If you're *alone,* you'll go out of your mind, like me. You behave as though you're mad already, so we have to go the same way together. Let's go!"

Sonia doesn't feel all this, though she merely answers "Why? Why are you like this?" and, "what can be done?" Raskolnikov swings back again and talks of smashing things and gaining power and then takes his leave, vowing to return and tell her who killed Lizaveta. Despite his hints she still does not suspect him; her reaction: "How terribly unhappy he must be."

The connection between Sonia and Lizaveta has been established in these passages; they are both "holy fools," they give everything away, they have the same childlike faith and trust. It is significant that Raskolnikov says he will tell her who killed Lizaveta, rather than the pawnbroker, Aliona. He is going to reveal his murderous attack on a version of her; this will be the ultimate test of her love and capacity to accept him.

He approaches his confession with a jumble of contradictory feelings: he is terribly excited, he will *"have to tell her,"* yet he foresees "his own terrible anguish." And then he feels "helpless and afraid" and wonders, "Do I need to tell who killed Lizaveta?" He begins by again trying to provoke her anger. They are fresh from the incident in which Luzhin falsely accused Sonia of stealing, and Raskolnikov asks her if she doesn't think Luzhin should be done away with. He is posing the question to which his theory leads, the theory that rationalized the killing of the pawnbroker. In other words, he is asking Sonia if she, too, doesn't feel the world should be rid of such unscrupulous villains. She responds,

"Why do you ask what shouldn't be asked? Why these empty questions? How could it ever depend on my decision? And whoever made me judge of who was to live and who not to live?"

She will not play the angry avenger, even as a game. He feels a flare-up of "bitter hatred" for her, looks, sees the love in her gaze, and the "hatred disappeared like a phantom." Now he must confess and he hints more and more directly who the murderer is:

"I must be a great friend of *his,* since I know," Raskolnikov said, looking steadily at her face, as though he no longer had the power to take his eyes away. "He didn't want to kill this Lizaveta. He killed her accidentally. He wanted to kill the old woman, when she was alone, and he came, and then Lizaveta came in, and he was there, and he killed her. . . . can't you guess?" "N-no" Sonia whispered. . . . "Take a good look." As soon as he said it another old, familiar sensation suddenly turned his soul to ice: he looked at her, and suddenly he seemed to see in her face the face of Lizaveta.

What we see is not just the confession of the murder but the overcoming of Raskolnikov's splitting; he is confronting a version of the idealized woman with his murderous deed. The dread he feels is what the splitting has served to protect him from, what the child must feel when it wants to kill the very mother whose love its life depends on.

Sonia's reaction is crucial, of course. She takes his hand and looks him in the eyes.

"Enough, Sonia! Don't torture me!" he begged. . . .

"Why, why did you take this upon yourself!" she said in despair. Rising from her knees, she threw her arms around his neck and hugged him very tight. . . .

"How strange you are, Sonia. Embracing me and kissing me after I've told you *about that.*"

"No, no, there is nobody, there is nobody anywhere in the world now unhappier than you!" . . . A feeling he had not known for a long time surged into his soul and softened it at once. He did not resist. Two tears started from his lashes. He said almost with hope as he looked at her: "then you won't leave me, Sonia?"

The splitting has been bridged, rage and his need for love have been brought together in one relationship, his primitive fear of desertion confronted—"you won't leave me?"—Sonia has responded with acceptance, empathy for his pain, and physical affection.

His confession and her loving acceptance mark the turning point for Raskolnikov. He is not reborn on the spot, there will be more testing, but he has taken a significant new direction. Immediately after the confession, Raskolnikov swings back to pride and anger. He runs through a variety of reasons and explanations for the crime but Sonia does not get caught up in any of these intellectualized justifications. Her reactions: "You're in pain, aren't you?"; "It's better I should know—much better!"; and "Talk, go on, talk! I'll understand, I'll understand it all *inside!*" Her final message: he must admit to the world he has killed, bow down and kiss the earth he has defiled, and then God will send him life again. He leaves, the Svidrigailov drama is played out, and he comes to her a final time before turning himself in.

In this visit, before Raskolnikov makes his public confession, Sonia's love and the trust he feels for her have the upper hand, though his other reactions are still active. He can even recognize the sadism that he directs toward her:

"Do I love her? Surely I don't? I drove her away like a dog just now. . . . What I wanted was her tears; I wanted to watch her fear; I wanted to see her aching, suffering heart! I had to have something to hang on to, a chance to linger and watch a human being suffer! . . . What a beggar I am, what a nobody! How vile, vile!"

This is an accurate insight, yet the guilt does not disrupt their connection. Sonia takes two crosses, hers and Lizaveta's, and they each put one on. "She's going to be my nursemaid," he thinks. And then, still hesitantly, he goes to kiss the earth and confess to the police.

Raskolnikov's rebirth—has final emergence from isolation—does not occur until he has been in prison for some time. Sonia has accompanied him to Siberia, lives nearby, and visits him whenever possible. In the prison camp, Raskolnikov, both literally and symbolically, lets himself drift toward death. He avoids the other prisoners, and they come to dislike him. Their response to Sonia makes a sharp contrast; they recognize her gentle, loving nature and greet her with "You're our tender, aching mother!" Raskolnikov is silent for days on end, eats little, and finally becomes quite sick.

During his illness he has a final dream. In it the whole world suffers a plague, everyone except a handful of the chosen are doomed to die. The plague is caused by a new germ that infects the soul as well as the body. Its effects, interestingly enough, are unconscious: those infected consider themselves clever, scientifically correct, and above the morality of others. This is the madness caused by these germs of the mind, by these destructive ideas. Once infected, each man believes in his own truth, no one understands anyone else, war, chaos, and senseless rage overtake the world, and civilization breaks down in an orgy of self-centered destructiveness.

The dream is a commentary on the ideology behind Raskolnikov's crime; it shows him where he will end if he continues in his withdrawn state, nursing his anger and grievances, trying to exist without human contact. The dream foreshadows the end of this path. That self, and everything associated with it, has run its course; the way is finally open to a new mode of life. Sonia does not visit him for a while and he realizes how much he misses her. He begins to see nature and the people around him in new ways, and he lets feelings of hope enter his soul. Sonia returns, and he finally experiences the full force of their love for each other:

Tears came. They were both pale and thin; yet in those pale, sickly faces there already glowed the light of the renewed future, resurrection to a new life. Love resurrected them; the heart of one contained infinite sources of life for the heart of the other. . . . He knew that he was born again. . . . He could not think very long or steadily about anything that evening or focus his mind on anything; nor did he come to any conscious decision; he had merely become aware. Life replaced logic, and in his consciousness something quite different now had to elaborate and articulate itself.

CHAPTER 4

Associations to the Novel
and the "Scene"

A sound psychoanalytic interpretation of a dream rests on the dreamer's associations. Wouldn't it be nice if we could ask Dostoevsky himself for his associations to the many elements in *Crime and Punishment?* Where did he get the names for his characters, the repeated image of the cramped room with dirty yellow wallpaper, the idea of a self-destructive alcoholic husband (Marmeladov), the suffering horse? While we cannot ask him, we can treat the material that is available—*The Notebooks,* ideas expressed in his correspondence, information about his childhood, and recurring themes and images in the other novels—as if they all were associations. To put it another way: the analysis of *Crime and Punishment* in the last chapter is based entirely on the novel itself: here, this analysis can be confirmed by bringing in these "associations," the surrounding material.

A central interpretation is that Dostoevsky expresses his conflicts toward women through a series of female pairs—the pawnbroker and Lizaveta, Raskolnikov's mother and Dunia, Katherine Marmeladov and Sonia, the landlady and her maid, Martha and the young girls of Svidrigailov's dreams—who represent two sides of his ambivalence. One is the depriving, hated and the other the giving, loved mother figure. How do these characters link up with his own life? Katherine Marmeladov is modeled fairly directly on his first wife, Maria. She represents the angry-guilty connection with a sick and dying woman: Katherine's half-mad state in the final stages of her tuberculosis is drawn directly from Dostoevsky's observations of Maria. Since, as we have already seen, the marriage was an unconscious reenactment of Dostoevsky's relation with the first Maria, his mother, this extends the link back into childhood.

There are additional associations along this path: Maria's first husband, the man she was with when Dostoevsky met her in Siberia, was an alcoholic who drank himself to death. Dostoevsky's own father turned to heavy drinking after his wife's death; drunkenness played a role in his murder by his serfs. In the article in which he recounts the horse and courier memory, Dostoevsky gives, as an example of the internalization of cruelty, the way beaten-down husbands turn to drink and abuse their wives and children. An early plan for *Crime and Punishment* was called *The Drunkards,* it was to have been an exposé of alcoholism. All these associative lines eventually found expression in the Marmeladov subplot of the novel. Marmeladov is the alcoholic who passes cruelty down the line, not by beating his wife, but with more complex masochistic aggression.

Many commentators on *Crime and Punishment* have called attention to the symbolic meaning of the character's names. Dostoevsky, like Dickens before him, had fun with this literary device.[1] Raskolnikov comes from the Russian *raskolnik* meaning *schism* or *religious schizmatic*. It is appropriate, I think, both in terms of the splits in his personality, and his separation from God and Christian morality. The name of his sensible and down-to-earth friend, Dimitry Razumikhin, comes from *razum,* meaning *good sense, intellect,* and *Demeter,* which suggests the earth. Marmeladov is from the Russian *marmelad, marmelade, jam*—an appropriate enough title for his wobbly character.

Other names have more personal associations. I think it particularly significant that Dostoevsky gave the name Aliona to the old pawnbroker. While the deaths of several of the other women in the novel are brought about by indirect means, she is the object of a violent attack: she is the depriving, guilt-inducing mother figure in pure form. Why did this name come to him when he created her?

It was a name he knew well throughout his childhood: Aliona Frolovna was the family nurse. She came to the Dostoevskys when Varvara, the sister born after Feodor, was an infant, and was still on hand, caring for the youngest siblings, at the time of the father's death. Dostoevsky was originally nursed by a peasant woman whose name is unknown, a wet nurse who was brought from the countryside for that purpose and then sent away. From the point of view of the infant Feodor, this woman who nursed him was his mother and weaning was accompanied by an actual loss. He then had his own mother, Maria, only to lose her to Varvara, the first of many sibling replacements. Aliona then joined the family and shared caretaking with Maria for the remainder of his childhood years. I spell out these details to make clear that Dostoevsky experienced a series of losses early on in the sphere of maternal care. The pattern of multiple mothers also shows that his predisposition to splitting does not just stem from the good and bad aspects of one mother, but has a background in reality.

It would be convenient for the present interpretation if the real Aliona, like her namesake in *Crime and Punishment,* was a cruel and depriving woman. But, what evidence is available (see Coulson 1962, 3–5) suggests a more complicated picture. She was very tall—like Lizaveta—with an immense appetite and an equally immense belly. She was not a serf but a Moscow townswoman who, like Katherine Marmeladov, found it necessary to stress her higher status in relation to the other servants and wet nurses.

Dostoevsky seems to have felt affection for this alternate mother, judging by comments he made in later years. Grossman reports that he "often recalled his own nanny, a Moscow girl, an 'unassuming woman,' amazingly noble in spirit, hired from among the petite bourgeoisie, who with dignity called herself 'citizenness'!"

Dostoevsky speaks of her in a letter to his mother, written when he was fourteen: "I am so sorry for Aliona Frolovna she suffers so much poor thing, soon she will waste away to nothing from the consumption she has caught."

Aliona was still living three years later so her consumption was probably just a cough, but Maria did, in fact, come down with tuberculosis at about this time. It was she who wasted away to nothing before the eyes of her grieving son, as his wife did many years later.

To sum up, there were various features associated with the real Aliona that led Dostoevsky to use her name for that figure in the novel who personifies the negative side of his maternal ambivalence. She was one of his two principal mothers and was tied to those aspects of his real mother that most aroused his helpless rage and guilt: tuberculosis and loss. In fact, the final loss of both these women occurred at the same time. Since she was a servant and the subject of his father's cruelty, she was a more acceptable target for aggression than Maria who—especially after her early death—was idealized by everyone. In addition, she seems to have been a living caricature of deprivation and oral greed, with her "wasting away" and huge stomach, words and sights that make strong impressions on young children.

While Aliona came to symbolize the hated mother in *Crime and Punishment,* the name Maria or Mary was a natural symbol for the idealized, loving mother. The Dostoevsky family were believing Christians and the young Feodor had a good deal of exposure to pictures of Christ and the Virgin Mary. The relationship between the biblical Mary and her perfectly loving son—as Dostoevsky imaged him—became an abiding ideal, a goal he strove for to the end of his life, as an analysis of the later novels will reveal. His daughter reports that he always kept a print of Raphael's *Madonna and Child* on his writing table.

As we have seen, *Crime and Punishment* presents an intense struggle with both sides of the maternal ambivalence. There is a major resolution in the novel, though versions of the conflict continue in other works. In *The Possessed,* Fedya—Dostoevsky's nickname as a child—murders Maria; who is a Lizaveta-figure, a loving, simple, woman.

It is intriguing to trace these associative links, but it can also lead to overinterpretation. Let us return to the horse and courier, an image connected with the rage and guilt that stand at the heart of *Crime and Punishment.*

As we saw in the Prologue, Dostoevsky places his memory of the horse and courier scene on the journey from Moscow that began just a few months after his mother's death. The departure for school marked the abrupt end of his childhood and the loss of the home in which he and his brothers and sisters grew up. Within two years his father would be dead—he never saw him again after he went to the academy—and the younger children dispersed among various relatives. Father was scheduled to take his two oldest sons to Petersburg, shortly after the mother's death, but the journey was delayed when Feodor developed a "mysterious illness . . . a throat or chest ailment whose diagnosis was uncertain." Dostoevsky's younger brother, Andrey, later wrote that, from the time of their mother's death and the strange illness, Feodor's voice always retained "a curious throaty quality which never appeared quite normal."

Dostoevsky himself does not mention his mother's death in relation to the horse-courier memory—nor anywhere else in his writing or correspondence as far as we know—though he does make much of his mourning for Pushkin. It is my view that his idealized love for his mother was displaced onto Pushkin, whose death coincided with hers. This would explain why, of all writers, he idolized Pushkin to the end of his life. Pushkin was a great poet; he stands at the beginning of the masterful literature of nineteenth century Russia and many later authors felt a strong allegiance to him. Dostoevsky drew both inspiration and specific content from his work. (See, for example, the dream scene in Pushkin's *The Captain's Daughter* as a predecessor of the horse-beating dream.) Yet, while Dostoevsky was a discerning critic of most other authors— including those such as Gogol whom he admired—his praise of Pushkin seems one-sided, suggesting a leftover idealization. (See the speech he gave in 1880 at the unveiling of the Pushkin monument in *The Diary of a Writer*.)

Dostoevsky's mother's death had a profound impact on him and the emotions and images related to it were active when the horse-courier scene so impressed itself in his mind. What additional evidence suggests that this might be so? First, the death of a young mother is likely to have a strong impact on any fifteen-year-old. This was particularly so in this family where the father was the demanding authority and the mother the main source of affection. Her death marked the loss of the primary loving figure in his life. Yet, while outwardly idealizing her, there is much that indicates his powerful ambivalence: strong longings for her love, frustration over not obtaining enough, and a great deal of unconscious anger and guilt. All of these emotions would have been activated by her death; a prime indication is his throat and chest ailment, which sounds like an unconscious identification with his dying mother's tuberculosis. That is, it is an instance of how she was symbolically kept alive within him in an attempt to block the pain of loss and also punish him for his anger. Much is suggested by this somatic reaction to her death, including his capacity to experience external relationships vividly as if they were other selves, living within him.

The throat and chest symptom is not the only evidence that ties the horse-courier memory to the mixture of love, anger, and guilt stimulated by his mother's death. There is abundant material from the relationships with women later in his life, along with the way women are depicted in his fiction, in which these same emotions are played out. The analysis of *Crime and Punishment* has shown how Raskolnikov is driven by a powerful mixture of love and rage. The violence that breaks through so clearly in the horse-beating dream is the underside of Dostoevsky's feeling for his mother, the rage and frustration aroused by her illness and death. At the same time, the dream captures his horror at this feeling, his love for her, and his identification, the way he must also suffer her fate.

While fathers have almost no place in *Crime and Punishment,* they do in Dostoevsky's other novels. His father played an important role in his actual development and a complete account of the horse-courier memory must include some comments on their relationship. At the time he witnessed the scene, he was being taken to the Academy of Military Engineering by his father, to be forced into a career that was completely foreign to his own interests, talents, and sympathies. The father, a former military physician, was by all accounts a most difficult man. Within his family he was moody and irritable, jealous and begrudging of his wife's time and affection, rigid and demanding with his sons. He never beat them physically, as far as we know, but did subject them to a great deal of verbal abuse and criticism. Like the mother in *Crime and Punishment,* the pawnbroker, Luzhin, and other hateful figures, Dostoevsky's father was a great inducer of guilt; he never tired of letting his children know how much he suffered on their behalf. From early in their lives, the Dostoevsky boys were subjected to strict academic demands; they had to learn Latin, geometry, memorize long passages, and perform for their father, and small mistakes brought forth his rage and insults. Of course, they were not allowed to react openly to this treatment; he was the authority and demanded obedience and respect. The placement in the academy was the culmination of their father's control of their education; he had decided, largely on the basis of his own insecurity about money and status, that military engineering was safe and profitable, and, with his characteristic lack of understanding of his sons' interests, was forcing this career upon them.

It is reasonable to assume that these emotional currents concerning his father were active on the trip to Petersburg and played their part in Dostoevsky's reaction to the horse and courier scene. He was being abused and insulted psychologically and could do nothing about it. He was filled with anger that he could not directly express at the authority who was running his life, as the courier ran his driver, and this reinforced his identification with the scene.

Dostoevsky's reaction to the scene illustrates several important aspects of his personal style. There is the capacity for powerful identifications, the way in which he experiences his own conflicts and feelings in and through the people and events around him. These identifications are multifaceted: he feels himself to be both horse and courier, victim and oppressor, as well as, and perhaps most, the driver, the one in the middle who is "insulted," knows what it means to suffer, yet cannot help passing the hurt down the line. We have seen this clearly in Raskolnikov's vacillation between sympathy for victimized women and the urge to attack them, and it is an abiding theme throughout Dostoevsky's fiction. An additional feature of his style is the way in which personal reactions are generalized into broad themes: social, national, even universal. He responds to the scene not only with his own feelings—which may have been too painful to think about directly—but also in terms of the Russian people. Both the capacity for identification and the universalization of the personal, in evidence at age fifteen, were to prove important when he later took up literature as the primary means of expressing his ideas and feelings.

Now, let us return to the associations that surround the horse and courier line in *The Notebooks for "Crime and Punishment."* Here is the complete passage:

First Part: Beginning
Boulevard. Young Girl.
My first personal insult, the horse, the courier.
Violation of a child.
Why does that old woman, who has outlived life, continue to live?
Mathematics.

He came home: letter from his mother. He loses his temper with the landlady because of the soup.

Having explored the horse-courier association in some detail, let us look at the others.

Boulevard. Young Girl.   This refers to a scene, early in the novel, set between the letter from Raskolnikov's mother and the horse-beating dream. He encounters a drunken young woman on the boulevard, being followed by a well-dressed, older man—a "Svidrigailov," as he calls him —intent on sexually accosting her. Raskolnikov connects her with his sister, for mother's letter has just informed him of the attempted seduction in the Svidrigailov household and the plan to prostitute Dunia by marrying her to Luzhin. At first, he intervenes and attempts to save the young girl on the boulevard. Then his feelings turn and he leaves her to a fate that he thinks she deserves. This little vignette nicely captures the two sides of his feeling: his identification with and wish to help the victimized woman, and his anger and identification with the attacker. He will, much later in the novel, try "Svidrigailov's way." This same pattern is played out much more fully in the relationship with Sonia, of course.

Violation of a Child.   This is a central preoccupation of Dostoevsky's; one that runs throughout the major novels. In *Crime and Punishment,* the young woman on the boulevard is "only a kid" as is, more centrally, Sonia. Svidrigailov's final nightmares chronicle his sexual violations of young girls, and the Marmeladov children, victims of their father's alcoholism and their mother's illness and instability, are clear child victim figures. Most important, I think, is Raskolnikov himself, who feels like a violated child; this is the source of his—and Dostoevsky's— primary identification with those who are victimized. My guess is that, at the time of the horse-courier scene, Dostoevsky's anger at his mother was projected into his father. It would be easy to see him—he was eleven years older than his wife—as her exploiter since he was irritable and demanding and this could have deflected awareness of Feodor's own anger at her. His own feeling of victimization was displaced onto his younger siblings. As his correspondence with Mikhail makes clear: they, not he, are seen as the poor orphans who will have a hard time in the world. The image of a violated child, most often a young girl subject to sexual abuse, occurs again and again in Dostoevsky's novels, most strikingly in the banned chapter of *The Possessed* (Stavrogin's confession). A fuller exploration of its origin and meaning will be presented later when more evidence is at hand.

Why Does that Old Woman, Who Has Outlived Life, Continue to Live? This is a direct reference to both the source of Raskolnikov's rage and his rationale for killing the pawnbroker. She is depicted, through his eyes, as a worthless creature, she has nothing to "give"; like the nag in the dream, she is useless and has outlived life. Katherine Marmeladov is also a useless mother and, as she dies of tuberculosis, her final words are "They've overstrained the old nag." Naming the pawnbroker Aliona is not the only way Dostoevsky links her with the actual women in his life. At the time of his wife and Mikhail's deaths, when he was desperately trying to raise money to keep *The Epoch* afloat, he was forced to ask for money from his Aunt Kumanin, an old woman who controlled a fortune. Like the pawnbroker in the novel, she planned to give her money to a monastery so that prayers would be said for her soul while, in Dostoevsky's eyes, Mikhail's poor orphans were in need. The Kumanins, his mother's relatives, had become substitute parents for the younger Dostoevsky children after their mother and father died so that, both literally and symbolically, this "old woman" controlled the supplies that the children needed. Aunt Kumanin "lent" him ten thousand rubles, as she had Mikhail a short time before, loans that were never expected to be repaid. She may have seemed an ungiving old nag but, in reality, she gave when asked. This connects with the other side of the maternal image, realized in the novel through the series of open and giving women: Aliona's half sister Lizaveta, the landlady's maid, Nastasia, and Sonia, counterposed with her stepmother, Katherine Marmeladov.

Mathematics. Two lines branch out from this association. It refers, as do related comments in *The Notebooks,* to Raskolnikov's logical, intellectual preoccupations, his belief that his plan will succeed. A central feature of the novel, of course, is Dostoevsky's demonstration of the undoing of this rational plan by emotion and unconscious need. Raskolnikov's schemes and reasons are, again and again, revealed as covers for the underlying feelings that drive him. The second theme—rebellion against paternal authority—is not pursued in *Crime and Punishment,* though it finds ample expression in other novels. Many of Dostoevsky's interactions with his father, during the period before the father's murder, centered on guilt-related requests for money. His father espoused the careful, stingy, and rational control of funds, while his artist-son could never seem to manage his finances. The one course that Dostoevsky flunked during his first year at the academy was algebra and his father responded to the news of this failure with "a stroke." Money, numbers, mathematics, and rational schemes for living all aroused Dostoevsky's active disidentification with his father's values and this theme, universalized, is connected with his furious opposition to Positivists, utopians, and others who advocated a rationally planned or controlled society.

He Came Home: Letter from His Mother. He Loses His Temper with the Landlady because of the Soup. This association ties several strands together. "Letter from his mother" refers, of course, to the letter in the novel that makes Raskolnikov suffer with tormenting rage and guilt. The mother and landlady-as-mother-figure are directly linked here and the idea of bad feeding referred to. In the novel, Raskolnikov does not "lose his temper with the landlady because of the soup," but he does live in her house in a state of anger over bad feeding or, more precisely, over the way what is needed—food, money, acceptance, and love—is given in a manner to arouse a sense of indebtedness. Raskolnikov's psychological state throughout the novel is one of rageful guilty deprivation, and it is significant, I think, that he never shows any sexual interest in women: in his eyes they are sources of supply.

At this point, the pathways and associations have become so complicated that the reader may have lost his way, though such complications are typical of both Dostoevsky's life and his fiction. Let me attempt to summarize. Dostoevsky's relationship with his mother left him with intense and contradictory emotions: a great longing for love, much frustration, rage, and guilt. Consciously, he idealized her, the anger and guilt were experienced in split-off forms: in fantasy or displaced onto scenes and other people. His mother's death heightened all sides of his feelings. Here was the final blow to his hopes as well as an enactment, in reality, of his rage. His vivid response to the actual horse-courier scene at age fifteen derived from these emotional currents as he identified with both victim and aggressor.

While this theme finds some expression in the early novels, it was largely dormant in his life until after his release from prison. It was then that he experienced his first great romantic passion, his love for Maria Isaeva, which proved to be an unconscious reenactment of the relation with his mother. Maria became the idealized loving woman he longed for and, initially, he contrived to overlook the many ways she did not fit this image. The actual marriage and, ultimately, her illness and death, undid the splitting. He was, once more, faced with his own disappointed hopes, rage, and guilt.

But he was, by this time in his life, a novelist of great skill; he was able to take all these conflicts and feelings and work them through in his writing. *Crime and Punishment* is like a laboratory in which many different relationships with women are explored. Katherine Marmeladov plays out the possibilities of a sadomasochistic attachment to a tubercular woman, just as his first marriage did. The murder of Aliona enacts the full rage at the hated depriving mother. The "accidental" killing of Lizaveta shows that one cannot kill the hated woman without destroying the loving woman at the same time. Like Dostoevsky's actual mother, Lizaveta is described as "always pregnant," a nice touch that brings in one of the central sources of Dostoevsky's rage. And Raskolnikov's rebirth with Sonia displays the need for the perfectly loving, accepting woman. Just as Katherine Marmeladov resembled his first wife, there are parallels between Sonia and Anna Snitkina, the woman he married shortly after finishing this novel.

The interpretation of *Crime and Punishment* to this point has been so focused on the theme of maternal ambivalence that I fear the reader may see it as old-fashioned psychoanalytic reductionism. That is, it may seem as if I were implying that this multilayered novel were *nothing but* an expression of Dostoevsky's unconscious "mother complex," whatever that might mean. Several points need to be made in clarification. First, while the novel contains many other themes, psychologically it *is* centered on the theme of maternal ambivalence; it is one of the most focused of Dostoevsky's books. My guess is that this results from its position at the most "regressed" point in his self-exploration. There is a resolution in the writing of this novel and a parallel resolution in his life. Ambivalence toward women—or even hatred culminating in murder—does not disappear in the works that follow, but none of the later novels are characterized by the atmosphere of deprivation, rage, and guilt that pervades *Crime and Punishment*. The feeling for women moves to an adult sexual level and a wider array of conflicts and relationships are explored in later works.

Second, the writing of *Crime and Punishment,* far from being unconscious, represents a process of developing awareness; it is not a dream, but a dream analyzed. In the course of the novel, Dostoevsky shows the full consequences of giving way to hatred and rage; he exposes idealizations and undoes splits. And, finally, it is hardly a case of nothing-but-a-mother-complex. The conflicts explored in the novel are those found, to one degree or another, in all relations of love and intimacy, whether between children and their mothers, men and women, or any of their many variants. One reason for the wide and lasting appeal of *Crime and Punishment* is Dostoevsky's treatment of the theme in a way that is both highly individualized—his own life transformed into Raskolnikov-Marmeladov-Svidrigailov—and universal. Readers with backgrounds very far from nineteenth-century Russia are drawn into the emotional world of the book because of the direct connection with their own experience.

Dostoevsky was a man of many parts; he had the capacity to form relationships on many levels. He lived in a male autocracy and suffered both the cruelty and beneficence of the tsar. His father was much involved with his upbringing and exerted a complex influence on his character. Of great importance were the "brothers" in his life: Mikhail and a series of male friends who shared his intellectual and artistic interests. It is no accident that the novel many consider his greatest is *The Brothers Karamazov.* He felt much love for his younger sisters. It is time now to move on from the maternal world that so colors *Crime and Punishment* and explore this wider human network.

CHAPTER 5

The Dostoevsky Family

Many authors of conventional biographies idealize the parents of their subjects; it must seem like bad form to say anything negative about the families of famous men and women. In addition, much of the evidence that the biographer relies on comes from earlier historical periods when an uncritical acceptance of parental authority was widespread, reinforcing this tendency. At the other extreme are those early psychoanalytic biographies, which focused on pathology. Psychoanalysis had its origins in work with disturbed individuals and its language is overweighted with descriptions of symptoms, traumas, fixations, perversions, and neuroses. At its worst, this distorts the individuality of the artist by forcing him into some general pathological category. Analytic experience has demonstrated the great formative importance of the childhood years, but this needs to be carefully spelled out in a way that does not conflate creative artists with neurotics, a way that does justice to the unique individual.

Dostoevsky's life and art abound with health and disturbance, with strengths and symptoms. We should expect to find the roots of all these in his family. He had a solid core to his sense of identity as a writer, an identity that was not derailed by the innumerable obstacles that life threw in his path. He was enormously productive, often under very difficult circumstances; he survived severe traumas—deaths, losses, and imprisonment—that crushed many lesser souls. He had a capacity to love, great generosity, and continued to grow and develop throughout his life, both as an artist and as a man. At the same time, he was plagued by fears, insecurities, petty prejudices, and anxieties. He came close to a nervous breakdown in his twenties, was for some years a compulsive gambler, could fall into an epileptic seizure in the most unlikely circumstances, and had difficulty getting along with many people. There was something of Raskolnikov, Svidrigailov, and the Underground Man in him, along with Prince Myshkin and Alyosha Karamazov.

An account of the family must show the origins of all sides of Dostoevsky's character, his strengths and disturbance. The fact that his family was not simply a breeding ground for pathology is evidenced by the lives of his brothers and sisters: they turned out, for the most part, to be healthy and productive individuals. It will be a test of our skill at avoiding idealizations and projections—at not taking the easy road of splitting—if an account of the family can be constructed that is true to the many sides of his complex personality.

A word about evidence: how do we know what went on in the family during Dostoevsky's childhood? This is a more complex question than at first appears; it goes to the heart of the difference between the conventional and psychoanalytic approaches to biography. Dostoevsky himself gave almost no direct account of his childhood and family years. In *The Diary of a Writer,* or in correspondence and conversation—with both relatives and friends—he rarely mentioned his parents. On those occasions when he referred to his mother, it was with the same overly idealized terms that he used for the Russian people. Evidence about the family consists of a few letters between the parents and some bits of historical material, but the main source, relied on by all the biographers, is the *Reminiscences* of Feodor's younger brother Andrey.[1]

Andrey was fifty years old when he first wrote out the recollections of his childhood and, clearly, the long gap in time leaves much room for distortion of memory. He was three and a half years younger than Feodor and, as his later life and reminiscences reveal, a very different sort of person. He became a civil engineer, raised a family, and seems a pleasant if somewhat ordinary fellow. All this is to say that his memories of the family—the way he experienced it—were no doubt different from the way similar events impressed themselves on his volatile and imaginative older brother. With all these cautions, some of Andrey's descriptions still have the ring of truth. This is especially so when they are consistent with what I consider our most reliable source of information about the family: Dostoevsky's novels.

As must be clear by now, my position is that Dostoevsky's fiction is a literary transformation of his personal experience. Not every old woman in every novel represents his mother; not every male authority his father; but repeated patterns and themes show the way his early life was encoded in the form of emotion-laden memories and images. In this sense, *Crime and Punishment* gives the best picture we have of the way he experienced maternal care. The conventional biography relies on evidence that is seen as more objective: letters, diaries, memoirs—though all of these are subject to personal bias—or on suppositions based on typical social practice of the period, of the sort, Dostoevsky's father must have done such and such because that is what Russian fathers did in the 1830s. While reasoning along these "objective" lines is of some value, it frequently takes one far from the truth of individual experience. Let me illustrate with an example.

Dostoevsky's novels are filled with abused and victimized children, yet he came from a respectable middle-class family where he and his brothers and sisters were never beaten or hungry. What is one to make of this? The conventional biographer tends to put it down to the novelist's overactive imagination or to trace it to events in his adult life. This does not sit well with psychoanalytic experience: the images and emotional tone come from childhood, the repetition of the theme is what one sees all the time in patients who transform the traumas of their childhood into specific sexual fantasies and perversions. (See references in chap. 3, n. 4.) The connection of the literary theme and childhood experience need not be a literal one, of course; there are many ways to be victimized other than physical beating. The prevalence of the theme in the novels leads the psychoanalytic observer to search out these less-direct forms of victimization. A number of them are there, as we will see.

What I shall attempt in this chapter is something that combines the traditional biographical and psychoanalytic approaches. I will put together a picture of family life from the usual historical sources, but the novels will serve as a template to test the truth of this material. In other words, in trying to construct a picture of the family I will be guided by those images of maternal care, paternal authority, and sibling relationships that are found repeatedly in the fiction.

Fedya's World

Feodor Mikhailovich Dostoevsky was born on 30 October 1821, the second son of Dr. Mikhail Andreyvich Dostoevsky, a former military physician then serving on the staff of a public hospital for charity cases (the Mariinsky Hospital for the Poor). Two years before, Dr. Dostoevsky, age thirty-one, had entered into an arranged marriage—as was then the custom—with the nineteen-year-old Maria Nechaeva. She came from a family of Moscow merchants, and her wealthy sister and brother-in-law, the Kumanins, were destined to play an important role in the family's later life. Maria's first child, Mikhail, preceded Feodor by a year. He was the only one that Maria nursed herself, and, reportedly, he remained her favorite. Fedya, as Dostoevsky was called as a child, was followed a year later by the first daughter, Varvara and, three years after that, by the future memoirist, Andrey. These four were the first set of siblings. There was then a gap of four years until the birth of twin girls Vera and Liubov—the second died shortly after birth—followed by the final two children, Nikolay and Alexandra. Dostoevsky was, thus, the second of seven surviving children and, throughout his childhood, his mother was—like Lizaveta in *Crime and Punishment*—"always pregnant."

Fedya spent almost all of his early years in the hospital apartment or, weather permitting, on the surrounding grounds. The apartment was small for the burgeoning family and their few servants. He and Mikhail came to share a low-ceilinged, windowless room, the original model for Raskolnikov's "cupboard." (Did it have faded yellow wallpaper?) The atmosphere was close, crowded, with parents and babies around and about; there was little privacy, and everyone was involved in everyone else's life. Father was frequently in and out of the apartment and his oppressive presence was felt by the children.

The family received few visitors and went out infrequently; the children were educated at home and Dostoevsky himself did not attend school until he was thirteen. Until he was ten, and trips to their newly purchased country estate began, his only playmates were his brothers and sisters, his teachers were a few tutors, and his mother and father. All of this contributed to the hothouse atmosphere within the family; conflicts and emotions had few outlets and reverberated between the members of this closed-in world. One gets a sense of city life—the feeling of a world filled with people—which pervades the novels.

The apartment was on the grounds of a hospital for the poor, and the young Fedya, whenever he went outside, saw these unfortunate creatures, the bottom strata of a hierarchical society. Did his contact with them shape his sympathy for victims and the downtrodden? It may have to some degree, but I suspect the origins of this theme, so prevalent in the fiction, has a more personal basis.

The family constituted its own miniature world; it was quite isolated from the larger world outside the hospital grounds. The mother's relatives would visit occasionally—there was no contact with the father's family—and there were infrequent forays to Moscow. Fedya spent almost all his early years in the confines of the family. There was, of course, a window to the larger world: literature. Andrey's *Reminiscences* make clear that this was a family of readers. In those days, without movies, stereos, and television, the parents would read aloud to the children in the evenings. Mikhail and Fedya always had their heads buried in books, reading, memorizing, reciting passages for their father, and arguing over who the best poets were. They read and reread Karamzin's *History of the Russian State* and memorized most of Pushkin's poetry. Fedya had a special fondness for the novels of Walter Scott. In this way, they escaped the cramped and isolated apartment through the imaginative world of romance and adventure. The dreamer surrounded by mundane reality, the hero who knows the world of books but not that of real people, is a repeated theme in the novels, from the shy clerk, Devushkin, in the first published work, *Poor Folk,* to the Underground Man.

The young Fedya was the most imaginative, active, and energetic of the Dostoevsky brothers. Though a year younger than Mikhail it was not long before he became inventor and leader of their games with "the little tail," Andrey, trailing behind. His parents called him "a perfect flame," and his father jokingly warned that he would one day "wear the red cap"—become a convict—because of his difficulty submitting to rules and control. He was emotional, high-strung, and powerfully open to imaginative impressions:

I used to spend the long winter evenings before going to bed listening—for I could not yet read—agape with ecstacy and terror, as my parents read aloud to me from the novels of Ann Radcliffe. Then I would rave deliriously about them in my sleep.

Later, when there were trips to the country, it was Fedya who invented their games of savages and Robinson Crusoe; Mikhail painted the makeup and Andrey played the part of Friday. But such outdoor play did not start until Feodor was ten and was confined to a few summer months. Most of family life was spent in the apartment where his energy and emotions were forced inside, into imagination fueled by reading.

Dostoevsky is the only one of the great nineteenth-century Russian writers who was not born into the landed gentry. His father was a self-made man and his mother came from the newly rich merchant class. The family's struggle for status and money, and the psychological effect of this struggle on the children, has a very modern ring to it. The issues that preoccupied them are more ours than are those of Tolstoy, Herzen, Turgenev, and Dostoevsky's other literary contemporaries. The father felt himself to be a poor man who only received from the world by drive and hard work. He was much involved with the education of his two oldest sons and repeatedly let them know that their worth depended on their achievements. They were nothing—lazy, stupid beings—except what they produced by study and effort. They were, thus, imbued with a very modern sense of guilt and self-doubt. How different from the self-view of the born aristocrat who is told of his innate superiority or who may even be taught that he is lowering himself if he works too hard! In this way, Dostoevsky, and many characters in his novels, look forward to the psychological conflicts of the twentieth century, in contrast to the characters in Tolstoy's *War and Peace,* for example, who personify the fading values of nineteenth-century gentry life.

The family was very insecure about its status. They would use their few servants in multiple roles so as to seem wealthier than they were. Along with such pretensions went a general air of falseness, a facade of respectability that played its part in repression and the distorted expression of emotion. There was much in all this that made the family itself a version of the horse and courier: father, feeling insecure and oppressed from above, passed down his pain and outrage to his wife, the servants, and the children. Fedya, recipient of his father's criticism and coercive control, no doubt felt like passing his hurt down the line to the siblings beneath him. The impulse to do so is one important source of the child abuse that he places in the heart of his Great Sinners. He probably did mistreat his younger siblings to some degree—what older brother does not?—what is clear is that any direct aggression was fairly early stifled, and he became, outwardly, identified with, and helpful toward, those smaller and weaker than himself.

While outward aggression was blocked in the family, there was a great deal of indirect hostility. This took several forms including attempts to make others feel guilty, control and discipline in the name of education, and the use of illness and symptoms of many kinds. As is true for so many upwardly striving families, money was a flexible symbol, involved in many forms of communication and emotional exchange.

The Mother

Fedya had three "mothers." From birth until age one or so, he was suckled by a wet nurse, a peasant woman brought from the country for this purpose. A nurse or nanny, Aliona Frolovna, joined the family after Varvara was born and remained with them until the father's death. His natural mother, Maria Feodorova—we see he was named after her father—was always present and, as he grew past infancy, she no doubt came to represent "mother" in his mind. Still, it is important to note this actual division of the maternal function, so common in middle- and upper-class Russian and European families; it is one origin of the propensity to split the mother figure into good and bad versions, a ubiquitous feature of the depiction of women in the novels.

We know almost nothing of the wet nurse. Maria did nurse Mikhail, her firstborn, who reportedly remained her favorite, but was not able to nurse her second son because of a "chest ailment," according to one biographer. It is possible that, from the very beginning, his mother's illness interfered with Fedya's reception of her care. From the infant's point of view, the wet nurse who feeds and cares for him is mother and her abrupt disappearance at the time of weaning is a source of unhappiness and anxiety. Dostoevsky, like so many other children from this social stratum, lost his first mother.

Aliona Frolovna joined the family when Fedya was between two and three years old; she seems to have had a good deal to do with the feeding and care of the children in their early years. She was not a serf, but a member of the Moscow petite bourgeoisie who worked for wages, though the father kept her money on account and she did not receive any until the estate was settled after his death. She addressed the parents and children by their first names and made a point of differentiating herself from the wet nurses and other servants who called them master and madame. She thus played her role in the social striving—the horse and courier atmosphere—within the family itself.

We know of this woman largely from Andrey's recollection. Nevertheless, the image—and I stress the word *image*—that emerges is a significant one. Like the appearance of the split mother figures that populate the novels, the picture of Aliona is an exaggeration of certain maternal qualities. She is described as very tall and enormously fat with a belly that hung almost to her knees. She had charge of the children's meals before they were old enough to sit at the family table and, while Maria would limit their portions, Aliona always gave more. She considered it a sin to eat anything without bread and seems always to have been stuffing it into herself and the children. Once a year she was bled and the father insisted she fast. On these occasions she would complain that she was "wasting away" and this became an oft-repeated family joke: "How are you Aliona?" "Oh, I'm wasting away!" The mother referred to her as "our two-ton weight" and father, known for his cruelty to his serfs, made jokes at her expense. The overall image is of a female Falstaff, a personification of the bountiful breast, of uninhibited oral greed.

Maria Dostoevsky was nineteen when she married the doctor and twenty-one when her second son was born. All observers agree that she was of a cheerful disposition, well liked by others in the small society of the hospital, and, later, by the peasants on the country estate. She was a believing Christian and an effective manager of her complicated household, of the affairs of the estate, and of her difficult husband. Her letters to him show intelligence and a literary flare. While her parents were merchants, there was education and a love of reading in her background. At the same time, her life was not an easy one. She was pregnant seven times in the eighteen years of her marriage, was sick early on and eventually succumbed to tuberculosis. Added to this were the difficulties of keeping up a front of affluence and respectability that strained their resources and dealing with her husband's suspicions and inability to get along with others. Her life had its full share of frustrations and unhappiness, and she must have had ways of expressing anger and dissatisfaction. The image of her as cheery and loving is surely an idealized exaggeration of one side of her nature.

Maria taught Fedya to read from a book of illustrated bible stories. She was a sincere Christian and there were memories of a once-a-year pilgrimage to a monastery and churches outside of Moscow on which she took her children. One can speak of his inheriting an artistic and literary bent from her. She loved music, as he did. These memories of close, enjoyable times with his mother—associated with reading, literature, the Bible, and Christianity—are all part of Dostoevsky's image of the loving mother. It is an image composed of feeling and memories associated with all three "mothers" yet it came to be centered on Maria. It is no accident that, in the crucial scene in *Crime and Punishment* when Raskolnikov allows a loving relationship to penetrate his angry isolation, he asks Sonia to read the Bible, just as his mother did for the author when he was a young boy. (Another literary scene that draws on these early images is Alyosha's memory of his mother in *The Brothers Karamazov*.)

The association of mother, reading, and Christianity continued throughout Dostoevsky's life. Romantic literature became the great love of his late childhood and writing the core of his adult identity. His search for Christian belief, and the attempt to create a "positively good" man, can be seen as efforts to recreate the relationship between the well-loved little Fedya and the believing Christian mother who introduced him to the world of books.

Feodor was ten when the family purchased its country estate. For several months each summer, mother and children would go to the estate while father stayed in Moscow, attending to his patients. We must remember that, apart from occasional walks and outings in Moscow, this was the children's first sustained exposure to the world outside the hospital grounds. Summer in the country with their mother—and without their father's demands—was a real release for them. There were games, made up by Fedya, play in the woods and fields, and contact with the serfs and their children. Clearly, Dostoevsky's feelings for the Russian people relate to these contacts, which reinforced the earlier positive feeling for the common people derived from his wet nurse and nanny. His famous *Peasant Marey* (to be analyzed in chapter 9) is a fantasy-memory that draws on the images from this period of his life.

In sum, there is a set of memories and feelings all associated with happiness, freedom, love, and acceptance that define a loving-mother configuration. These include images of his wet nurse, his nanny Aliona, and of a happy young Maria. She is associated with reading, literature, music, drama, and artistic pursuits; with Christian beliefs, as embodied in Christ's love (as contrasted to the moralistic, religious structures associated with his father); with nature and beauty; and with simple peasants who exemplified what is best in the Russian people. All these images, memories, and ideas are associated with the mother herself, time spent with her, places connected to her, and things she loved and believed. A letter written when Feodor was twelve captures both his love for Maria and the unhappiness associated with her absence:

[Moscow, Spring 1834.]

Dear Mama,
When you went away from us dear Mama I felt terribly sad and now when I think of you dear Mama such sadness comes over me that I can't get rid of it anyhow if you knew how much I want to see you I can't wait for that joyful moment. Every time I think of you I pray God to keep you well. Let us know dear Mama whether you arrived safely kiss Andryushinka and Verochka for me I kiss your hands and remain your obedient son.

F. Dostoevsky

In later childhood, Feodor became deeply immersed in romantic literature; this reading was a kind of "transitional" activity in which the loving mother was kept alive. One can see the many ways in which he pursued this ideal in his later life and fiction. The search for woman's love is perhaps the single most prevalent theme in his work, from his first novel, *Poor Folk*, to the final, *The Brothers Karamazov*. His idealization of the Russian people and, of great importance, his attempt to write about and, in some ways to be, a positively good man—the way he took Christ as his ideal—were also associated with this idealized image. In effect, he was attempting, in figures such as Prince Myshkin and Alyosha Karamazov, to create a "good boy"—one without hatred —worthy of his mother's love. This always remained an ideal out of reach; the image of an unsullied loving union was never attainable. In his remarks following the death of his first wife, he notes how his own egotism and selfishness prevented his achieving a Christlike love with that Maria, along with the feeling that he must continue to strive after the ideal. This goal was never achievable in Dostoevsky's adult life and, indeed, from early childhood it was only one side of his feeling for his mother.

From the very first, an idealized union with his mother was disrupted by rivals. Mikhail came first and was her favorite. He was a placid boy and it was not long before the energetic Fedya took control. Later, the brothers became soul mates in their love of literature—and compatriots in their opposition to the father's values—a relationship that lasted all their lives. This does not mean that Fedya did not feel rivalry toward his older brother but that he was able to express it effectively in dominant activity. I suspect that most of his jealousy was aroused by the babies that came after him. Such reactions are often among the most powerful forces in a child's life. It was his experience from the earliest years to be repeatedly ousted by a new baby, a competitor for his mother's time and attention. These rivals aroused his anger and, like any jealous child, he must have imagined getting rid of them. There was also anger at the mother who kept betraying him in favor of still-another intruder. These reactions, typical of a young child who is replaced by siblings, would be more intense in the Dostoevsky family, which was characterized by the father's extreme insecurity and jealousy toward rivals for his wife's love. He was both another competitor and someone who created an atmosphere of scarcity: the feeling that there was never enough of the mother to go around and whatever someone got was at someone else's expense.

I am suggesting, in short, that Dostoevsky's idealized love for his mother was disrupted by rivals who aroused his selfishness, his rage, and the wish to kill them and her. What evidence is there for this idea? First, we know that this sort of reaction is very common. The power of sibling rivalry is easy to verify by observation of young children.[2] But this only makes Dostoevsky's reaction probable, what evidence is there for his actual feelings and fantasies? Here we must turn to the novels. There are certain scenes possessed of a vividness and emotional power that seem to come out of the core of the author's being. They are often dreamlike, again suggesting their roots in his unconscious. Such a scene is the murder of the old pawnbroker and her sister in *Crime and Punishment*. Why does the innocent Lizaveta appear, why is she described as "always pregnant," and why is it her murder that Raskolnikov feels he must confess to Sonia? The answer is that she represents the mother whom he felt like killing in a rage of deprivation and jealousy induced by her repeated pregnancies.[3] This is the ultimate crime against the innocent mother and it is what must be atoned for to reestablish union with the loving woman, represented by Sonia.

Another vivid scene in *Crime and Punishment* contains Svidrigailov's final dreams, dreams that refer to his rape of a girl, her death, and the mixed wishes to care for and sexually abuse another, very young girl. The theme of the abuse of young children, and specifically the sexual abuse of young girls, had a strong grip on Dostoevsky's imagination—it is at the center of the suppressed chapter of *The Possessed* (Stavrogin's confession) and appears in *The Eternal Husband,* and other places. Dostoevsky was drawn to it with fascination and horror, it represented the ultimate crime and source of guilt. I suggest this was because it symbolized the most powerful source of rage and guilt in his own life: the wish to attack his own mother and the children who were rivals for her love. If this is so, why does the attack take a sexual form. Why is it rape? Svidrigailov, Stavrogin, and Valchaninov (in *The Eternal Husband*), are impulse-ridden types who drink, whore, and display their angry dependence on women. In the end of *The Possessed*, Stavrogin asks one of the women who loves him if she will not be his nurse shortly before his suicide, and Svidrigailov's dependence on his wife—and his angry neediness for Dunia—are evident. The rape of a young girl is an image that fuses all these elements: the wish for physical closeness and pleasurable gratification with the woman/mother, anger and the need to revenge the frustration of this desire, the wish to attack the child rivals who have taken the mother away, and identification with the victim. All of this brings on the most intense guilt, and both Svidrigailov and Stavrogin kill themselves.

On a more speculative note, one wonders if, as a child, Dostoevsky did not act/play out his feelings of desire and rage with one or more of his young sisters. In the closed-in world of the hospital, Varvara, one year younger, might have been a likely partner for games that expressed both his need for physical-sexual contact and his anger. The evidence for this comes from several sources, mainly in the novels. There is certainly a tone of sexual feeling between Raskolnikov and his younger sister, Dunia, and part of his rage at her fiancé, the older Luzhin, comes from jealousy. There are other suggestive images in the novels; both Stavrogin and the father (the dual character of Trusotsky-Valchaninov) in *The Eternal Husband* cause the death of young girls, and, in both novels, the girls raise their "little fists" in a gesture of hurt and helpless anger. One wonders if this repeated image does not come from Dostoevsky's own sexual/angry games with a young sister?

Murderous fantasies involving mother and siblings are extremely difficult for a young child to deal with, yet they do not always lead to the intense guilt and need to suffer that one finds in Dostoevsky and his characters. There were several additional factors, however, that turned things in this direction. The family strove to maintain an idealized facade, and it is unlikely that either parent would tolerate or empathize with such unseemly reactions in their children. On the contrary, a major pattern of communication in the family—seen in the letters between husband and wife and father and son—was the expression of hostility by accusation and the attempt to make the other feel guilty. Given this atmosphere, it seems most likely that the young Dostoevsky would have experienced his angry impulses as unacceptable and dangerously threatening to his acceptance by mother and others: they would have to be radically disassociated from himself, split off.

Greatly compounding the threatening nature of his anger toward his mother was her illness. She seems to have been sickly from early in his life, and her illness was aggravated by the repeated pregnancies and babies. She died of tuberculosis at age thirty-seven, when he was fifteen. Maria's death was one of a series of sudden losses going back to infancy, when he lost the wet nurse. Then, Aliona's bountiful feeding gave way to increasing adult demands, and his mother's loving education was replaced by his father's harsh and critical methods. Her final illness and death were one more way in which he was deprived of her love.

From an adult point of view we can feel sympathy for someone who is ill and dying; from the self-centered perspective of the child it is simply another enraging deprivation. But such anger is an almost reflexive source of guilt; how can one feel justifiably angry at the loved one who is sick and dying? Evidence for these complex reactions can be found in both Dostoevsky's life and his fiction. Recall that he internalized his sick mother in the form of a throat and chest ailment, a somatic symbol that served to both maintain the attachment to her and punish him for his anger. In addition, there was the marriage to Maria Isaeva, an unconscious reenactment that combined the wishes for love, revenge, restitution, and self-punishment. There is the picture of the dying Katherine Marmeladov in *Crime and Punishment,* modeled on this same Maria, which manages to be both angrily satirical and compassionate. More generally, one sees his dual response to victims, especially women. On the one side is rage at them for accepting their lot—Raskolnikov shows this toward Sonia—and, on the other, compassion. This reaction derives from the dual feelings aroused in him by his mother's illness: sympathy and anger.

An additional source of the compassion/rage that Feodor felt toward his mother was stimulated by his father's treatment of her. Fedya was identified with both the victim and the tormentor; he was hurt and outraged at his father's treatment of his mother—the miserliness and accusations—angry at her for putting up with it, yet aligned with his father as an attacker of women. In *Crime and Punishment* this duality comes out in the novel's most hateful character, Luzhin, who plants money on Sonia and then accuses her of stealing it. In this scene Luzhin is the bad father mistreating the idealized woman. But, even here, Raskolnikov's outrage has a false ring since he himself has murdered women, including Sonia's "twin," the innocent Lizaveta.

Maria bore the burdens of her life like a good Christian woman. Yet she was ultimately worn down by her many pregnancies and her difficult and demanding husband and fell victim to her disease. The mixture of rage, compassion, and guilt that Dostoevsky expressed in his fiction around the images of sick, unfortunate, and victimized women must come from the similar reactions stimulated in him by his sick and dying mother.

The mother is the first and most important love object in the child's life. Her love and care are vital for the earliest feeling of trust and for a coherent and stable sense of self. Because she is so important, the child's rage poses a dangerous threat to the mother-child bond. This is widely recognized in the clinical literature: preoedipal ambivalence, the coexistence of love and rage toward the mother, is implicated in many forms of severe disturbance. Because it is so threatening, and because it occurs early in life when the vulnerable child does not clearly distinguish fantasy from reality, the defensive measures adopted to deal with this ambivalence are primitive. It is from the conflicts of this period that one finds splitting and projective identification. The very young child does not have other means of dealing with his overwhelming emotions except by attempting to "get rid" of them, by projecting them onto others and by concretizing them in other "selves" who are, at once, him and not him.

I am suggesting, in sum, that Dostoevsky's own tendency toward splitting—seen in both his personal life and his novels—has its origins in the adjustment that the imaginative Fedya worked out with the mother he loved and hated. To state this another way, we can look at the long-term impact of his relationship with his mother. There was a basis of love and positive identification that gave him strength to endure the many obstacles of his life, to persevere in the face of adversity, and that lay at the core of his identity as a writer and man of letters. In both life and novels he could identify with mothers; he was very maternal in his attachment to babies, and he was, in his work, a creator, one who brings new life into the world. Along with this positive identification was a split-off side that was enraged at women, as seen in acted-out relationships and many examples in the fiction. The power of his rage—which did not diminish for years because of its fermentation "underground," its existence in a split-off state—is seen in the fury with which the old mare is beaten to death in Raskolnikov's dream. Such fury is also extremely frightening; it arouses the child's fear that his rage will destroy the world for, in the early years, the mother is the world. Much of Dostoevsky's most disruptive anxiety comes from this source. And, finally, it is the origin of a primitive sense of guilt, which is a direct turning of anger against oneself. Out of this complex of feelings, imagination, and primitive defense a pattern evolved. The split-off, sinful Dostoevsky took revenge on the hated mother figure by whoring, gambling, unfaithfulness, neglect, taunting, and other means. This was followed by guilt, and the seeking of forgiveness, his attempt to restore the relationship between the saintly Fedya and the loving mother. This pattern was established in childhood and then formed the unconscious basis for its repetition through the adult years.

The Father

Dostoevsky's father, Mikhail Andreyvich, was born in the Ukraine, the son of a nonmonastic clergyman, a member of a minor religious faction. While there were aristocratic connections in the distant past, for at least several generations the father's family had sunk to a low level; it belonged to what one biographer calls "the despised priestly class." Mikhail Andreyvich was destined, by the rules of his caste, to become a priest like his father before him, a fate that he apparently shunned. After graduating from the seminary at age fifteen he ran away to Moscow and never returned home nor had any further contact with his family.

In Moscow, he made his own way and took training as a doctor, serving in army hospitals during the Napoleonic campaigns. It is important to remember that doctors, at this time, while certainly of higher status than village priests, commanded neither the respect nor income that they do today. Medicine in the early nineteenth century was not very advanced and Dr. Dostoevsky's service in the military consisted largely in amputating diseased limbs and attending to the dying. The experience had an understandably depressing effect on him. A more important source of the depression, anxiety, and insecurity that plagued him was the complete loss of all contact with his parents, siblings, and childhood home.

Dr. Dostoevsky was a man who pulled himself up the social and economic ladder by his own efforts; he had both the virtues and scars of a self-made man. There was a striking contrast between the outward persona—the respectable doctor, terribly concerned with how the world perceived him—and the insecure volatile man beneath this facade. Many official versions of social mobility ignore the price that is paid when one tears oneself loose from home and family and struggles to success in a foreign milieu. Dr. Dostoevsky was never comfortable with himself or his life. The biographers portray him in more or less favorable ways but they all agree that he was irritable, moody, jealous of his wife's affection, suspicious of almost every one, and difficult to get along with.

Maria's family was an important connection with the social world outside the hospital; the wealthy Kumanins, her sister and brother-in-law, were the contacts through which the doctor built his private medical practice. Yet he was envious of them and disparaged their lack of culture. His personality made relations with Maria's family difficult. For example, her brother used to visit and they would play the guitar and sing together. This charming young uncle was caught having an affair with one of the housemaids. There were words, the doctor slapped his face, his visits were permanently ended, and they never spoke again. This incident seems typical of Dr. Dostoevsky's inability to get along with people and of the way his personal limitations curtailed the lives of his wife and children.

The father's background and personality can be summarized in the following terms. His own family life must have been decidedly unpleasant since he ran away from home and never returned. It left him with a legacy of anger, anxiety, and depression, which he attempted to counter with work, social striving, and a rigid moral religious code. His adjustment was tenuous, anger was always close to the surface, as were anxiety and unhappiness. He was afraid that the servants or his superiors were taking advantage of him. In his correspondence with his wife he urges her to count the spoons for fear that some may have been stolen and, on a more serious note, accuses her of having conceived their last child with another man. His jealousy and suspicions could take paranoid forms and he required a great deal of reassurance from her. He suffered, as well, from various physical complaints and moods that required her attention and care. There was much about him that was infantile, he was like another baby in competition for Maria's time and affection.

Dr. Dostoevsky was very ambitious for his children, especially his two oldest sons. They were set to studying at an early age, and, later, he was their tutor in Latin, mathematics, and other subjects. His methods reflected both his own need for control and the underlying anger that this control was directed against. His young sons were made to stand at attention and recite passages in Latin that they had memorized. Any mistake or lapse led to the father's criticism of them as sluggards or fools. Discipline of one's children, in the name of education and advancement, has always been considered a legitimate outlet for the suppressed anger of the self-made man. Andrey reports that the boys were never allowed to go out alone. They could walk on the hospital grounds but were forbidden to speak with the patients. The father was very tight with money, and his sons were not given any of their own until they went away to school in Petersburg. Even then, as a seventeen-year-old cadet, Feodor had to plead with his father for funds.

Here are some additional examples of the father's style: he would sometimes take the children for walks and use the occasion to improve their minds with a geometry lesson, pointing out the angles formed by streets and paths. Thus was nature turned to material advantage (it is no wonder that the Underground Man rebels against $2 + 2 = 4$ and that the adult Dostoevsky always valued the aesthetic over science and reason). Dr. Dostoevsky was also a miser, he referred to himself as "a poor orphan"—which is, no doubt, how he felt—and never gave freely to his family; they were always made to feel the burden he was bearing. The biographer Joseph Frank, who strives to show the father's virtues as well as faults, speaks of him as

self-righteous and pharisaical, so intolerant of the smallest fault, so persuaded that only perfect obedience from his family to all his wishes could compensate for all his toil and labor on their behalf.

(For an additional description of the father's oppressive control of his children, see Rice 1985, 15.)

What was the effect of his father on the young Fedya? As we might expect, the impact was twofold, the relationship of father and son was characterized by positive and negative emotions and both reactions were incorporated in the son's character. While it is relatively easy to look back and see the father as a very insecure man and something of a petty tyrant, his children did not have the benefit of such distance and objectivity. In the closed world of the hospital apartment he was the unquestioned authority, respected—at least outwardly—by his wife and the servants. His children shared this respect and, in the early years, must have looked up to him. Fedya worked at his lessons, tried to please and gain approval, and was vulnerable to criticism. We might think of a first layer of internal conflict in which the wish for father's approval, and the sense of being a good boy, existed along with feelings of inferiority and guilt, inculcated quite directly by being told he was stupid and at fault.[4] At the same time, there were positive sides to the relationship. The father was interested in his son's education and career, took time with him and was *the* authority of the early years.

Illness was central to the life of this family whose very home was on the grounds of a hospital. Fedya must have seen that sick people were the legitimate objects of his father's attention. More important, the father, like many depressed persons who must outwardly deny their own neediness, relied on illness to express his unhappiness and wish for love. His son incorporated this tendency into himself, as his later history of hypochrondriacal symptoms demonstrates. Did the father, as a doctor, care for Fedya when he was ill? We don't know, but sickness played an important role in Dostoevsky's later life, and there are several important relationships with doctors—real and fictional—that suggest this as a positive aspect of his feeling for his father.

Fedya was an extremely sensitive and perceptive child and, as he grew older, became increasingly aware of his father's inconsistencies and faults. He felt anger at his father's tyranny, anger that could not be expressed openly. The letters he wrote as an adolescent are filled with praise, protestations of love and respect for his father—almost to the point of caricature—and requests for money phrased in a way to make his father feel guilty:

My Dear Good Father:
Can you really think that your son is asking too much when he applies to you for an allowance? God be my witness that not for self-interest, nor even in actual extremist need, could I ever wish to despoil you in any way. How bitter it is to have to ask my flesh and blood a favor which so heavily oppresses him? I have my own head, my own hands. Were I but free and independent, I should never have asked you for so much as a kopeck—I should have inured myself to the bitterest poverty.

He goes on to ask for money so he can at least buy tea—does his father want him to freeze when he returns from the field cold and wet? —and, please, send enough for extra boots and a decent uniform so he won't be humiliated in the eyes of his fellows. His father sent the money, along with a letter describing his hardships and suffering. Clearly, communication by the mutual induction of guilt was well ingrained. This was an important family pattern: love and suffering were constantly tied together as they so often were later in Dostoevsky's life and fiction.

It seems likely that by adolescence, if not sooner, Feodor had incorporated into his own personality the several sides of his relationship with his father. Part of him complied, submitted, and wished to please, and part rebelled, wished to attack and revenge the insults he had suffered at the tyrant's hands. The intensity of this conflict was such that these opposing parts were sometimes experienced as separate selves—each with the power to take over the whole personality—something that appears in various places in his character and fiction. Outwardly, of course, these were not apparent. He had learned, very early, to hide his feelings and he remained, in some ways, secretive and evasive all his life. But the inner conflicts remained; as an adult he was both a rebel against his father and—in ways that he did not like about himself—similar to the very father he disliked. The rebellion is easy to see: while the father was a doctor and a military man, rigid, careful with money, and concerned with appearance, his son became an artist, lived a disorderly life, threw money to the winds, and had difficulty complying with rules and etiquette. In contrast were the ways in which he incorporated his father into himself: they were both moody, irritable, and prone to hypochondria, at times violently jealous, sensitive to social slights, and in need of a young wife to idolize and care for them.

The underside of the father's personality became clear after his wife's death, and, although Feodor was no longer a child nor living with him at the time, his knowledge of what happened brought the impulsive side of his father more clearly into the open and influenced his own identification with it. Following the death of his wife and the placement of his two oldest sons in school, Dr. Dostoevsky gave up his position at the Moscow hospital and moved to the small country estate that he and his wife had bought some five years earlier. The purchase of this estate was made possible by the doctor's promotion into the lowest rank of the nobility; the money was borrowed from Maria's wealthy relatives. Buying the estate was clearly motivated by social ambition. Now the family name could be restored to its lost glory and inscribed on the lists of the hereditary gentry. The land itself was marginally productive and the serfs poor.

Dr. Dostoevsky was no better able to get along with his peasants than he was with anyone else and this final move proved disastrous. Without the support and reassurance of his wife, his respectable moral persona crumbled. He drank heavily, took a young peasant girl as his mistress, and turned his cruelty loose on the serfs. All this was bad enough but his mismanagement of the estate was even more serious. Never very productive, and ravaged by fire and drought in recent years, the land produced barely enough to keep the peasants alive. Dr. Dostoevsky's drunkenness and incompetence threatened their very lives and the lives of their families. A group of them, in response to some cruel provocation of his, fell on him and finished him off. The details of the murder will never be known for certain; it is possible that one of the killers was the father of the young girl he was carrying on with. While some recent biographers have raised questions about the father's death,[5] it seems fairly certain that Dostoevsky and the other members of his family all believed that he was murdered by his own peasants. Nobody was particularly surprised, given their knowledge of his personality, and nobody was ever punished for the crime; to do anything to the serfs—then the property of the surviving children—would have endangered their inheritance.

His father's murder affected Dostoevsky in several ways. Coming two years after the death of his mother, it meant that he and his siblings were now truly orphans. The mother's rich relatives helped out with the younger siblings, and a marriage was arranged between his sister Varvara and an older man—Peter Karepin—who assumed the role of manager of the family estate. Feodor's share of the estate was not large and he was left to make his own way in the world. He makes little mention of his father or his death in the correspondence with Mikhail; there is one brief reference in a letter written after the murder. In later life, he almost never spoke of him; clearly the memories were too painful. He does not directly take up the theme of fathers and parricide in his fiction until *The Brothers Karamazov*—Father Karamazov displays much of the impulse-ridden side of Dr. Dostoevsky—the novel he wrote at the end of his life.

Given the ambivalence that Dostoevsky felt toward his father, it is certain that his death—especially his murder by the victims of his cruelty

—produced a dual effect on Feodor. On the one side, he must have felt glad: finally justice was done, revenge taken, on the tyrant who had oppressed him. At the time of the murder, he was having an intensely unhappy time of it in the school his father had forced him into, and, with the death, he could see his way out of an unsuitable career in engineering. On the other side, he must have felt guilty over the actualization of his own murderous wishes. His last correspondence with his father had been an exchange of guilt-inducing letters and shortly before the murder he wrote Mikhail that "our poor father's tears . . . burned into my soul." This was over his having flunked algebra and been kept back a year at the academy.

In sum, he identified with his father's murderers and was punished by his conscience for this wish. (This is the heart of Freud's well-known analysis of Dostoevsky.) Dostoevsky's oedipal crime left its legacy of guilt, though I suspect this was not nearly as painful as that arising from his mother's death. He seems to have been conscious of his anger at his father, even if he preferred never to speak of it, but it is not likely that he was aware of the ambivalence toward his mother, even though his fiction—and his life—is filled with women who are experienced in precisely this way.

The father's final disintegration was clear evidence of the dual nature of his own personality. In the end, the moralistic authority was revealed as a cruel drunkard and a debaucher of young girls. It was one of several splits within the family that formed the background for Dostoevsky's own duality. The family was greatly concerned with keeping up appearances, with presenting a respectable image to the outside world. They attempted to appear wealthier than they were, and the purchase of the country estate, which strained their means, showed the lengths they would go to in order to achieve status. When such concern for appearance takes an extreme form, it poses problems for sensitive children. The false front of the family is a predisposing condition for a false self in the child. In other words, the family's propensity for pretending to feel differently than they did, for extremes of idealization, reinforces these tendencies in the child. As we have seen, there was much professed love between the parents that coexisted with hostility. Father scorned the wealthy Kumanins as uncultivated merchants—an attitude that his son shared—while simultaneously borrowing their money to advance his own desperate ambitions. The myth of the ancient nobility of the Dostoevsky name was put forth while at the same time the father had no contact with his real family. The doctor's respectable veneer was everywhere belied by the emotions and actions that contradicted the image he attempted to maintain, a contradiction made even more apparent by the disintegration of his last years. And, finally, there was an unrealistically exaggerated difference between the personalities of the father and the mother. His tradition-supported role as the hard, demanding authority, and his obvious faults, made it relatively easy for the father to become the prime target of his children's dislike. The mother, who was outwardly cheerful—"natural gaiety" was her own phrase—was easily idealized, a tendency supported by several other factors including her illness and early death. (Since the pictures of the father and mother are based largely on Andrey's memoirs and the reconstruction of biographers, it is likely that these splits and idealizations are perpetuated in the very descriptions that have come down to us.)

Siblings

The seven Dostoevsky children, largely isolated from the outside world, were a universe unto themselves. There was much love and closeness between them along with jealousy and competition. Feodor's brothers and sisters were the prototypes for many of the friendships and rivalries of his later life. The most important and long-lasting of these relationships was with his older brother, Mikhail. They were only one year apart, shared a room, and were educated as a pair. One has the impression of a sort of twinship that, from very early, possessed a common passion, literature. Judging from the intimacy of their later correspondence, one can imagine Fedya and Mischa engaged in endless talk about stories, authors, poems, and life. Mikhail was more the passive dreamer, even as a child drawn to poetry, whereas Fedya identified with the heros of Walter Scott's romantic adventure novels. In competition, the younger brother almost always prevailed. When they left home it was Feodor who gained admittance to the academy of engineers; Mikhail went to the academy with him, but failed the entrance examinations and had to settle for a school in the provinces. Much later Mikhail was business manager for their literary journals, while Feodor did the real editing and writing, and, of course, we know only one writer named Dostoevsky; the older brother's poetry has not survived. From his successful competitive play with his brothers, Feodor acquired a sense of confidence in his own abilities, which, along with the love of his mother, sustained him through the difficult times.[6]

The friendship with Mikhail lasted until the older brother's unexpected death when Feodor was forty-three. Even before that loss, Dostoevsky had shown the capacity for intimacy with a series of male friends who shared his literary and intellectual interests. During the academy years it was Ivan Shidlovsky; in the prearrest period there was Dr. Stepan Yanovsky; in Siberia after his release from prison, Baron Alexander Wrangel; in the later Petersburg years, Nikolay Strakhov and the poet Apollan Maikov. There are many examples in the fiction: in *Crime and Punishment,* Raskolnikov's friend Razumikin and, most obvious of course, the brothers Karamazov in the novel of that name. While Dmitri, Ivan, Alyosha, and Smerdyakov represent the split-up attributes of a single self, they also come alive in the novel as real brothers who love each other, share a troublesome father, and are rivals for the same women.

There were three girls in the family: Varvara, one year younger than Feodor; Vera, eight years younger; and the last child, Alexandra, who was only two when her older brothers left home. Fedya's most sustained contact was with the two older sisters. Little girls can be attractive, innocent, and loving creatures and I suspect there was a good deal of genuine affection between Fedya, Varvara, and Vera. In addition, the girls were identified with Maria in his mind, both as female love objects and because they literally spent a good deal of time in close proximity to her, preparing for their future roles as wives and mothers. From these experiences, Feodor derived an image of the innocent young child-woman, an image composed of feelings for both his young mother and his sisters. This image was central to the loving-mother side of his split version of women. In both his later life and literature it can be seen as part of various mother-daughter, sister-sister pairs, where feelings of incestuous love, jealousy, and guilt are at play. Here are some examples.

The heroine of Dostoevsky's first novel, *Poor Folk,* is a desirable young woman named Varvara who the dreamer hero loves but cannot have. At the novel's end, she is married off to a rich, unsavory older man. This theme is derived from Dostoevsky's experience with both his sister and his mother. In reality, after the death of the parents, a marriage was arranged between the seventeen-year-old Varvara and a forty-four–year–old widower, Peter Karepin. Whatever the real Karepin may have been like—and other reports indicate that he was not a bad sort—Feodor took an instant dislike to him. In the imagination of the aspiring young writer, this older man fitted the niche of the miserly controller of money and exploiter of innocent females just vacated by his father. Much later, in *Crime and Punishment,* Karepin became the model for Luzhin, the wealthy older man whose proposed marriage to Dunia so enrages Raskolnikov. Raskolnikov betrays his incestuous feeling for Dunia and his jealousy at the older man who may possess her. The attraction and jealousy brought out in this relationship come from Dostoevsky's own image of the innocent young woman, derived from Varvara and Maria. In other words, behind the real Karepin and the fictional Luzhin, lives the original miserly old man who exploits the young woman: Dr. Dostoevsky.

Vera, eight years younger than Fyodor, seems to have been his real favorite. She is probably the original model for the innocent young girl who loves without reservation. She married a doctor named Ivanov and had seven children. In his forties, while writing *Crime and Punishment,* Dostoevsky spent some months in the midst of this lively, happy family. His love for Vera was also transferred to her daughter Sonia, and he even proposed marriage to one of Sonia's friends. There was an incestuous tone to his feelings for this young niece and it is likely that Sonia in *Crime and Punishment*—the clearest literary example of the young woman who loves without reservation—was named for her, as was, a bit later, the first child of his second marriage.

The various mother-daughter and sister-sister pairs in the novels are too numerous to list here. In *Crime and Punishment* alone there are Aliona and Lizaveta, Katherine Marmeladov and Sonia, Raskolnikov's mother and Dunia, Svidrigailov's wife (Martha Petrovna) and the young girls of his dreams. In Dostoevsky's life there was a regular pattern of attachment, as friend and confidant, with the sisters of the women he was in love with. This happened with Varvara Constant (sister of his first wife, Maria), Nadezhda Suslova (sister of Apollinaria, his mistress), and Sophia Kovalevskya, (to whose sister Anna Korvin-Krukovskaya he proposed between his two marriages). In all these ways we see the lingering effects of his sisters—blended with his mother—as models for the loving woman. His jealousy, anger, and guilt are apparent, in both fiction and life, in the many images of child abuse, particularly the crime he considered most foul: the rape and destruction of the innocent young girl.

Summary

The Dostoevsky family was in transition between the traditional religious values of previous generations and a new urban, bourgeois way of life. They were part of that upwardly mobile, ambitious class whose competitiveness and anxiety were inculcated in their children, who were pushed hard academically and could gain parental love and approval with their success. The family contained a complex mixture of qualities: old and new values, love and closeness along with rivalry and competition, gratification and deprivation, idealism and corruption. Dostoevsky emerged from his years in the family with all these complexities contained in his own personality. There was a solid core to his sense of self, derived from the love and care of his mother and peasant mother figures, intimacy and affection between the many siblings, and his leadership and successful competition with Mikhail and his other brothers. For all the rigidity of his father's demands, he had the satisfaction of meeting and mastering them, further building his self-esteem. The family was oriented toward literature, reading and learning, influencing his positive identification in this area.

Yet, Dostoevsky's was also a character with significant inner divisions. Powerful ambivalence in the relationships with mother, father, and siblings led to inner splits and an acute sense of guilt, played out in later life in relation to women, authority, and a variety of brother and sister figures. He loved literature and strove after a Christian ideal, yet tormented women, wrote of their murder, and symbolically incorporated his mother's tuberculosis into his own body. He rebelled against his father's values yet was, like his father, irritable, moody, and hypersensitive to social slights. His personality had a permeability to it; he absorbed aspects of his mother, father, and siblings into himself where they lived on as partially integrated inner selves.

Of course, there is something more: Dostoevsky was not only a man whose early years produced serious conflicts and divisions, he had the imagination and creative capacity to express these conflicts in novels that deal with the problems of ambivalence, splitting, and projection. He worked hard all his life to give truthful expression to the many emotional currents, conflicts, and selves that surged within him. The lasting quality of his novels, and their profound impact on so many persons, is testimony to his success.

CHAPTER 6

The Engineering Academy:
Poor Folk

Social awkwardness, fantasized superiority, and feelings of inferiority were all active when Dostoevsky began school at age thirteen. He was divided into an outwardly compliant persona and an inner self, protectively secreted away, where his most cherished fantasies and ideals were kept alive. This inner self was nourished on literature; from early on he was most alive when reading, imagining, and discussing books. The most consistent image of the outer boy through the school years is of a misfit, an isolate, someone who kept largely to himself.

Feodor and Mikhail attended a dayschool (Souchard's) and then boarding school (Chermak's) in Moscow. Dostoevsky's sense of alienation and inferiority at Souchard's is indicated by a thinly veiled reference in his novel *The Adolescent* (1874) where the school is named Touchard's. There the hero is picked on and ridiculed for his family background. In reality, he was not totally isolated and the contacts he did have with other boys are revealing. He was always horrified by the mistreatment of the smaller and weaker children and one of them recounts how Feodor rescued him from bullies, consoled him in his loneliness, and told him exciting stories. This sympathy for the underdog, consisting of maternal warmth and a genuine identification, along with a reaction formation against his own sadistic urges, is a central part of his character, already in evidence in these early years.

When Dostoevsky was fifteen life took a tragic turn. His mother died, his father, in the words of Andrey, "was totally destroyed," Feodor developed his throat and chest symptoms, and he and Mikhail were taken off to the Academy of Military Engineering on the journey of the horse and courier incident. On the trip, Mikhail wrote three poems a day while Feodor was preoccupied with a novel, set in Venice, that he composed in his mind. They arrived in Petersburg for a period of preparatory study and entrance examinations, and here he suffered yet another loss. He passed the examinations—doing extremely well on the academic subjects—but Mikhail did not; the older brother was sent off to a lesser academy in the provinces. Thus was the young Feodor cast into an uncongenial milieu, suffering the recent death of his mother, bereft of home and family, and separated from his closest companion and soul mate.

Life in the academy was, in his own words, "one long torment." In a rare open criticism of his father's decision he says, "We were taken, my brother and I, to Petersburg and to the Academy of Engineers and thus our future was spoiled. In my opinion, it was an error." What was it about the academy that he found so repugnant? The whole enterprise stood in opposition to his own deepest interests, values, and sympathies. Military harshness, endless hours of drill, the demanding study of subjects, particularly mathematics, in which he had no interest, strict discipline, and physical violence confronted the dreamer of romances, the seeker of all that is "beautiful and sublime." The romantic idealist was saddened to see "children of thirteen already reckoning out their entire lives: where they could attain to what rank, what is more profitable, how to rake in cash and what was the fastest way to get a cushy, independent command." He was also deeply troubled by the corruption and abuse of position found among the officers. In these ways, his anger, fueled from many sources, found an outlet in moral outrage.

The academy was a living version of the horse and courier: upperclassmen, suffering under the restraints and discipline of their superiors, engaged in merciless hazing and tormenting of the students below them. The authorities looked the other way, and if the victim complained he was liable to mass beatings. Dostoevsky was particularly horrified by these cruelties. He did not take part in them, and, with a few friends, attempted to aid the victims. Again, we see the central character trait of his deep sympathy and identification with the victims of unfairness and oppression. In his later years at the school he raised money for deprived peasants.

He felt himself to be, in his own words, a "foreign presence" in the academy. A fellow student describes him: "His uniform hung awkwardly, and his knapsack, shako, rifle—all those looked like some sort of fetters that he was obliged to wear temporarily and that weighed him down." Another notes that he already then exhibited traits of unsociability, stayed to one side, did not participate in diversions, sat and buried himself in books, and sought a place to be alone. He was often to be found late at night, sitting by a window reading or writing while the other students slept.

The capacity to divide himself, to withdraw to an inner world of imagination and literary identification—already developed in the years at home—served him well at the academy, as it would later in prison. He complied with the demands, did his work, passed his courses, but did not allow the place to touch the core of his being. Here the lonely sixteen-year-old speaks in a letter to Mikhail:

I don't know if my gloomy mood will ever leave me. And to think that such a state of mind is allotted to man alone—the atmosphere of his soul seems compounded of a mixture of the heavenly and the earthly. . . . This earth seems to me a purgatory for spirits who have been assailed by sinful thoughts. [He talks of ending it all.] . . . How terrible! How petty is man! Hamlet! Hamlet! When I think of his moving wild speech, in which resounds the groaning of the whole numbed universe, there breaks from *my* soul not one reproach, not one sigh.

We see how his personal unhappiness is tempered by placement in a universal context, how his involvement with a fellow sufferer from Shakespeare takes him out of his misery. The rest of the letter discusses other authors with enthusiasm: he has been reading "the whole of Hoffmann in Russian and German and nearly all Balzac. . . . Balzac is great! Goethe's 'Faust' and his shorter poems . . . Victor Hugo." The depressed mood is lifted.

He was not entirely alone; there was always at least one friend—and sometimes two or three—who shared his passion for books and ideas. There were the letters back and forth with Mikhail and a few courses— Russian and French literature, history, drawing, and architecture—that captured his interest. He was, as well, editor of and chief contributor to a student newspaper. Religion was very important, especially during the early years, and one student recalled that he "zealously performed all the obligations of the Orthodox Christian faith" and could be seen engaged in long conversations with the priest.

Of real importance was a sustaining friendship with a slightly older man—Ivan Shidlovsky—who worked at a minor government post in Petersburg. Shidlovsky was a philosopher-poet, a romantic who provided many hours of inspired conversation on topics close to the young Feodor's heart. Like Dostoevsky, he valued the emotional life over the rational and, in his later years, became quite unstable. Shidlovsky filled an important need in the young cadet's life: he was a model, an ideal, a positive father-brother figure with whom he could identify. This was particularly important since Dostoevsky was so alienated from his own father, as well as from his father's values and those of the academy and the majority of the other students. This older friend—along with a few fellow students—supported the commitment to his inner image. As a successful author in his fifties, he looked back and spoke warmly of Shidlovsky's importance.

Two events from the academy years deserve special notice: Dostoevsky's failure the first year and the death of his father. As much as he inwardly hated his situation, he applied himself hard to his studies. He had an intensely competitive side to his nature, so competitive, in fact, that be wished to redefine all the rules he was forced to live under. Since he could not change the world, he worked hard to succeed in it. As an example, we know that he studied diligently for the entrance examinations, did extremely well, and was greatly offended when some students, whose parents could afford bribes, were admitted ahead of him. As a student he was dutiful and respectful—even timid—in relation to the instructors but there were some subjects that strained the limits of this pretense. One was algebra, mathematics—$2 + 2 = 4$ as he refers to it in *Notes from Underground*—was a life-long area of rebellion against his father's control. He apparently made a rude remark to the algebra instructor, who then flunked him. His other grades were good the first year, though he did poorly in military drill, for obvious reasons. In a letter to Mikhail describing this event he says:

The failure would not have worried me so very much, if our poor father's tears had not burned into my soul. I had not hitherto known the sensation of wounded vanity. If such a feeling had got hold of me, I might well have blushed for my-self. . . . But now you must know that I should like to crush the whole world at one blow.

There is a breakthrough of his underlying rage—"crush the whole world"—as well as guilt in relation to his father. The doctor, learning of his son's failure, suffered something like a stroke and had to be bled. Dostoevsky himself was "ill and miserable." The incident must have underscored the necessity of keeping his rebellious feelings under control and intensified his depression and alienation from most of what the academy required of him. There is also a self-analytical note to the letter, he is aware of his "wounded vanity"—what we might today call narcissitic rage—he analyzes his reaction as well as suffers it.

The father's murder occurred while Dostoevsky was in his second year at the academy. Much has been written about this event. Freud puts it in the center of his analysis, and all the biographies discuss its obvious importance. In some ways, it is surprising that the murder did not have more disruptive results. The ambivalence was so marked, the failure of the first year had just occurred, along with his father's stroke, and their last letters contained the guilt-inducing pleas for money and protestations of suffering. There is no question that his father's murder did feed into Dostoevsky's sense of guilt, but I suspect that the pattern of their relationship had been set for so long—and a well-developed defensive style evolved—that it was not as disruptive as one might expect. The only information we have concerning Dostoevsky's immediate reaction is contained in a letter to Mikhail:

I shed many tears over our father's end, but now our condition is even worse. Is there anyone in the wide world more unfortunate than our poor brothers and sisters? The thought that they will be brought up by strangers devastates me.

The younger Dostoevskys were to be brought up by the wealthy Kumanins, and it was those "paltry souls" who became targets of anger as Feodor identified with his father's dislike of them. What is most striking is the ease with which his reactions are projected outside him-self: the younger siblings became the poor unfortunates, and the wealthy relatives the villains. One is reminded of similar reactions in Raskolnikov, who projects his feelings of deprivation into the Marmeladov orphans and whose rage is directed at Luzhin, a man of crass materialistic values. (Did Dostoevsky have an epileptic attack—or a precursor, a fainting fit—when hearing of his father's murder, as Freud's reconstruction would have it? The evidence now available indicates that he did not. See the Appendix.)

Dostoevsky seems to have been conscious of his anger at his father, and his life was not unduly disrupted by the doctor's murder. In fact, he experienced it as something of a liberation. In the same letter to Mikhail he goes on to speak of his faith in himself and of a growing sense of peace and freedom from turbulence and agitation. His soul, he writes, is "like the heart of a man concealing a profound enigma," and his aim will be "to study the meaning of life and man." He will do this by delving into the "characters in the writers with whom the best part of my life is spent freely and joyously. . . . Man is an enigma [that] must be solved, and if you spend all your life at it, don't say you have wasted your time; I occupy myself with this enigma because I wish to be a man."

Several things are worth noting about these remarks, made at the time of his father's death. First is the obvious commitment to his identity as a writer, one who lives "freely and joyously" in literature. Whatever guilt he felt at the time of the murder, it did not turn him away from this primary identity toward one more in line with his father's wishes. Second, there is an increased sense of freedom. While he was still to spend several years in the academy, his father's death weakened what little hold that career may have had on him. Finally, and of special interest, is the self-analytical direction suggested by these comments. Dostoevsky not only dedicates himself to literature, but also to solving the riddles of man's existence. The murder and his own complex and tumultuous inner life posed enigmas that needed to be deciphered, a task that he would work on through writing.

There is an interesting parallel between the lives of Dostoevsky and Freud. In the 1890s Freud was moving out of his original career in neurology and it was the death of his father, and all that it stimulated within him, that brought forth his self-analysis, the writing of *The Interpretation of Dreams,* and the full assumption of his new identity as psychoanalyst. Dostoevsky, too, speaks with confidence and conviction of the identity he projects for his future. While both these creative geniuses seemed destined to become explorers of the unconscious and man's emotional life, the death of their fathers focused conflicts and guilt while, at the same time, giving them the freedom from old models, values, and constraints with which to analyze these same conflicts.

Dostoevsky passed through his years at the academy as a foreign presence, for the most part isolated, unhappy, chafing under the discipline, and deeply at odds with his fellows. During these years he pursued his own parallel education. He learned from those few courses that fit his interests: literature, of course, but also drawing and architecture. *The Notebooks* for his later novels are dotted with evocative character sketches and gothic buildings. He read voraciously and never tired of discussing authors, ideas, characters, and style with those friends who shared his passion. There was also something else that was acquired—or strengthened—during these years: discipline. He abhorred working at subjects he disliked, but emerged from the academy with the capacity for sustained effort that he would shortly focus on his real vocation. While other sides of his life would show signs of haste and disorder, this was not true of writing. For example, at the start of his career he produced several pieces in the romantic mode but was not satisfied and never published them; going on to create a new form to express his own inner truth. The later novels were often worked and reworked. He wrote a long draft of *Crime and Punishment* in the first person and then, unsatisfied, burned it and redid it in its present form. *The Idiot* went through no fewer than eight drafts. In summing up the years at the academy, we see that he had the inner strength and commitment to his own ideals and goals to resist its influence, to take what he could and go his own way.

Dostoevsky spent—or as he would say, wasted—five years at the academy. During the last two he was promoted to the rank of field ensign, which enabled him to live in an apartment in Petersburg. He graduated in 1843—for his final project he submitted a design for a fortress that had no doors, either as an unconscious mistake or a joke—and was assigned to a modest post in the city doing drafting. The job captured no more of his interest than work at the academy did, but it paid a salary, which, along with money from his inheritance, allowed him to live a relatively free life in the exciting capital. He went to plays, concerts, and ballets, enjoyed cards and other games of chance, and indulged in the pleasures of sex: "The Minnas, Claras, Mariannas, etc. [prostitutes] have got amazingly pretty, but cost a lot of money. Turgenev and Belinsky lately gave me a talking to about my disorderly way of life."

A young doctor named Riesenkampf—a friend of Mikhail's—lived with Feodor during this period and his account reveals the underside of Dostoevsky's personality, already in evidence in his early twenties. First there was money. No matter how much he had, he spent it like water. He paid liberally for amusements; enjoyed games of chance—where he was an archsucker, once allowing himself to be taken by a billiard shark for a thousand rubles—and let himself be fleeced by his soldier-servant who supported a mistress and her family on pickings from his pockets. He gave money away to Riesenkampf's poor patients, ostensibly while gathering information about Petersburg life. He was often in debt, borrowing from his brothers and friends, from pawn brokers, and attempting to extract more money from his brother-in-law, who now managed the family estate. We see, in all this, the familiar pattern of rebellious disidentification with his father—Feodor gives freely to the needy ones, he is not the miser—guilt, and self-punishment by humiliation.

Riesenkampf, living at close quarters with Dostoevsky, was also witness to his mood swings and peculiar symptoms. Mikhail was placid and agreeable but Feodor had trouble controlling his emotions, being liable to bursts of enthusiasm and anger. He was easily carried away in discussion and could become quite abusive. In addition to difficulty controlling his temper, there were periods of depression and insomnia. Though sleeping alone, he would complain that the sound of someone snoring kept him awake and would stay up reading and writing. These sleepless nights were followed by periods of irritability. There was also a fear that he would fall into a deathlike state and mistakenly be buried alive. He would be compelled to guard against this by leaving notes specifying that he not be entombed for a certain number of days. Some of these symptoms may have been early signs of the epilepsy that made its full appearance in the years in prison (see the Appendix).

As he worked his way free of his career as a military engineer—he formally resigned in 1844 and wrangled a lump-sum settlement of his share of the family estate that same year—he more and more lived the life of a creative artist, a bohemian, one not constrained by conventional rules and mores. He had always been more open to fantasy and emotion than most, even his compulsions and symptoms show this. As he himself expressed it at various times, he was a man of extremes: "Everywhere and in everything I go to the limit. All my life I have crossed the last line." His personality was a vehicle, as it were, for conflicts, feelings, and fantasies; these were lived through him and then funneled into his writing where they were given organized expression. In the end—with all the excitement and turmoil of his life—he lived to write.

Dostoevsky's early efforts took the form of romantic dramas. In the period of transition between the life of a student/engineer and that of a full-time author he wrote two plays: *Maria Stuart* and *Boris Gudunov*. He never published these—their existence is only known from references in letters—but they were apparently in the romantic mode of Schiller that so entranced him in his youth. There were several reasons why this mode was no longer suitable, some external and some internal. Russian literature in the 1840s was undergoing a renaissance, the new style of the day was social realism. Literary magazines published sketches of Petersburg life and the protagonists in fashion were people of contemporary Russia and not legendary historical figures. Having cashed in his inheritance and resigned his commission, Dostoevsky had to earn a living with his pen and this need kept him clearly focused on his audience. While he would always write from inner necessity, this was balanced by a concern with what he could publish and sell. In addition to such practical considerations, he was drawn to social realism by two masterpieces that had just been published: Gogol's influential short story *The Overcoat* and his novel *Dead Souls*. Dostoevsky's correspondence reveals his preoccupation with Gogol. He and his friends would read *Dead Souls* aloud and one of them reported how Feodor loved to recite passages from memory. The impact of Gogol is clear, especially in the first two novels.

The rise of social realism and the influence of Gogol were important in Dostoevsky's move away from the romantic form and they gained force from other sources within him. In part, his fiction always remained romantic: his heroes seek the love of virtuous women, he attempts to create perfectly "good" men, and characters are idealized (or he tries to idealize them). Perhaps the most powerful romantic strain is the commitment to emotion over reason: truth for him is always truth of the heart;

men delude themselves with logic. Yet access to his own rich emotional life revealed the coexistence of ideal and far-from-ideal feelings. The emotions that he found in himself—and observed in others—were romantic and hateful, sublime and grubby, exhalted and mundane. He needed a literary form in which he could express the full range of this emotional experience, in which he could move beyond splitting and idealizations, and he created this form by combining his earlier romantic predilection with social realism.

Dostoevsky's first published work was a translation of Balzac's novel *Eugénie Grandet* a work, interestingly enough, that chronicles the conflict between a virtuous young girl, and her miserly father. In 1845, at the age of twenty-four, he published his first novel, *Poor Folk*. The year before he had a vision: "In some dark corner I saw the honest and pure heart of a ninth-grade civil servant, and with him I saw a girl, insulted and sorrowing, and their whole story tore deeply at my heart." The years he worked on this novel were those of his disorderly life in Petersburg, with money squandered and practicalities mismanaged. Discipline was confined to writing: he wrote and rewrote—and rewrote again—as he worked to realize his vision.

Poor Folk is a novel in the form of letters between a middle-aged copy clerk, Makar Devushkin, and a young girl, Varvara Dobroselova. They are timid and obedient souls who love and struggle amidst poverty and low social position. The basic plot is simple, though, already in this first work, we see the introduction of subthemes and subsidiary plots that enrich the narrative. Varvara has lost her parents and a procuress, posing as a friend, attempts to sell her off to a wealthy older man, Bykov. Devushkin tries to help her, sends presents and money, but is too poor himself and she must marry Bykov. In the end, as she leaves for her new husband, Devushkin discovers the depth of his love for her.

The surface of the novel shows the reality of Petersburg's poor; they too can love, show pride, be hurt, and suffer. The unfairness of wealth and the humiliation of poverty are clear. But the novel does much more than this. The reader comes to know the two central characters from their own points of view; they express themselves directly and their creator is identified with both of them. This is an important way in which Dostoevsky goes beyond Gogol, for, while Gogol wrote about poor clerks and ordinary Russians, he did so from an outside perspective. Dostoevsky not only knows his characters from inside, but he places parts of himself in both the male protagonist and the young girl. Devushkin is involved with literature—at one point he criticizes Gogol's *The Overcoat* for not showing enough sympathy for its hero—and mainly relates to the object of his love by writing; he shies away from actual contact. In these ways he resembles his creator, a man always more comfortable in the world of books. On the female side, it is known that an early plan for the novel was centered on Varvara; it was to have been an account of the misadventures of a young girl in the big city. This initial idea is retained in *Poor Folk* in a long autobiographical section where Varvara tells of her family and past. This account is closely modeled on Dostoevsky's own family background, he writes of himself through her. For example, she works hard at her studies to please her father, who loves her but is moody and irritable and makes her feel guilty. Her loving mother dies of tuberculosis. Dostoevsky's insight into his own father's inability to have empathy for his children is revealed in his writing that Varvara's father makes her feel

that I alone was at fault, and that I must answer for everything. Yet this did not arise from any *want of love* for me on the part of my father, but rather from the fact that he was incapable of putting himself in my own and my mother's place. It came of a defect of character.

Devushkin's name is derived from the Russian word for maid or young girl, again pointing to the mixture and complexity of the author's identification with his creations, his capacity to express aspects of himself through both male and female characters. The most central identification, one that cuts across both protagonists, is with their status as victims. Indeed, the whole work is based on Dostoevsky's deep feeling for, and identification with, those who suffer, who have been unfairly treated.

Poor Folk is not a great novel; it would be of little interest today if it were not for the works that followed. But it is the first in that line and it is interesting to see how many of Dostoevsky's persisting concerns and themes are already present in it, if only in faint outline. It is, of course, a novel about the love of an older man for a young girl/woman. There are echos of sexual guilt: something dishonorable may have occurred in Varvara's past and she and Devushkin are distantly related, giving a hint of the incestuous love that comes out more forcefully in the later works. Dostoevsky's conflicted feelings and identification with his mother and sisters—including the real Varvara—are no doubt behind this theme. More striking is the way in which romantic love is despoiled by crass material motives: Bykov—the first in a line that will come to include Luzhin and Svidrigailov—has seduced and abandoned other girls and only marries Varvara so that he can sire an heir and disinherit a nephew he dislikes. The novel ends as these base motives triumph over sympathy and love. Varvara is the first of many sexually victimized young girls.

Other of Dostoevsky's themes are only hinted at in *Poor Folk*. For all his meekness, Devushkin shows some pride and rebelliousness—he goes on a drinking spree at one point—and, for all her sweet innocence, Varvara tortures him a little, sending him on errands in preparation for her wedding. They are by no means the divided souls that will appear later—in the next novel, in fact—but they show glimpses of duality.

Rarely has a first novel met with such instant acclaim as *Poor Folk*, a circumstance brought about by a confluence of factors: the talent of its author and its intrinsic merit; its fit with the newly popular social realism; and the response of Belinsky, the most influential critic of the day. Dostoevsky showed the completed manuscript to his friend and fellow writer Grigorovich who, in turn, showed it to the young poet Nekrasov. They were so taken with it that they stayed up all night reading it aloud and returned to Dostoevsky's apartment at four in the morning to convey their enthusiasm. Nekrasov took it to Belinsky the next day and he, too, was enthusiastic; he could not put it down and exclaimed to one and all, with much emotion, that this was the work of a brilliant new talent. Belinsky's position and prestige were such that Dostoevsky was quickly taken up by the Petersburg literary community and showered with praise and adulation. For a young man of limited social experience, prone to grandiosity—and one who always went to the limit emotionally—this instant success was to prove a very mixed blessing.

CHAPTER 7

Nervous Crisis:
The Double

Dostoevsky's experiences in the years after the publication of *Poor Folk* read like something in one of his novels. This is no accident; life imitated art in an unconsciously determined way. The instant success of the first novel did not last, as critical voices were raised. A rapid rise and fall took place on the personal side as well. Dostoevsky was initially welcomed into the Petersburg literary circle surrounding Belinsky, but soon antagonized most of the members of this group as a boastful, vain, and domineering side of his personality emerged. As this was going on, he published his second novel, *The Double,* which met with a much less favorable response than *Poor Folk.* Significantly, *The Double* deals with the disastrous effects that occur when "another" side of the hero's personality breaks out. The criticism and rejection of both his work and his person precipitated a severe "nervous disorder": he became intensely anxious, fearful of death, suffered a number of hypochondriacal symptoms, and a disturbance in his sense of reality. He was able to weather this crisis with the help of a supportive doctor and friends and a gain in insight. As always, his tumultuous personal affairs provided material for his writing. *The Double,* even though completed at the beginning of this period, provides important information about its author's psychological state.

Through the childhood and academy years, Dostoevsky kept his writer self largely concealed from the outside world. His dreams of glory, his identification with great authors, and his literary ambitions were only confided to a few trusted intimates. With the publication and success of *Poor Folk* this secret self was suddenly exposed to the world. The actual acclaim he received fit only too well with his grand inner view. Here, he writes to Mikhail after the initial reception of the novel:

Well, brother, I believe my fame is just now in its fullest flower. Everywhere I meet with the most amazing consideration and enormous interest. . . . Prince Odoyesky begs me for the honour of a visit and Count Sollogub is tearing his hair in desperation. Panaev told him that a new genius had arisen who would sweep all the rest away. . . . Everybody looks upon me as a wonder of the world. If I but open my mouth, the air resounds with what Dostoevsky said, what Dostoevsky means to do. Belinsky loves me unboundedly. The writer Turgenev . . . has quite lost his heart to me. Turgenev is a really splendid person! I've almost lost my own heart to *him*.

With this view of his glorious reception by his literary peers—and this was his perception, others did not see him in quite such a glowing light—more of his personality began to assert itself. In the words of one biographer: "It opened the floodgates of a boundless vanity which, up to this point he had kept tightly closed. His letters are now filled with a manic exuberance and self-glorification . . . exhibiting a dangerous lack of self-control."

The young writers and poets, centered around Belinsky, were like a band of brothers and Dostoevsky was impelled to dominate them. He tried to take revenge on them for the humiliation he had suffered. In other words, the situation became an unconscious reenactment of his years in the family in which his competition with, and domination of, his siblings was a central outlet for the rage engendered in him from above. During the period under consideration, this was enacted with his actual brother as well as in relation to Turgenev and his other "brother" writers. He writes to Mikhail:

A whole crowd of new writers have popped up. In some I divine rivals. Particularly interesting are Herzen and Goncherov. Herzen has published some things. Goncherov is only beginning; and has not yet been printed. Both are immensely praised. But at present I have the top place, and hope to keep it forever.

And with Mikhail himself:

Sometimes a nameless grief possesses me. I can't help thinking perpetually how moody and "edgy" I was when with you at Ravel [the city where Mikhail was living]. I was ill then. I remember still how you once said to me that my behavior towards you excluded all sense of equality between us. My dear brother, that was unjust. I have indeed, it is true, an evil repellent character. But I have always ranked you above myself. I could give my life for you and yours; but even when my heart is warm with love, people often can't get so much as one friendly word out of me.

At such times I have lost control of my nerves.

While explaining it away as illness and the evil side of his character, he does not deny Mikhail's charge that his behavior "excluded all sense of equality."

A central gathering place for the circle of young writers was the literary salon presided over the wealthy Panaev and his beautiful young wife. Madame Panaeva's *Memoirs* provide a fairly objective picture of Dostoevsky at this time. The contrast between her view and the picture he paints of himself is striking:

It was evident, from only one glance at Dostoevsky, that he was a terribly nervous and impressionable person. He was slender, short, fair-haired, with a sickly complexion; his small gray eyes darted somewhat uneasily from object to object, and his colorless lips were nervously contorted. He already knew almost all of our guests, but, clearly, he was disconcerted and did not take part in the general conversation. Everyone tried to involve him, so as to overcome his shyness, and to make him feel that he was a member of the circle.

Because of his youth and nervousness, he did not know how to conduct himself, and he would only too clearly express his conceit as an author and his high opinion of his own literary talent. Stunned by the unexpected brilliance of his first step in his literary career, showered with the praises of competent literary judges, he could not, as an impressionable person, conceal his pride vis-à-vis other young writers whose first works had started them modestly on the same career. With the appearance of new young writers in the circle, trouble could be caused if they were rubbed the wrong way, and Dostoevsky, as if on purpose, did rub them the wrong way by his irritability and his haughty tone, implying that he was immeasurably superior to them in talent.

Unfortunately for Dostoevsky, the other young writers were not the easily dominated siblings of his childhood; like him, they were men of talent and pride. His conceit and superior tone aroused their ire and they began to provoke and bait him. Turgenev, at first friendly, became the leader of these attacks. He would draw Dostoevsky into argument and lead him to take extreme and ridiculous positions—which the excitable young author was prone to do—and then mock him. Madame Panaeva describes how one evening Turgenev invented a story about a man in the provinces who imagined himself a genius and then presented a thinly veiled satire of Dostoevsky who, "white as a sheet and quivering from head to foot took flight." He never returned to the Panaevs' and wrote to his brother that "they are all scoundrels and eaten up with envy."

There was another aspect of the rivalry in the group; Dostoevsky was secretly in love with Madame Panaeva who, at this time, became the mistress of the poet Nekrasov. It is hard to know how deep his infatuation was but it is another way in which he lost out to a rival. Looking back on the incidents of this period, one suspects that he was unconsciously driven to bring about the attack of his brother writers. Gratification and triumph must be paid for—in the calculus of his personal psychology—with punishment and suffering. He wouldn't have been Dostoevsky if he had taken his success reasonably and with modesty.

The critic Belinsky, while the central figure in the group, did not join in the personal attacks. He was aware of the young author's emotional instability and felt sympathy for him. But the difference in their views of literature soon led to a break that was even more damaging to Dostoevsky's state of mind than his falling out with Turgenev and the others. Belinsky's praise of *Poor Folk* was of great significance to Dostoevsky who allowed himself to be "adopted" by the older man. This praise and acceptance of his first novel, along with similar reactions from others in the Belinsky circle, facilitated the emergence of the concealed aspects of his character: the view of himself as a great writer, his competitive and domineering side, and, in the next novel, the split nature of his own personality. Emboldened by the reception of *Poor Folk,* he plunged into work on *The Double.* His letters reveal that he was much more personally involved with this book, which he called "a confession"; "Golyadkin [hero of *The Double*] has gained something from my spleen," he noted. *The Double* wrote itself through its author as the following account, in a letter to Mikhail, reveals:

Golyadkin is a bad hat! He is utterly base, and I positively can't manage him. He won't move a step, for he always maintains that he isn't ready; that he's a mere nothingness as yet, but *could,* if it were necessary, show his true character;

then why won't he? And after all, he says, he's no worse than the rest. What does *he* care about my toil? Oh, a terribly base fellow!"

While this is partly tongue-in-cheek, it does show how Dostoevsky experienced the creation of this work; Golyadkin came out of him and gave expression to a troublesome side of his own personality. Just as his behavior at the Panaevs' revealed his domineering side, *The Double* exposed his inner division to the light of day. This was a great risk, and failure to appreciate this newly revealed side of himself was extremely damaging. Belinsky was, at this point in his own evolution as a critic, strongly committed to social realism. While still enamoured of Dostoevsky's gifts, he was out of sympathy with *The Double*. After commenting on "the power, depth and originality of Mr. Dostoevsky's talent" and "the immense power of creative genius," he goes on to say that the novel "suffers from another important defect: its fantastic setting. In our days, the fantastic can have a place only in madhouses but not in literature, being the business of doctors, not poets."

Dostoevsky's own evaluation of *The Double* vacillated: at times he thought it his best work and, at others, he agreed with those who complained of its stylistic deficiencies. But Belinsky's attack on its fantastic character—his charge that it belonged in a madhouse—was another matter entirely. What the influential critic was calling fantastic and mad was the author's revelation of a deep truth about himself. This line of criticism from his former admirer was a devastating blow to his emerging sense of self.

It was at precisely this time that he suffered his severe "nervous illness." The events that brought it on can be summarized as follows: the success and praise that greeted his first work encouraged him to expose more of the long-concealed aspects of himself to others. In doing so, he took the risk of exposing this fledgling inner self to damaging attacks. The falling out with Turgenev and the other young writers was troublesome but not unmanageable; there was always much competition among authors and he could turn to other friends. More of him was invested in his work than his social relations in any case, and much of his self esteem—his narcissistic pride—was tied up in *The Double*, a novel that revealed a good deal about his mental state. When this work was criticized—especially by Belinsky and especially as fantastic and mad—this was a staggering blow. He had exposed himself to the real world and this world was—like his family and those at the academy—uncomprehending, hostile, and critical. His reaction was a nervous collapse that was the most serious psychological crisis of his life. Part of the irony here is that *The Double* is the best work of his early period. It is a brilliant and darkly humorous study, far ahead of its time, and the only one of the novels from his preimprisonment days that is still widely read.

We can obtain a fuller understanding of the nervous crisis of 1846–48 by looking first at the details of Dostoevsky's symptoms and, second, at his portrayal of a parallel crisis in Mr. Golyadkin, hero of *The Double*. Some years later, Dostoevsky told a friend:

Two years before Siberia, at the time of my various literary difficulties and quarrels, I was the victim of some sort of strange and unbearably torturing nervous illness. I cannot tell you what these hideous sensations were: it often seemed to me that I was dying, and the truth is—real death came and then went away again.

At the core of the nervous crisis was a powerful anxiety, manifest in a variety of symptoms. There were many fears centered on his body, "nervous spasms of the throat," pains, dizziness, and trouble sleeping. There were paranoid distortions of reality centered around the quarrels with his literary rivals. That is, the real arguments took on an exaggerated form, at worst becoming a sort of persecution mania. At least one experience qualifies as a hallucination: in bed at night he would see death in the form of a "mystic horror." The fear of death was so strong and so real that he would leave notes warning his friends not to bury his body if he seemed to be dead lest he be buried alive.

A brief word needs to be said about the relation of these fears and symptoms to his epilepsy which was present in its early form at the time. While there is some dispute among the biographers, the best evidence points to a few incidents of temporary loss of consciousness and one or two mild seizures. Since these were not initially diagnosed as epilepsy, they no doubt fed into the general state of anxiety. I do not think that a dawning awareness of the epilepsy itself can account for the nervous crisis, but it was part of the physical-psychological constitution that made him susceptible to these sorts of experiences. The quote, above, in which he says that "real death came and then went away again" is from a later time in his life after the epilepsy had been diagnosed and he was familiar with his seizures. Clearly, he is referring to something more than the loss of consciousness of an epileptic attack, although, as we will see, the same thematic meaning that underlay the nervous crisis, was later tied to the seizures.

Let me attempt an interpretation of the anxiety, symptoms, and fear of death that draws on what we know of Dostoevsky's history and unique personality structure. As a young boy he struggled with a number of severe conflicts in his family: the loss of his loved mother to rivals and, eventually, to illness and death; a demanding, insensitive, and guilt-inducing father; and a general atmosphere of emotional strain, hypocrisy, and falseness. While the exuberant, creative, and spirited Fedya was in evidence in the early years, by late childhood and adolescence the most vital and lively part of him was withdrawn into a private world of fantasy. To the outside world, he presented a false self of compliance; his real self lived within. This split of his person was greatly intensified during late adolescence—the years at the Academy of Military Engineering—where the outward young man was secretive and isolated; he went through the motions of his role but held himself aloof from it.

Students of conditions such as this (Kohut 1977; Laing 1960; Winnicott 1965) note several of its regular features. The false self is associated with the body, which is often treated as a meaningless "thing," that is as if it were not alive. Many who knew Dostoevsky during this period note his apparent lack of concern about his body and his unhealthy appearance. The real self is tied to ideas and fantasies which may be kept entirely to oneself or shared with one or two others. This part of the person is experienced as "alive" though, paradoxically, it may have the least contact with the world of others. Because the fantasy or inner-self has existed in an isolated state it has not been tempered by reality testing. It is often heroic, grandiose, and possessed of great powers; destructive fantasies run to extremes. While such a divided state of existence evolves out of necessity it is a delicate equilibrium in two ways. First, people have a need for real contact and attachment to others; withdrawal into a fantasy world eventually leads to intense loneliness. Second, despite our rather amazing capacity for defensiveness, splits, and dissociations of all sorts, we are also motivated toward the creation of a coherent ego, a unified self. So the divided individual is impelled both to maintain his split existence and to heal it through contact with others.

When we look at Dostoevsky we must introduce an important modi-fication into this account; his real, or inner, self was not entirely nur-tured on fantasy: it was identified with books, authors, literature, and writing. Connections with others who shared these interests always offered a road back to reality. It was the main—and, at this time in life, the only—means of regaining a unified existence.

With the acceptance of his first novel and the praise of Belinsky and his circle, Dostoevsky began to express more and more of his inner self. He allowed those parts of him that always felt most *alive* into the public world. But, since he had long lived an isolated existence, he did not know how to behave in public. In psychoanalytic terms we would say that his personality contained a number of poorly integrated self frag-ments or introjects. There was a grandiose self, focused on its own power and insensitive to others, along with a self that deeply needed the praise and acceptance of these same others. There was a part of him that was generous, helpful and which felt at one with victims, and another part that was sadistic and impelled to dominate those beneath him. First one of the selves would be in control and then another; his own com-ments from this time show how he felt at the mercy of emotional states that were often at cross-purposes.

The self that emerged in the Belinsky circle was grandiose and egocen-tric in ways that offended others and brought forth criticism and hostil-ity rather than the adulation Dostoevsky desired. His literary peers were not a group of loving mothers; it was his poorly developed sense of reality that led him to expect anything other than the reaction he re-ceived. Their criticism and hostility felt like an attack on his very core. He had taken a chance on coming alive, on being reborn into this world of writers and lovers of literature, and they were killing him. Only the false, outer self was confirmed, the self of mediocrity and conformity, the part of him associated with his body, which he now experienced as sick and falling apart.

As Dostoevsky's correspondence makes clear, he imagined the Peters-burg literary world as an all-loving family. He would be the best-loved child, the one "who would sweep all the rest away," and "have the top place . . . and keep it forever." The power of this fantasy, and the extremes to which it ran, arose from the same capacities that made him a great imaginative novelist: his particular openness to identifications and his propensity to experience emotions and relationships vividly as parts of himself, including as parts of his body. The Petersburg literary world began, in his mind, as a loving mother that brought his writer self to life; when the members of this world turned on him, he felt it as a death like attack: his very body was in danger of dying, just at it was after Maria's death.

The divided existence of his childhood and adolescence was relatively stable; it was an adjustment that provided some security. He was left without this security when his inner self made its debut and—lacking his long-standing defensive adaptation and finding himself without an empathic milieu—he was precipitated into a state of intense anxiety. His fear of dying or, more precisely, the feeling that he actually experienced death, is the feeling of a person without inner or outer support; a person with no reliable defenses, identity, or relationships.

States of acute anxiety such as these are intolerable. A new adaptation is desperately sought. Dostoevsky fled the Belinsky circle and sought out others for support. Most important was a young doctor named Stepan Yanovsky. Dr. Yanovsky was interested in literature and was, at first, flattered to work with the famous young author. He successfully treated him for what sounds like a venereal disease but their work soon focused on the symptoms of the nervous illness. He would come every morning and Yanovsky would take his pulse, listen to his heart, reassure him that his hallucinations and other symptoms were due to nerves and that his physical health was normal. They became friends and would have tea and talk after the fears were calmed. Religion, literature, philosophy, and life were all discussed in these daily sessions that had some things in common with what today would be called psychotherapy. He appears to have relied on Yanovsky in this fashion daily for three years. The doctor's sympathy and calm reassurance were crucial in gaining control of the anxiety and symptoms. In addition, he was an important anchor in reality, someone that Dostoevsky trusted to check out his frightening ideas and distortions. Yanovsky was the only doctor he ever trusted and they remained friends for the rest of their lives. Dostoevsky also read many of the doctor's books dealing with nervous disease—then a poorly developed field—as he attempted to understand his own condition.

In addition to the friendship with Yanovsky, Dostoevsky became involved with a group of young writers, critics, and friends whose support and sympathy, on both the personal and intellectual levels, were very important. During the worst months, when he was, as he wrote to his brother, "almost in a panic of fear about my health," he took up with a former friend from the academy, a man named Beketov. Beketov, his two younger brothers, Dostoevsky, his friend Grigorovich, and some others moved into a spacious apartment where they shared meals and living expenses. Dostoevsky writes to Mikhail:

Brother, I am reborn, not only morally but also physically. Never have I felt in myself so much abundance and clarity, so much equanimity of character, so much physical health. I am indebted for much of this to my good friends, Beketov . . . and others with whom I live; they are sensible and intelligent people, with hearts of gold, of nobility and character. They cured me by their company.

In effect, he had found a band of accepting brothers to replace those of the Belinsky circle, where hatred and rivalry had gotten out of hand. The new group was compatible personally and shared a passionate indignation at the injustices so prevalent in their society. At this same time he also became friends with Valerian Maikov, who took over Belinsky's position as chief critic on one of the most important literary journals. Where Belinsky had dismissed *The Double*, Maikov was responsive to its merits and wrote about it with penetrating insight. Unfortunately, the talented young critic died prematurely. Dostoevsky transferred his affection to his brother, the poet Apollon Maikov, who remained a close friend and correspondent through the later years. In 1847, he persuaded Mikhail to move with his family to Petersburg—much to the annoyance of future biographers since there was, then, no need for the revealing correspondence between them—further bolstering his group of supportive brothers.

In all these ways, Dostoevsky was able to make use of his capacity for friendship with men his own age in overcoming the frightening symptoms that beset him. He also worked on his difficulties in another way; he examined himself honestly and, in his letters and novels, began to express the insights gained from this self-scrutiny. In 1846 he writes to Mikhail. "I was for some time utterly discouraged. I have one terrible vice: I am unpardonably ambitious and egoistic." The next year he wrote,

It is indeed true that the dissonance and lack of equilibrium between ourselves and society is a terrible thing. External and internal things should be in equilibrium. For, lacking external experiences, those of the inward life will gain the upper hand, and that is most dangerous. The nerves and the fancy then take up too much room, as it were, in our consciousness. Every external happening seems colossal and frightens us. We begin to fear life.

In this passage, he is describing the way in which his own unconscious side—his inner self—had gotten out of hand, with very frightening results. His self-analysis was a continuous process, of course, worked on throughout his career; here are some remarks in an article published in 1847:

When a man is dissatisfied, when he is unable to express himself and reveal what is best in him not out of vanity, but because of the most natural necessity to become aware of, to embody and to fulfill his Ego in real life, he at once falls into some quite incredible situations; one, if I may say so, takes to the bottle in a big way; another becomes a gambler and cardsharp; another a quarrelsome bully; another, finally, goes off his head because of ambition, at the same time completely despising ambition and even suffering because he has had to suffer over such nonsense as ambition.

(The Russian word *ambitisia* does not have the same neutral meaning as its English synonym. In Russian, the word has the pejorative sense of self-love, pride, and arrogance.)

These remarks are followed by a plea on behalf of "necessary egoism." What he says directly here is that it is absolutely necessary to express all sides of one's nature—"to become aware of, to embody and to fulfill his ego in real life" and that the inability to do so leads to pathology. When Dostoevsky himself attempted to express all that was in him, he almost went off his head with ambition—pride, arrogance— as these long surpressed emotions burst forth. Having weathered the nervous crisis, he does not shrink back and urge conformity and repression. On the contrary, he continues to advocate "necessary egoism" and to search for ways in which all of him can be expressed. The quotation ends with a typical piece of Dostoevskian irony, a reference to the man who "goes off his head because of ambition, at the same time despising ambition and even suffering because he has had to suffer over such nonsense as ambition." This describes his own dilemma in the Belinsky circle and, in a related way, the problem faced by Mr. Golyadkin, hero of *The Double*. The novel was written just before the nervous illness, yet it anticipates what shortly befell its author.

Dostoevsky: The Author as Psychoanalyst

The Double is about a man, Yakov Petrovich Golyadkin, who splits in two; he encounters another version of himself, his double, in a way that seems real to him. The novel portrays, in other words, a concretization of projection.[1] Many commentators have noted antecedents of the theme. Readers of English are probably most familiar with Robert Louis Stevenson's *Doctor Jekyll and Mr. Hyde*. Dostoevsky knew the works of Edgar Allen Poe and the German fantasist E. T. A. Hoffmann well, but was most influenced by his immediate predecessor, Gogol, especially his stories *The Diary of a Madman* and *The Nose*. In this last, the hero's nose vanishes from his face and assumes an independent identity, going about town in the uniform of an officer. *The Double* moves beyond these earlier works in several ways. Gogol's *The Nose* counterposes the fantastic with the banal to humorous effect, but it is narrated from an outside perspective, it does not arouse the reader's sympathy for the protagonist. Rather, one is amused by a grotesque and laughs at the odd contradictions. *The Double* has some of this humor but the narrator is closer to the hero, a closeness that grows as the novel moves along. In other words, the author is identified with his character and writes in a way that draws the reader into this identification. If we let ourselves, we feel his fear, shame, and confusion. Dostoevsky creates a mode of expression for Golyadkin that is just right for a man who is at once pretentious and terribly insecure. He talks in a mixture of clichés, obsessive repetitions, and vague generalizations; it is hard for the other characters—or the reader—to understand just what he is trying to say. Dostoevsky also conveys Golyadkin's difficulty distinguishing between fantasy and reality, a difficulty that increases as the novel draws to its end. The reader, too, feels this confusion; we are never certain just who or what the other Golyadkin is. Is he just a projection of the hero's imagination? If so, why do other characters relate to him in a normal fashion? Is he some other person that Golyadkin misperceives as his double? Possibly, but, again, the response of others leaves this uncertain. It is left unclear for us because that is the way it is for Golyadkin; we are made to share the experience of someone whose sense of a unified self is crumbling.

There is another aspect of the style that must be noted: the irony. Dostoevsky treats Golyadkin in a mock-heroic fashion; he is "our hero" and we follow his "adventures," though he is anything but heroic and the adventures consist of petty and insignificant matters. This tone brings out the contrast between Golyadkin's romantic fantasies and the world of reality on which they founder. Dostoevsky also mocks his own romantic illusions here, the ways in which he was "a Schiller," by this counterposition of romantic hopes with the mundane world of clerks and servants, of "Excellencies" and bribes, of noble aspirations and materialistic strivings. While Dostoevsky no longer dreamed of being a hero out of Walter Scott or Schiller at this time in his life, he did harbor grand ambitions as a novelist, in fact, for this very novel! In all these ways, he conveys the experience of the divided individual from an inside perspective. He did, after all, refer to the novel as a confession and one of his friends described him at the time as "extremely withdrawn, cautious, fearful and socially over-anxious," just as his "hero" is. Yet, it must be added, he is not Golyadkin; the novelist who creates the character, and who develops the innovative sytlistic devices to convey this experience, is an insightful outside observer. Dostoevsky is, in other words, both inside and outside, experiencing the Golyadkin in himself and getting the distance from this experience that allows him to bring it alive for the reader. The creation of this brilliant work is an example of the way in which he was most sane when turning his personal conflicts into literature.

Now, to the novel itself. Golyadkin is a middle-level clerk in one of those endless Petersburg bureaucracies. He lives in an apartment with his servant. Unlike Devushkin in *Poor Folk,* his problem is not poverty but psychological conflict. He is torn between grandiose aspirations— ambition—and extreme social timidity and ineptitude. As the novel opens, he is attempting to bridge the gap, to fulfill his aspirations in the real world. He has hired a carriage and outfitted his servant in livery, much as Dostoevsky's parents used to do in their social climbing days. He reassures himself by counting his money and sets out to crash the birthday party of the beautiful Klara, daughter of his superior, whom he secretly loves. He has his romantic dreams: he aspires, he can be as good as any of them, and maybe he will even win her hand or rescue her from some dreadful fate. Yet it is clear that she doesn't know who he is and that he has not been invited to the party.

The disparity between the inner dream and his outer performance is immediately brought forth as he rides through town in his rented carriage, dressed in his finest clothes. Andrey Philippovich "head of the section in the Department where Mr. Golyadkin was . . . assistant to the head of his subsection" drives by and sees him.

Mr. Golyadkin, seeing that Andrey Philippovich had recognized him beyond doubt and was staring with all his might, so that he could not hope to remain concealed, blushed to the roots of his hair. "Ought I to bow? Should I speak to him or not? Ought I acknowledge our acquaintance?" Our hero wondered in indescribable anguish. "Or shall I pretend it's not me but somebody else strikingly like me, and look as if nothing's the matter?" said Mr. Golyadkin, lifting his hat to Andrey Philippovich and not taking his eyes off him. "I . . . It's all right," he whispered, hardly able to speak, "It's quite all right; this is not me at all, not me, and that's all about it."

In this humorous yet poignant scene, the contradiction between aspiration and realization is forcefully illustrated. Imagining himself a dashing hero, he is ashamed to be seen by his superior and does not know how to manage a simple greeting. And, we see the beginnings of a solution to his painful dilemma: he will pretend to be someone other than himself. This pretense, carried to its logical end, will result in the most extreme disavowal: the appearance of another "him."

Sensing that something is wrong, Golyadkin stops to see his doctor, Christian Ivanovich Rutenspitz. The disparity between his inner state and the outside world is brought out in another way as he attempts, with little success, to communicate with the doctor:

"I was saying you must excuse me, Christian Ivanovich, I am not a master of eloquence, as far as I am aware," said Mr. Golyadkin, in a half-offended tone of voice, slightly losing the thread and stumbling a little. "In this respect, Christian Ivanovich, I am not like other people," he added, with a special kind of smile, "and I have not the art of talking at length; I never learned to beautify my phrases. On the other hand, Christian Ivanovich, I act; I act on the other hand, Christian Ivanovich!" . . . I, Christian Ivanovich, like peace and quiet and not fashionable hubbub. There, Christian Ivanovich, in society, I say you must learn how to polish the parquet with your shoes"—here Mr. Golyadkin scraped his foot lightly over the floor—"it's expected of you, sir, and you're expected to make puns, too, you have to be able to produce a well-turned compliment, that's what's expected of you. And I've not learnt to do all that, Christian Ivanovich, I've never studied all those clever tricks; I had no time. I am a simple uncomplicated person, and it isn't in me to shine in society. In that respect, I lay down my arms; I lower my sword, speaking in that sense. [To which the uncomprehending doctor replies,] "you appear to have digressed slightly from the point. . . . and I confess I couldn't quite follow you."

Golyadkin is trying to tell the doctor that he really doesn't know how to act in society—a problem faced by the young author himself at this time—but his confession is so mixed in with self-justifications, repetitions, and clichés that the communication is not heard.

The interview with the doctor ends to no good effect, and "our hero" moves on to the fateful party. He sneaks in through the kitchen, makes his appearance, tries to compliment the beautiful Klara, and even dance with her, but feels stared and laughed at by everyone as he stumbles and makes a fool of himself. The shame and humiliation are literally mortifying:

Everything was stillness and silence and expectancy; a little further away someone whispered, a little nearer, someone tittered. Mr. Golyadkin cast a humble, desperate look at Andrey Philippovich. Andrey Philippovich answered him with a glance which, if our hero had not been quite, quite dead already, would certainly have killed him again, if that were possible.

He is thrown out of the party, his aspirations totally shattered and, in this state, his precarious ego comes apart: he splits in two.

If some casual and uninvolved passer-by had chanced to give an indifferent side-glance at Mr. Golyadkin's melancholy flight, even he would immediately have been stirred to the depths by all the dire horror of his disastrous plight, and would infallibly have said that Mr. Golyadkin looked as if he was trying to hide from himself, as if he wanted to run away from himself. Yes, it really was so! We will say more: Mr. Golyadkin wanted not only to run away from himself but even to annihilate himself, to cease to be, to return to the dust.

This threatened death of the self requires desperate defensive measures:

He began to look around him with inexplicable anxiety; but there was nobody, nothing particular had happened and yet . . . and yet it seemed to him that just now, this very moment, somebody had been standing there, close to him, by his side.

This shadowy figure takes substance and Golyadkin comes face to face with another version of himself. There is, in other words, an increase in projection as he attempts to rid himself of the qualities that have led to his humiliating rejection: it is not he who is ambitious, not he; it is another Golyadkin. For all the mock horror of the style, Dostoevsky describes the experience of the disintegration of the self and loss of the sense of reality with great acuity.

Golyadkin junior appears at the office the next morning, a newly hired clerk. Golyadkin senior—the "real" Golyadkin as we are repetitively told—is shocked, but others see nothing amiss.

> "Anton Antonovich, I . . . here . . . I'm an employee here, Anton Antonovich. . . ."
> "Well? I still don't understand."
> "I mean, Anton Antonovich, that there's a new employee here."
> "Yes, there is; his name's the same as yours."
> "What?" exclaimed Mr. Golyadkin.
> "I said his name's the same as yours; he's another Golyadkin. Is he your brother?"
> "No, sir. Anton Antonovich, I . . . "
> "H'm! Then how is it . . . and I supposed he must be a close relative of yours. You know, there is some . . . what might be called family likeness."
> Mr. Golyadkin was dumb with astonishment; for a time he simply could not speak. To treat such a shocking, such an unprecedented subject so lightly, a matter really unique of its kind, a matter that would have astonished even an indifferent bystander, to talk about a family likeness, when there was no more difference between them than if they were two peas in a pod!

The disparity between Golyadkin's perception of his double and the reactions of others, who see nothing wrong, continues for the remainder of the novel. What Dostoevsky captures here is the frightening estrangement that a person such as this feels; it is Golyadkin's ego that is falling apart—it is his anxiety—so naturally he is agitated. To others, the world appears normal, and they show no concern. He cannot tell them; his attempts to talk with Anton Antonovich, like his earlier efforts to communicate with the doctor, are unsuccessful. The main reason he cannot communicate is his own lack of insight; he is driven to his defensive efforts by extreme anxiety, and he really doesn't know what is happening to him.

At first Golyadkin is on good terms with the double, he takes him home, gives him dinner, invites him to spend the night, and shares certain confidences. I think this represents the initial hope that this new form of projection will prove successful, that it will restore his equilibrium and sense of well-being. But it is doomed. The very next day at the office, Golyadkin junior does not acknowledge their friendship and begins to take over. He is busy, officious, and shows none of Golyadkin senior's shyness as he worms his way into the confidence of the authorities. This sets the course for the rest of the book. Golyadkin junior becomes more evilly ambitious and successful—he is continually seen mincing about, sucking up to supervisors, and pushing his timid counterpart aside—while Golyadkin senior becomes more frightened and paranoid—he sees "enemies" everywhere and is less and less able to deal with the world. Senior is the "real," the "honest," the "straight-forward" Mr. Golyadkin, we are continually reminded, but his ambitious double —the "nasty, dishonest and treacherous" Mr. Golyadkin junior—undermines him at every turn.

As Dostoevsky plays out the theme of the two personalities, the psychological insight that sets him apart from his predecessors becomes evident. The two Golyadkins do not represent good and evil—nor even ambition and timidity—in any simply way. Rather, we see what happens when a person is driven to extreme defensive efforts. Both sides of his conflict are increasingly exaggerated, neither is an acceptable identity, the personality is more and more torn, until it collapses entirely. The ambitious Golyadkin junior is successful, but only by becoming a toady; he is shown as dishonest and sickeningly ingratiating. As his success grows, Golyadkin senior becomes correspondingly frightened, ineffectual, and powerless. Dostoevsky conveys this widening gap with an increase of adjectives so that, by the end, we have our "noble, frank and open hero" and his "false friend's awful treachery." What is portrayed here is the failure of projection as it would be experienced by such a person. Golyadkin tries to get rid of his undesirable qualities by putting them in a split-off "other," but this only makes them more undesirable *and* they follow him around and ruin his life; he cannot get rid of them. Nor does the dissociation ease his pain; throughout, he remains ashamed and frightened, and, in the end, he makes a last barely coherent attempt to humble himself before authority:

"It's like this. As I say, I've come to explain. Your excellency."
"But . . . Who are you?"
"M-m-mister Golyadkin, Your Excellency, Titular Councillor Golyadkin."

"Well, what do you want?"

"As I say, it's like this: I look on him as a father; I stand aloof in the whole affair—and protect me from my enemy! There you are!"

"What is all this?"

"Everybody knows. . . . "

"What does everybody know?"

Mr. Golyadkin said nothing; his chin was beginning to tremble slightly.

There follows his final collapse and he is taken off to an insane asylum.

Let me attempt to sum up Dostoevsky's achievement in *The Double*. One can think of the novel as an experiment with projection, splitting, and dissociation; with what happens when these defensive efforts are carried to extremes. The underlying conflict is between ambition and social anxiety, between grand aspirations and the lack of skill to realize these in the world. Initially, we are presented with a character who sees himself as an important man of substance—if not a romantic hero—a vision that contrasts sharply with his subservient and timid behavior as a clerk. His pride is submerged and he is driven to assert it, he tries to fulfill his aspirations, just as the author was doing at this time in his life. But his inner self has been isolated too long, he has almost no skill with other people, and, when his efforts to act in the world go awry, he becomes more defensive. Instead of learning from his mistakes he is more threatened and blames others: projection increases. Golyadkin is close-mouthed and suspicious to begin with, and as the events unfold he more and more feels his enemies everywhere. There are several marvelously realized scenes in which we see him create his own persecution; attempting simultaneously to express his greatness and hide himself, he talks in vague and grandiose terms to some younger clerks who end up laughing at him.

There are two related ways in which Golyadkin attempts to rid himself of his own threatening and undesirable characteristics. There is projection of the familiar sort in which criticism and attacks on the self are experienced as coming from others: a vaguely defined group of "enemies." And there is the creation or experience of an entire, split-off self, the other Mr. Golyadkin, who contains all that the hero cannot manage within his existing identity. It is in the elaboration of the two selves, their relationship with each other, and their ultimate fate that Dostoevsky's psychological genius is apparent. The "real" Golyadkin—

who keeps maintaining that he is the real one, that the qualities represented by the other are not part of him—tries to be friendly, to the authorities who neglect and misunderstand him, as well as to his own disreputable "other." His persistent attempt to claim that he is the honest, straightforward, and real Mr. Golyadkin only serves to increase the distance between his two sides. Dissociation and projection become more entrenched and his perception of reality more distorted. The projection of all the nasty, dishonest ambition into the other Mr. Golyadkin leaves the original with no pride, no power, no strength, a crucial process that Dostoevsky brilliantly portrays as the original becomes more and more empty and anxious and his split-off self more vicious. In the end, the ability to function in the world is lost, the hero is left with no viable identity—he has been "killed," "utterly annihilated"—and he regresses into a state of helplessness.

At several points in this discussion of *The Double,* I have noted the connections between Dostoevsky's life and the novel. Like Golyadkin, Dostoevsky was insecure, anxious about other's perception of him, suspicious, and very sensitive to social slights. He had lived an isolated life, with a prideful inner self held in check, and did not know how to express this side openly in an effective way. The romantic aspirations of his "hero" had their counterparts in his own adolescent dreams of glory and, ironically, in his great hopes for this very novel. In all these ways, he was writing about emotional states that were his own. Golyadkin's final insanity is paralleled by his own nervous illness though he never reached the desperate state of his hero.

But, there are crucial differences between the author and his fictional creation. Golyadkin has little real inner substance; what is exposed when pride impels him to assert himself is the most petty ambition. Dostoevsky, of course, was a writer of great talent, a powerful intellect with interesting—if sometimes extreme—things to say on a wide range of topics. While he was unpolished and rude in his aspirations, there was a great deal of rich substance within. In Golyadkin, he exaggerates and parodies the problematic sides of himself. By doing so, he obtains distance and control over them. We can, again, see a parallel between the process of writing and psychoanalysis. Turning his conflicts and troubling emotional states into a novel required him to work this inchoate material into an organized form. As he wrote it out in a way that met his own demanding artistic standards, private preoccupations and concerns were transformed into understandable public communications. This was a way of bringing these sides of himself into contact with reality. In other words, as he wrote about the extreme and ridiculous aspects of Golyadkin, he gained some distance and objectivity—some insight—into his own related difficulties.[2]

The self-analytical potential of *The Double* was temporarily derailed by the hostile reception it received within the Belinsky circle. This led, as we have seen, to the nervous illness and the seeking of a new group of friends and critics who were more understanding. The setback was temporary, Dostoevsky reconstituted himself and pushed on in his quest "to become aware of, to embody and to fulfill his ego in real life." He always considered *The Double* an important work, it had a special significance for him and is one of the very few of his early novels that he rewrote. (The version we have today is a revision done in 1861, though the revising consisted mainly in cutting and shortening, the substance was all there in 1845.) Modern readers share his assessment: *The Double* is a small masterpiece; its reception in the 1840s was mixed because it was so far ahead of its time. Dostoevsky suffered the fate of many innovative geniuses: it took awhile for his contemporaries to catch up with him.

CHAPTER 8

Political Conspiracy:
The Possessed

We come now to one of the most dramatic episodes in Dostoevsky's life: his arrest for political subversion and his years of imprisonment in Siberia. A consideration of this period will sharpen our understanding of his political, social, and religious ideas. There is a popular view, mistaken in my opinion, that Dostoevsky was a socialist—even a radical or revolutionary—in the late 1840s before his arrest, and that his years in prison transformed him into a political conservative, a Russian nationalist, and Christian. This view is incorrect, he was never a revolutionary nor much of a socialist, to begin with, and he was a very unconventional conservative and Christian afterwards. Some biographers put forth the view that he returned from prison purified and humane. But Dr. Yanovsky, who knew him more intimately than anyone in the years before his arrest says he was *"just exactly the same* as he returned from Siberia and as he departed to the grave." As is always the case, he does not fit into the standard categories. The years in prison and Siberia had their effect on him—how could they not?—but it is also striking how his underlying character was untouched by these events. His writing picks up ten years later with the same themes and preoccupations that were interrupted by the arrest.

In 1847 Dostoevsky began attending Friday evening meetings at the home of Mikhail Petrashevsky. A number of writers, students, artists, and intellectuals came to these meetings to discuss the political and social events of the day. Petrashevsky was a dedicated follower of the utopian socialist Fourier, and he had a large library with many forbidden books. The group formed a loose association—part social club and part debating society—where issues such as atheism, the emancipation of the serfs, women's rights, and visionary socialist schemes were discussed. No one advocated revolution or violent attacks on the government; most of these intellectuals believed in spreading enlightenment through talk and the dissemination of written works.

After the European uprisings of 1848, the discussions at Petrashevsky's took on an increasingly political cast; this was not to the liking of some of the group, including Dostoevsky, who began holding their own meetings at an apartment shared by Alexander Palm and Sergey Durov. The Palm-Durov group was artistic as well as political. The evenings there included readings of poems and novels, musical performances, and much less talk of socialist schemes. The members of this group held quite diverse views, including artists with little interest in politics, Fourierist dreamers, and socialists and radicals.

Most striking of the radicals was Nikolay Speshnev. Speshnev was wealthy, handsome, cool, and aloof. He had lived in Europe, where he had associated with socialists, and was believed to be irresistable to women. In fact, he was thought to be, quite literally, a ladykiller: he had stolen a beautiful woman away from her husband and she was rumored to have poisoned herself as a result of their affair. His self-possessed air and the aura of romance and revolution made him an attractive figure. He came to have a special hold on Dostoevsky. Yanovsky, whom Dostoevsky continued to see at this time, quotes his patient as saying:

I have taken money from Speshnev [five hundred rubles] and now I am *with him* and *his*. I'll never be able to pay back such a sum, yes, and he wouldn't take the money back; that's the kind of man he is. . . . From now on I have a Mephistopheles of my own."

Just why Dostoevsky felt Speshnev had such a hold on him—it wasn't only because of the borrowed money for he was, as usual, in debt to everyone he knew—will become clear shortly. As always, the transformed version in a novel will be our best source; Speshnev is the model for Stavrogin in *The Possessed,* a work written many years later (in 1872) that draws on the events of this period.

Speshnev was no idle talker. He recruited a small group—including Dostoevsky—into a secret society whose purpose was to assemble a printing press in order to publish material without the permission of the government censor. All the members of this secret group attended the Palm-Durov meetings, along with many others such as Mikhail Dostoevsky—a committed Fourierist—and Dostoevsky's good friend, the non-political poet Apollon Maikov, who turned down Feodor's request to join the secret group.

What was Dostoevsky's participation in the meetings at Petrashevsky's and Durov's? For the most part he was withdrawn and said little. He felt a passionate indignation over the mistreatment of society's victims, as we should not be surprised to learn. Like most of the participants, he favored freedom for the serfs and the abolition of corporal punishment. He did not share the atheism of some members, such as Petrashevsky himself, nor was he critical of Russia or the government in any general way. He was sympathetic to the goals and ideals of the socialists—especially the vision of a life of unity, peace, and harmony—but remained skeptical concerning the practical implementation of these goals. He was never drawn to those aspects of socialist ideology that favored a planned and controlled society organized along "rational" lines. On the contrary, he spoke out on behalf of artistic freedom and he disagreed with Petrashevsky, as he had with Belinsky earlier, over the political uses of literature. Where they put political and social concerns first and saw art as an instrument of social change, he argued forcefully that literature must be free to develop in its own way; the artist should never be subject to political control.

Shortly before his arrest, Dostoevsky read aloud Belinsky's famous open letter to Gogol. This act was to serve as one of the specific charges against him. Since this letter involves two figures who had important influences in his earlier career, we need to be clear as to just what it contained and why he chose to read it in public. Toward the end of his life, Gogol—who had himself long struggled with the censorship of the repressive government—had become a frightened sycophant. He published *Selected Passages from My Correspondence with My Friends,* a politically conservative book that attempted to justify and rationalize the status quo. Belinsky wrote a stinging attack on this book in the form of an open letter, an attack that laid bare government abuses and deficiencies. He argued eloquently for three points: freeing the serfs, the abolition of corporal punishment, and the strict enforcement of the laws (essentially to control widespread favoritism and bribery). The letter was not a call for illegal action or the overthrow of the tsar, though it was, of course, branded revolutionary and banned by the government. It's main points were in line with Dostoevsky's own sentiments, and this, along with its literary merit, led him to bring it to the attention of his friends and to read it aloud at Durov's and Petrashevsky's.

In April of 1849, Dostoevsky, along with more than twenty others— including Petrashevsky, Durov, Speshnev, the members of the secret group, Mikhail, and others—were arrested and charged with crimes against the government. Petrashevsky's meetings had long been attended by a government spy who supplied the authorities with full reports of the activities there. What followed gives a clear picture of the police-state in which Dostoevsky lived and worked. He was placed in solitary confinement for some eight months, for the first four cut off from all contact with the outside world, and not allowed to write. The charges against him were taken up by a military commission. There was no question of a trial with legal rights and safeguards as we know them, nor even as they existed in Russia some fifteen years later. He was informed of the charges and was required to write out a statement and to answer the commission's questions. They would decide on his guilt or innocence. The charges of which he was ultimately convicted were having read the Belinsky letter at several meetings, having taken part in conversations questioning the severity of the government censorship, having listened to readings of various articles at Durov's, and, having knowledge of a plan to establish a secret printing press (The press itself was not found by the government).

In his written and oral response to the military tribunal Dostoevsky showed great courage. While he attempted to minimize the illegal side of his activities he did not back down from his convictions. He spoke out against the censorship in favor of free literary expression. He tried to protect his friends even when this meant taking responsibility for acts that could lead to severe punishment. The record justifies Leonid Grossman's conclusion: "Dostoevsky's testimony is striking for its intellectual power, its independence and truthfulness, its dignity and nobility." This was one of those rare occasions when a person is put to a public test of his convictions. Dostoevsky showed the strength of his character.

All of this was in vain, of course. The tsar had decided to make an example of the Petrashevskyites and most of them were convicted (Mikhail and some others were released). Dostoevsky's punishment was to be four years of penal servitude and then "into the ranks" as a private in the army, all to be served in Siberia. As an added piece of cruelty, the tsar directed that all of the "conspirators" face a mock execution. This was, in fact, carried out. After eight months in solitary confinement, he and the others were taken before a firing squad and the death sentence was read to them. The first group of prisoners was prepared—he was in the second group—and then, at the last moment, an announcement was read that the tsar, in his infinite mercy, had spared their lives and they were informed of their actual sentences. For a brief period, Dostoevsky believed he was about to be killed. The harshness of the sentence, the added cruelty of the mock execution, and the complete lack of legal rights, all remind us that Dostoevsky's preoccupation with brutality and victims was not an internal matter. He lived in a sadistic society, run by a king (father figure) whom everyone was required to love and respect, and who could torture his "children" in ways such as this.

Many biographers and commentators make a great deal of the effect of this dramatic episode on Dostoevsky's character and later beliefs. It is certainly a striking event, but I don't believe as important an influence as is sometimes assumed. Dostoevsky thought he was going to be executed for about one hour before the "reprieve" was announced. Studies of such situations show that the initial response would be one of shock and *disbelief*. Before Dostoevsky could have moved beyond these reactions, the threat was removed. Life-threatening events must be of much longer duration if they are to have the profound effect on the personality that some attribute to the mock execution.

In order to get a complete picture of Dostoevsky's political activities and beliefs before his arrest we need to examine, at least briefly, the literature he produced during this time. He wrote several stories and short novels after *The Double*—*Mr. Prokharchin, A Weak Heart, White Nights,* and *The Landlady*—and was at work on a longer novel, *Netochka Nezvanova,* which was interrupted by his arrest and never completed. During the months of solitary confinement he wrote a story, "A Little Hero," that is almost pure romantic escapism. A young boy rides the wild horse that frightens others, returns the lost love letters to the beautiful woman of his fantasy, and is rewarded with a kiss. It is a good example of the comfort Dostoevsky could draw from imaginative work in harsh surroundings. A striking fact about all these works is that they have have no "political" content whatsoever. The familiar themes are all there: victimized children, frustrated love, madness and, in *The Landlady* and *Netochka*, we see him progressing toward the themes of the great novels of the post-imprisonment period. *The Landlady* has two men romantically/sexually involved with the same young woman. One of them may be her father. At one point the "father" tries to kill his rival and falls into an epileptic seizure. All the characters are on the verge of madness. *Netochka* also contains themes of incestuous love between a young girl and her stepfather, the father's hostile treatment of his wife— from which she eventually dies—and other instances of sadism and masochism. There is not a word about socialism, atheism, or any of the burning issues discussed at the Petrashevsky meetings. This lack of manifest political content in the fiction is consistent with Dostoevsky's disaffection with the Petrashevsky meetings and his move to the Palm-Durov group with its focus on literature, poetry, and music. Those political concerns that did captivate his interest—freeing the serfs, and the abolition of corporal punishment—fit with his abiding preoccupation with victims and brutality. All of this makes a coherent picture, with one exception: the involvement with Speshnev's secret society. This was a bit of direct political activity that was out of character, and it requires a special explanation.

We can approach such an explanation by looking at the particular attractiveness that Speshnev held for Dostoevsky—why he felt that he had found his "Mephistopheles" in this man. I would guess that the political participation was secondary to the special personal meaning with which he imbued Speshnev. Speshnev's own demeanor, and the rumors about his past, allowed Dostoevsky to see qualities in him that fit with his own unconscious preoccupations. Speshnev appeared to be violently antiauthority—he was the most radical in the group around Petrashevsky—and he had a fatal attractiveness for women. What is more, his cool and aloof manner made it look as if all this were done without anxiety or guilt. This made him an enormously attractive figure: he appeared to be someone who could carry rageful wishes into action —to rid himself of all authority and to kill women—without having to suffer the tormenting guilt and punishment that accompanied these same impulses in Dostoevsky himself. In other words, Dostoevsky imagined him as a version of the evil or murderous self. This character type—and this moral issue—was to become a major focus of the later novels. Again and again Dostoevsky was to explore the question of what happens when the most violent immoral impulses are carried into action. In several novels, he explores characters modeled on the Speshnev configuration: Bronze Men, Great Sinners, men of demonic will who seem beyond guilt and conventional morality, the type that Svidrigailov seems to be and that Raskolnikov tries to be. The character most directly modeled on Speshnev himself is Stavrogin in *The Possessed*. I will conclude this discussion of Dostoevsky's political beliefs with a brief examination of him.

The Possessed (also translated as *The Devils*) is Dostoevsky's most explicitly political novel. He wrote it during the years 1870–72, that is, more than twenty years after his own "political" participation with Speshnev, and his correspondence reveals that his conscious purpose was to expose and attack the left-wing revolutionaries and "Nihilists" then active in Russia. Part of the plot is woven together from newspaper accounts of a contemporary political murder by the members of a revolutionary cell led by one Nechayev, together with details from Dostoevsky's own earlier participation in Speshnev's secret group. In the novel, the revolutionaries, while spouting high-minded ideas and socialist schemes, are portrayed as a group of petty, troublesome nonentities whose vision of a harmonious future society is satirically contrasted with their inability to agree on anything. Their leader, Peter Verkhovensky, is essentially a scoundrel. While posing as a revolutionary, his real goals are the acquisition of personal power and the use of others for selfish ends. The part of the novel centered on him contains some perceptive observations of revolutionary characters, and some devastatingly satirical scenes, but it rarely rises above the level of caricature. As is always the case, beneath Dostoevsky's conscious intentions are other currents that give the novel added depth and power. At the core of *The Possessed* is the character of Nikolay Stavrogin, a man of wealth and great personal attractiveness. Everyone is drawn to him, including Peter Verkhovensky and the novel's two heroines. Stavrogin seems to be the embodiment of power, self-will, and antisocial impulses of a primal kind. Through him, Dostoevsky reveals the universal force that his revolutionaries and Nihilists only dimly project. A close look at Stavrogin will help us understand what it was in Dostoevsky himself that lay behind his preoccupation with the Great Sinner type and what, at an earlier time, made him feel that Speshnev was his Mephistopheles.

Stavrogin's immoral and antisocial acts may be grouped into three categories: attacks on authority and conventional society; attacks of various kinds on women; and, in a remarkable passage—the famous banned chapter ("At Tikhon's: Stavrogin's Confession")—a penetration to the deepest source of hatred and guilt, his sexually sadistic relation with a young girl. Stavrogin comes into the novel from a wild and dissolute past life, a life of whoring, gambling, fighting, and murderous duels. More recently he has behaved bizarrely: he has pulled the nose—literally—of a minor official and bitten the ear of the provincial governor. These apparently trivial acts demonstrate his contempt for the simplest social rules; in both large and petty ways he is a man whose strength and will seem to set him above the herd. In his dissolute days he carried on numerous sexual affairs, including simultaneous liaisons with a rich woman and her maid. On a drunken whim, he married Maria Lebyatkin, a lame half-wit—she is another good soul, a "holy fool," like Lizaveta in *Crime and Punishment*—as a further gesture of rebellion and contempt. The marriage is an insult and affront to his proud and wealthy mother. Though married to Maria, and flouting the marriage publicly, he later gives money to an assassin, Fedya, who murders her. (One can't help noting the names here: a Fedya, Dostoevsky's nickname as a child, kills an innocent Maria.) The novel's two attractive young heroines—Liza and Dasha—are both in love with him and he rejects, seduces, and betrays them in turn. Liza is eventually killed by a mob because she is "Stavrogin's woman." All of this shows his disregard for convention and morality and his destructive relations with women. And it is done, it seems—and I stress *seems*—without guilt or sympathy for the others involved. Yet, more and more, Stavrogin feels bored; he can find no meaning in life.

A deeper layer of his character is revealed in his confession to the monk Tikhon. This chapter was too strong for Katkov, the publisher, and he refused to include it in the book, despite Dostoevsky's urging and attempts at revision. Fortunately, it was preserved and is available to the modern reader. Here is what Stavrogin confesses: he has sublet a room in the apartment of a poor family, a room that he occasionally uses for his sexual liaisons. The family consists of a passive, failed father; a twelve-year-old daughter, Matryosha, who is strongly attracted to him; and the mother, a woman who has much in common with Katherine Marmeladov. She is a woman of good intentions, driven to distraction by her poverty. She cannot help taking out her frustration on her innocent daughter. One day, Stavrogin happens to mention to the mother that he cannot find his penknife. She accuses the daughter of stealing it and beats her until she is covered with welts. The girl bears this in silence, turning the blame on herself. Stavrogin later finds the penknife on his bed, where he had mislaid it, and, rather than setting the situation aright, he says nothing and throws it away, feeling that he is doing something that is simultaneously "despicable" and "pleasurable." A few days later he finds himself alone in the apartment with the love-starved and mistreated Matryosha. He sits down next to her, and kisses her hand, and she laughs "the way a baby laughs" and then responds to his affection by throwing her arms around him and kissing him back. He ends by seducing her and then silently leaving, knowing that she will feel extremely guilty "that she had committed an unspeakable crime, that she was guilty of a mortal sin that, indeed, she had 'killed God.' " He returns the next day with a mixture of emotions: there are flashes of hatred and he is afraid of the little girl. She is terribly upset, appears feverish, and shakes her little fist at him in a gesture of pitiful anger. As in the incident of the penknife, he deliberately does nothing to alleviate her suffering. She goes into a small storeroom; he sits in his room, acutely conscious of the smallest details—a fly buzzing, the minutes ticking by, a tiny red spider on the leaf of a plant—while she hangs herself. He lets more time pass, arranges the room as if he had not been there, looks in the storeroom, sees her dead, and leaves. No one ever suspects his complicity in her suicide. While a variety of feelings come and go in him at the time of the incident—and when he later confesses —what is emphasized is his lack of guilt or concern:

"I neither know nor feel what evil is. It wasn't simply that I had lost the feeling of good and evil, but that I felt there was no such thing as good and evil—I liked that—it was all a convention; that I could be free of all conventions; but that if I ever attained that freedom, I'd be lost."

Nevertheless, the image of the tiny red spider recurs and, at the novel's end, he hangs himself.

In the character of Stavrogin, Dostoevsky captures the psychological essence of an alienated, divided personality. Stavrogin does not know how he feels and, much of the time, he seems emotionally detached from others and the action that swirls around him. He is as likely to act with generosity, tenderness, and kindness as he is to commit acts of brutality and violence. All of this reveals a deep split in the self, a lack of integration and coherence in the personality. In addition to this insightful description of Stavrogin's character, Dostoevsky provides him with a childhood that helps us understand how he was formed.[1] Stavrogin's mother, the wealthy and powerful Madame Stavrogin, only loves him as an object through which she hopes to gratify her own needs. From the novel:

The boy knew his mother loved him, but he didn't seem to feel very much for her. She didn't talk to him much and hardly ever prevented him from doing what he wanted, but somehow he felt the intensity with which she watched him, and that made him feel painfully ill at east.

Her care is minimal; she largely turns him over to Stepan Verkhovensky, his tutor. By the time he is fifteen she sends the "puny pale and strangely withdrawn" boy off to boarding school. When she later hears of his success in Petersburg as a young man she becomes interested in him again, for now she can once more attempt to use him as an object: "her great love for her son dated from the time of his success in Petersburg society. . . . [He represented] her new hopes and even a daydream of hers."

Stavrogin's father is largely missing from his life and Stepan Verkhovensky—who could, as tutor, fill the paternal role—is like a child himself. He lives in a state of financial and emotional dependence on Madame Stavrogin and needs the boy as a target for his poorly controlled emotions: he can neither function as a parent nor serve as a model of an adult male. In addition, because Mr. Verkhovensky stands in a dependent relationship to Madame Stavrogin—because he is her other "child" —Dostoevsky's picture of the way she treats him provides further evidence for the kind of mother she is. She dominates Mr. Verkhovensky and alternately feeds off his intellectual and artistic pretensions to satisfy her own needs for status and punishes him for the frustrations and disappointments in her life. As was the case with her son, she relates more to her image of him than to the real man: Stepan Verkhovensky

had become, above all, a sort of son for her—a creation, her own invention. . . . She had invented him, and she was also the first to believe in her own invention. He was a bit like a part of her private day dream. Consequently, she made great demands upon him, almost making a slave of him.

Madame Stavrogin's failure to love or respond to her son, Nikolay, as a real person—along with the lack of a father or any other figure to meet this vital need—shows us how his character was formed. As an adult, Stavrogin keeps himself hidden behind a mask; there is a false self. The real self behind the mask is deeply split between a childlike need for the love and recognition that he never received, on the one hand, and untempered rage, on the other. Both of these poorly integrated sides of his personality come forth most strongly in his relations with women: he seeks their love—with Liza and Dasha—or they become the objects of his murderous rage—Maria and Matryosha. In the end, he hangs himself in his mother's house.

The relationship between Stavrogin and his mother has, at its psychological core, much in common with the relationship between Raskolnikov and his mother.

Many of the dimensions of *The Possessed* resonate with *Crime and Punishment*. It is as if Raskolnikov and Svidrigailov were taken apart and the pieces rearranged in a new mosaic: Stavrogin. Each of these three characters attempts to live beyond conventional morality. They all feel a combination of need and rage toward women, and there is the special sexual attraction of the older man for young girls, something seen in Svidrigailov, Stavrogin, many other fictional characters, and in Dostoevsky's own life. More specific similarities include the murder of the "holy fool"—Lizaveta and Maria Lebyatkin—and the confessed crime itself: the sexually sadistic attack on a victimized young girl, along with the guilt and selfpunishment this engenders. Svidrigailov's memories and dreams of such acts lead to his suicide; Raskolnikov must confess and make reconciliation with Sonia for the murder of her innocent "twin," the victimized Lizaveta; and Stavrogin, ultimately, hangs himself after causing the death by hanging of Matryosha. The scene of the sadistic act contains all the elements of Dostoevsky's own deepest emotional conflict: the need for a woman's love—an innocent baby's need for good maternal care—mistreatment of a child by a disturbed mother; sympathy and identification with the innocent child victim; and the powerful need for revenge, the irresistible urge to pay back a hurt with more hurt, to pass cruelty down the line.

In the earlier analysis of *Crime and Punishment* I looked at the different characters as experiments in which Dostoevsky tried out, in the form of extreme types, solutions to his own conflicts. Svidrigailov, for example, was a possible solution for Raskolnikov's dilemma after the murders, a dilemma compounded of his "rational" plan to be a man unaffected by ordinary laws and morality and the feelings of guilt and need for self-punishment that arose within him. Stavrogin is an experiment of the same kind on a larger scale. Dostoevsky was still drawn to the idea of a powerful man who could carry out his own hostile and antisocial fantasies without feeling the guilt, fear, and need for punishment that tormented him. A lesser writer would have simply indulged himself—and his readers—in the fictional gratification of such fantasies, as many best-selling authors do. That is, Dostoevsky could have made Stavrogin into a one-dimensional superman or devil figure. But his commitment to personal and artistic truth did not allow this. He may have begun with the idea of a Great Sinner who existed in a realm beyond good and evil but, as the character unfolds, the counterside of his personality and the consequences of such a way of life are revealed. Stavrogin does not seem to feel guilt—and he is certainly not an outwardly insecure and volatile man like the author who created him—yet his depression is present in the form of boredom and alienation from life. He must ultimately punish himself in a most violent fashion.

There are two additional things that the experiment with Stavrogin reveals. First, is the idea that, when one lives beyond conventional rules, one pays the price of isolation and alienation. The more he expresses his individual will at the expense of others, the more empty and meaningless does his existence become. Most critics speak of this when they see Stavrogin as representing the fate of man cut off from God. This is accurate if one keeps in mind that, for Dostoevsky, *God* most often means a loving connection and sense of belonging: Christ's love is the most frequent image. The second and more subtle message is the progressive revelation of Stavrogin's comic or ridiculous side. Liza is attracted to him as a great evil "spider" that she associates with all sorts of dark horrors. But, after she runs off and spends a night with him, she is disappointed, hints that he is impotent, and his evil side now appears like a ridiculous insect, like the little red spider that became fixed in his mind at the time of his crime with Matryosha. There is a subtle but profound bit of insight at work here. For what are Stavrogin's great crimes? He has attacked a helpless young girl and had his poor half-witted wife killed, pathetic acts requiring no great courage. To put this another way, the exposure of his nasty sexual perversion undermines the fantasied power of his evil nature. It is a direction of insight that continues and expands into Dostoevsky's final work, *The Brothers Karamazov*, where the self-willed characters—the father and Dimitri—seem comic and immature, without the aura of evil power that surrounds Stavrogin.

This discussion of *The Possessed*—a complex and multidimensional work in itself—has taken us far from our starting place: a consideration of Dostoevsky's attraction to Speshnev in the period just before his arrest in 1849. I would suggest that this attraction was motivated by exactly the same forces that drew him to Stavrogin and the other Great Sinner types that he worked and reworked in the late novels. In other words, he works out, through the fictional development of Stavrogin, what would happen if he gave his antisocial and perverse impulses free reign. With insight he sees—and shows the reader—that the result would be empty depression, alienation, and self-destruction. People need the love of others and must be connected by a shared set of beliefs and ethics even as—and especially because—they are driven by selfwilled rage. The universal version of this personal message comes through clearly in *The Possessed:* it is dangerous to tamper with rules and laws; people—

especially his beloved Russians—have a great capacity for violence and revenge. Well-meaning movements for social reform may unleash these violent forces, which easily run out of control.

This discussion of *The Possessed* brings us to a consideration of Dostoevsky's political and social ideas, both as these were forming in the late 1840s and as one finds them in the later novels. This is too broad a topic to explore with any completeness here; let me just offer a brief observation. While in his letters, articles and, to some extent, his fiction, Dostoevsky was concerned with politics, social movements, and systems of belief, in the novels, especially, these concerns are always subordinated to a focus on the individual personality. To put this in different words, for Dostoevsky, a social scheme or political idea is brought to life in the form of characters who, at their best, have all the complexity and quirkiness of real people—including the stubborn refusal to fit neatly into social or political categories! He could not consider Christian or revolutionary ideas apart from the people who espoused them, people whom he saw with all their virtues and failings. This does not mean that he was free of illusions; he was always striving to idealize someone or something—Christian love, pure women, the Russian people, and Great Sinners—yet a major fact of the novels is that the reality of human life continually intrudes on such attempts at idealization. Myshkin in *The Idiot*—an explicit attempt at a positively good man, a "Prince Christ"—brings about one disaster after another with his passive "goodness." Stavrogin, meant to be a personification of evil self-will, is shown, in the end, as powerless and somewhat ridiculous. In all the great novels there are very few one-sided characters. What this means, I think, is that Dostoevsky's political and religious ideas exist in two forms, one in his correspondence, casual conversation, and journalism—in portions of *The Diary of a Writer* for instance—and the other in the novels. The first is the least thought through: here we find his idealizations, his wishes for a harmonious Christian world, his glorification of the Russian people—many of whom he couldn't get along with or bear to be around—and the indulgence of his petty hatreds of foreigners, Jews, Westernizers, Nihilists, social planners, and other writers. This "ideological Dostoevsky" is superficial and commonplace. He lavished most of his creative energy, time, and thought on his novels and, not surprisingly, it is the "ideological Dostoevsky" that one finds there that is profound; there are the ideas and conceptions of lasting value. A central aspect of these ideas is the portrayal of political, religious, and social themes in their realistic human form. Dostoevsky's greatness as a psychologist—his insight into the complexities of human action, fantasy, and motivation—underlies his greatness as a political and social thinker. What the novels show, again and again, is how social, political, and religious schemes and beliefs are manifested in real life, with all their human complexities and contradictions.

The Possessed was published in 1872, more than twenty years after Dostoevsky's arrest and imprisonment. A reasonable question to ask is what effect the years of exile in Siberia had, both on his personality and on the themes and characters of his literature? Many commentators believe that these years were of great significance, that Dostoevsky's beliefs underwent a transformation during this time. I have suggested, on the contrary, that, for all the outward dramatics, this period had relatively little effect. To substantiate this claim let us return now and pick up where we left off in 1849.

CHAPTER 9

Prison, Exile,
the Second Maria

Following the mock execution, Dostoevsky was allowed to see Mikhail one last time. In this meeting, he seemed calmer than his brother, who had been released from confinement shortly after the arrests, he even spoke of looking forward to the future. The prisoners were prepared for the trip, ten-pound irons were fixed to their legs and he, Durov, and one other left Petersburg on Christmas Eve for the two-thousand-mile trek to Siberia by horse-drawn sled. An important encounter with a group of women, the Decemberist wives, occurred shortly before their arrival at the prison. In December of 1825, a group of army officers had staged an abortive revolt against the tsar. Most of the members of the Decemberist Insurrection were exiled to Siberia for life, and many of their wives followed them there and shared their hard lot. It was three of these women who met with Dostoevsky and the other political exiles, gave them food, clothes, advice on how to get along in prison, and a Bible with a ten-ruble note secreted inside. For Dostoevsky, the kindness of these self-sacrificing women fit his image of the loving mother. He later corresponded with one of them, Madame Fonvizina, and kept the Bible as a treasured object.

Dostoevsky and Durov arrived at the military prison in the frozen wastes of Omsk, Siberia, in January 1850. (The other "conspirators" were dispersed to different locations.) The tsar had ordered that they be treated in the same manner as the common criminals who made up the majority of the prison population. This was to be the novelist's life for the next four years. The prison was a former military fortress in bad repair. He slept packed between thieves and murderers on wooden planks in a crowded barracks. The floors were rotting wood, covered with slop, the rooms were freezing in winter, too hot in summer, and poorly ventilated. The ten-pound irons were exchanged, upon arrival, for somewhat lighter shackles made of iron rods, which remained on for the duration of the imprisonment. Flogging was administered as discipline; prisoners were regularly beaten with wooden sticks—sometimes to death—and, while Dostoevsky himself seems to have escaped this particular cruelty, it was ever present as a threat.

He lived amidst a motley of criminals: some were violent and some friendly and helpful. The officials and guards were also a mixed crew ranging from the sadistic major Krivtsov, who was in charge when Dostoevsky first arrived, an erratic alcoholic who had prisoners beaten for meaningless infractions of the rules, to a sympathetic doctor who allowed him to rest in the prison hospital on occasion and kept some of his notes and writings. These notes were eventually used when he wrote his account of these years, *Memoirs from the House of the Dead*.

The House of the Dead is the single most important source of information regarding the prison experience. Anyone interested in seeing these years through Dostoevsky's own eyes should read this fascinating book. Its scene in the bathhouse is an evocation of hell on earth that has few equals. The book is a fairly straightforward account of prison life, and most commentators and biographers have viewed it as such. Dostoevsky does tend to soften his own rage and conflicts. His letters, written immediately after his release, and the observations of others, are useful correctives to the account in this work.

Life in prison was not an unremitting horror. The severe rules and discipline were casually administered; those with access to money, and those of greater strength and talent, managed to obtain special favors. There was a thriving underground economy: the men made crafts and clothes, smuggled in vodka and got drunk, gambled, and occasionally slipped prostitutes past the guards. The spark of life could not be extinguished, even in these bleak surroundings. The prison was a forced-labor camp and, by Dostoevsky's own report, the hard manual work helped the time pass in a meaningful way. The aesthetic and physically passive author got plenty of vigorous exercise and he emerged from these years stronger than when he entered.

What was Dostoevsky's personal reaction to the years in prison? Most of his own remarks reveal deep hatred for what he had to endure. In a letter to Madame Fonvizina, written shortly after his release, he says,

> to be alone is a natural need, like eating and drinking; for in that kind of concentrated communism one becomes a whole-hearted enemy of mankind. The constant companionship of others works like poison or plague; and from that unendurable martyrdom I most suffered in the last four years. There were moments in which I hated every man, whether good or evil and regarded him as a thief who, unpunished, was robbing me of life. The most unbearable part is when one grows unjust, malignant and evil, is aware of it, even reproves one's self and yet has not the power to control one's self. I have experienced that.

This passage is interesting in several ways. It indicates that, for the sensitive and secretive author, the lack of privacy was a major burden. Sometimes, when he spoke of the prison experience, there was a tendency to idealize the common Russians he met there. He wrote to Mikhail, "Believe me, there were among them deep, strong and beautiful natures, and it gave me great joy to find gold under a rough exterior." But his remarks also reveal enormous rage, going at times, to paranoid extremes, of which the letter to Madame Fonvizina suggests he was partly aware. In the same long letter to Mikhail—his first communication with his brother in more than four years—he describes his relations with the other prisoners:

> They are rough, angry, embittered men. Their hatred for the nobility is boundless; they regard all of us who belong to it with hostility and enmity. They would have devoured us if they only could. [They were] a hundred and fifty foes [who] never wearied of persecuting us.

I call this paranoid because the reports of others suggest that this sense of persecution was largely of Dostoevsky's own making. Several naval cadets, active in the political movements of 1849, had been exiled to duty at the prison fortress. They describe Dostoevsky in the following terms:

The character of Dostoevsky was not attractive, he always looked like a wolf in a trap, and avoided all the prisoners; even the humane treatment shown by his superiors and their efforts to be useful to him and alleviate his lot, he took as an injury. He always looked gloomy, and amid the noise and animation of the prison held himself aloof from all; only of necessity did he ever speak a word. . . . Every expression of sympathy he met with mistrust, as if he suspected some secret purpose.

The prisoners did not like him, though they recognized his moral force; they looked askance at him, but with no malice, and would tacitly avoid him.

The cadets go on to contrast Dostoevsky with his fellow political inmate Durov, who was outgoing and friendly: "He [Durov] treated each individual prisoner amicably and cordially, and they all liked him." Needless to say, Dostoevsky conceived a deep hatred for Durov and would not speak to him.

One of the most galling aspects of the imprisonment was the blow to his pride and sense of self. Prior to his arrest, Dostoevsky was striving to realize his enormously high literary ambitions. His early success gave impetus to a grand version of himself. The tsar, in punishing the Petrashevskyites, wished to humiliate them by treating them like common criminals. They were forced to wear the same filthy clothes, had their heads shaved, wore shackles on their legs, and were subjected to the same brutal regimen as the criminals. The humiliation in all this was a personal blow, added to the more obvious rigors of prison life. This attempt to undermine his pride and sense of specialness was a further stimulus to rage; it posed an extremely difficult dilemma for the sensitive author. He reacted by projecting his anger into those readily available objects, his fellow prisoners. While there were, no doubt, many violent and immoral men among them, some of what Dostoevsky saw in "them" was, judging by material in the later novels, aspects of himself. In other words, the convicts in *The House of the Dead* are a blend of observations of others and projections of his own impulses. His principal means of coping with the threat posed by his humiliation and rage was to avoid any identification with the other convicts in prison. It was crucial that he isolate himself; "they" could then be seen as the containers of his rage, "rough, angry, embittered men . . . [with "hatred" that is] "boundless . . . a hundred and fifty foes [who] never wearied of persecuting us."

In sum, the injustice of his imprisonment, the small and large cruelties to which he was subjected, the lack of privacy, and deprivation of what was most important in his life—writing and involvement with the literary world—the humiliation and threat to his sense of specialness, all aroused a primal rage that he could only contain by withdrawing into an inward, tightly controlled state. As he wrote to his brother Andrey shortly after his release, he felt he was "shut in my coffin, buried alive for four years." But he had been through similar versions of this death-like existence before—in his family and at the academy of engineering, —and he could adapt. The living self was withdrawn inside, into a world of thought and literary plans, protected by a cold and aloof exterior. "Still the eternal concentration, the escape into myself from bitter reality, did bear its fruit. I now have many new needs and hopes of which I never thought in other days," he wrote to Mikhail. He never lost the hope that he would be reborn, that he would write, publish, find love, and live in the world once again. He had an abiding inner strength and self-confidence that saw him through an ordeal that crushed many lesser men.

Dostoevsky's withdrawn state in prison was not an escape into an unrealistic fantasy world. While he spent part of the time comforting himself with daydreams, he also stored up impressions for use in future literary work. One is reminded of Bruno Bettleheim's account of his time in a Nazi concentration camp. Bettleheim was trained as a social scientist before his incarceration and he survived the horrors of the camp by becoming the detached observer of the other inmate's psychological reactions. "He" became identified with an observing self while the "him" of his body—which was subject to the same abuses and threats as others —became less real. This sort of schizoid reaction, pathological in other contexts, proved highly adaptive in the "extreme situation" of the camp. So it was with Dostoevsky; while hostile and withdrawn from his fellow prisoners, he absorbed and remembered the details of prison life, as his later composition of *The House of the Dead* shows.

Finally, one may ask whether the contact with so much violence— living with murderers and seeing men brutally flogged—did not influence the later direction of his fiction? I think much less than is usually supposed. There is more overt violence in *Crime and Punishment, The Idiot,* and *The Possessed* than in most of the preimprisonment works, but it is not the violence of common criminals. The main impact of the prison years was an exposure to a powerful dose of his own capacity for hatred. As he says of himself in the letter to Madame Fonvizina: "The most unbearable part is when one grows unjust, malignant and evil, is aware of it, even reproves one's self, and yet has not the power to control one's self." This is more the sort of conflict that he and the characters of the great novels struggle with, and it was already present in such earlier works as *The Landlady* and *Netochka Nezvanova*.

His reactions to the arrest and imprisonment were a continuation of, rather than a sharp break from, what had gone before. All his life he had struggled with assaults on his individuality and autonomy. On many past occasions he had felt victimized by unfair authority, and since his youth, he had grappled with the inner legacy of this struggle: his own destructive rage in conflict with the wish and need for love. He discusses this conflict in the same letter to Madame Fonvizina in which he reveals the awareness of his "malignant and evil" self:

I want to say to you, about myself, that I am a child of this age, a child of unfaith and scepticism, and probably—indeed I know it—shall remain so to the end of my life. How dreadfully has it tormented me—and torments me even now—this longing for faith, which is all the stronger for the proofs I have against it. And yet God gives me sometimes moments of perfect peace; in such moments I love and believe that I am loved; in such moments I have formulated my creed, wherein all is clear and holy to me. This creed is extremely simple; here it is: I believe that there is nothing lovelier, deeper, more sympathetic, more rational, more manly, and more perfect than the Saviour; I say to myself with jealous love that not only is there no one else like Him, but that there could be no one. I would even say more: If anyone could prove to me that Christ is outside the truth, and if the truth really did exclude Christ, I would prefer to stay with Christ and not with truth.

This passage lights up Dostoevsky's central struggle, sometimes phrased in terms of an evil or hate-filled against a loving self and, at others, in terms of religious scepticism versus the longing to believe. It is a specific religious longing: a wish to believe in a perfectly loving Christ. The letter makes clear the attempt to identify with such a figure, to attain those "moments of perfect peace" in which "I love and believe that I am loved." He does not long for an omnipotent patriarchal God; there is no involvement or struggle with religious dogma, rules, or rituals, he does not feel himself a sinner because of his blasphemous thoughts or deeds; in other words, these—and many other versions of religious doubt that have assailed others—are of no importance to him. He strives after an ideal Christ, a figure without his own doubts, scepticism, hatred, and need for revenge.

Dostoevsky's religious ideal may be traced to the experiences of his childhood. His longing to believe in Christ is a symbolic version of his wish to recapture the relationship that existed between the loving young Fedya and his deeply religious mother. This is the relationship that was disrupted by the procession of rivals, who aroused his jealous rage, by his demanding and irascible father, and by his mother's eventual illness and death, all of which corrupted the idealized relationship with hatred and guilt. Abundant evidence for this interpretation can be found in the novels and his life, much of it already reviewed. Here, let me just mention two additional observations. In later years when he lived in Dresden with his second wife, Anna, he was fond of going to the art museum. His favorite artist was Raphael—a creator of calm, peaceful, and harmonious scenes—and his favorite painting the *Madonna and child*. He would stand in front of the picture of this "Maria" and her son for long periods of time, absorbed in the good feeling it gave him. His daughter Liubov reports that he kept a copy of this painting on his writing desk to the end of his life.

The second observation concerns Madame Fonvizina, the audience for the passage, just quoted, in which he describes his longing for faith. She, along with other of the Decemberist women, served as idealized loving figures during the years of imprisonment. Not only was she deeply religious like his mother, but a picture of her (see Frank 1983, 74) bears a resemblance to Maria. It should be clear that Madame Fonvizina was largely a creature of his invention; he only met her for one hour on the trip to Omsk. He needed to have a current representation to keep his hopes alive during the angry withdrawn years of his imprisonment. The Decemberist women were ideal candidates; they were, like him, victims of the father-tsar's injustice and cruelty, and they had sacrificed themselves out of love for their persecuted husbands.

In 1876, more than twenty years after his release from prison, Dostoevsky published a brief reminiscence in his *Diary of a Writer* entitled *The Peasant Marey*. All the biographers comment on it, and some, such as Frank, see it as central to the transformation of political-religious beliefs that they assume he underwent in prison. While I don't think

there was such a profound change in his beliefs, it will be worth review-
ing this incident; it sheds light on an important aspect of his later views:
his idealization of the Russian people. Needless to say, I view the anecdote as an imaginative construction, a story, made up of memories,
dreams, wishes and fantasies. It is remarkable how the specific images
confirm the interpretation we have been considering.

The Peasant Marey begins with Dostoevsky's memory of a crucially
difficult time in prison. It was Easter week, the convicts were free from
work and were engaged in drinking, singing, and fighting: "All this had
exhausted me to the point of sickness. Never could I stand without
disgust drunken popular rakishness." He flees the barracks with anger
in his heart and encounters one of the Polish political prisoners who
mutters what he himself is feeling: "I hate these bandits!" He goes back
inside and encounters a scene of still-greater violence: a group of peasants are beating the drunken Tartar Gazin—one of the most brutish of
the prisoners—almost to death. Dostoevsky lies down and pretends to
sleep as an escape from all the horror around him with the Pole's words
—and his own hatred—hammering in his head. Interestingly, at this
point he mentions the fictional disguise he used in writing *The House of
the Dead*: (He had published it as the memoirs of a man sent to prison
because he "killed his wife in the very first year of his marriage, killed
her out of jealousy.") "In passing, I may add, by way of detail, that since
that time many people have been under the impression, and are even
now asserting that I was exiled for the murder of my wife." I think this
reference to the murder of a woman is aroused at that point when his
whole being is suffused with hatred. He must find an antidote, and does
so in his imagination.

Lying on his plank bed he "became absorbed in reminiscences. . . .
They invaded my mind of their own accord. . . . I used to analyze these
impressions, adding new touches to things long ago outlived, and—
what is more important—I used to correct, continually correct, them."
He remembers a time when he was a young boy playing happily in the
fields and forests of his parent's country estate. Suddenly he hears a cry,
"a wolf's running!" He becomes very frightened and runs to Marey, a
peasant who is plowing with his "little filly" in a nearby field. Marey
comforts him and assures him there is no wolf. "What's the matter with
you? What wolf? This appeared to you in a dream!" He strokes the

cheek of the young Fedya, says, "Christ be with thee," and looks at him "with a long motherly smile." Again and again these words appear in the story: " 'I shall not surrender thee to the wolf!' he added with the same motherly smile, 'Well, Christ be with thee' "; "that tender, motherly smile of a poor peasant serf"; and "The meeting was a solitary one, in a vacant field, and only God, maybe, perceived from above what a profound and enlightened human sentiment, what delicate, almost womanly, tenderness, may fill the heart of some course, bestially ignorant Russian peasant serf."

Dostoevsky concludes the anecdote by describing how the memory of Marey took him out of his hate-filled state: "I could behold these unfortunate men with a wholly different outlook, and, suddenly, by some miracle, all the hatred and anger completely vanished from my heart." Thus were his violent fellow convicts transformed into loving "Mareys." All this supposedly occurred on Easter Eve, the time of the resurrection of Christ, and a favorite occasion, in Dostoevsky's later life, for the staging of unconscious death-rebirth rituals.

What Dostoevsky presents, in the form of a reminiscence, is a symbolic account of the central personal conflict with which he struggled in prison, along with his principal means of overcoming this conflict. His hatred is aroused to an almost unbearable degree. He sees rage and destructiveness all around him, observed in and projected into his fellow convicts. The dream-memory-story takes the conflict back to childhood where the wolf—he later realized it was a hallucination—serves as the symbol of his rage. "Marey" then appears as the loving mother: that central image to which he turned in so many ways to counter his rage. At his most desperate moments in prison, he had felt just like his fellow convicts, one of a group of immoral, depraved beasts. In Marey, they become transformed into Christlike loving mothers and he, as one of them, is reborn into this new form. The story of Marey shows how the many images associated with mother and love sustained him in prison. It also illuminates his later idealization of the Russian people: they had become part of this image. Is the very name a play on *Maria?* My Russian-speaking colleages tell me that *Marey* is an old peasant nickname derived from *Mark* which would not necessarily remind a native speaker of *Maria.* Still, the assonance may be enough for the language of fantasy and dreams.[1]

Prison, Exile, the Second Maria

To sum up, Dostoevsky's main response during his four years of imprisonment was an angry withdrawal into himself. This was not total —he formed relationships with some of the Polish political prisoners for a time and with some of the Russian criminals—but it was the most general feature of his adaptation. He allowed his real self to be buried alive—he went into a sort of suspended animation—with the hope of a later rebirth. In this inward state the novelist-observer remained active, storing up impressions for later use, as did the thinker. His prison experiences sharpened the awareness of his own capacity for rage and revenge and, at the same time, the presence of these destructive impulses made the need for love, life, and rebirth all the more necessary. He kept his hopes alive in various ways: with the image of the Decemberist women, with the revival of the Christian feelings of his childhood, with memories of his brother Mikhail, and with an attempt to idealize the Russian people. But the most direct route to rebirth would be to revive a version of the relationship with Maria, to find a woman to love and be loved by. And this is just what he will do in the next period of his life, his years of service at a Siberian army post.

Dostoevsky completed his prison sentence in 1854 and was forced into the army as a private, stationed in Semipalatinsk. He lived there for the next five years. Semipalatinsk was a small backwater Siberian town with few educated citizens. The inhabitants occupied themselves with gossip, gambling, and drinking. The army service itself was not very taxing, and, though he was under political surveillance, this, too, was not burdensome. Siberia, under the reign of Nicholas I, was filled with so-called political criminals and, since they were sincere, educated, and liberal individuals, they tended to be accepted by the members of the local towns. Dostoevsky was soon able to secure lodgings away for the barracks, in a hovel of a rented room in a poor section of town. There, by candlelight in the long night hours, he returned to writing. From the first days of his release he began to plan and work toward the rebirth of his career, he had to find a way to be published again.

The years at Semipalatinsk were the time when he came back to life from the house of the dead. We can discuss this rebirth in three spheres: his relationship with a new brother figure, Baron Wrangel; his writing and return to the literary world; and his falling and love with, and eventual marriage to, Maria Isaeva.

Baron Alexander Wrangel had, as a young student, witnessed the mock execution of Dostoevsky and the other "revolutionaries" in 1849. In 1854 he went to Semipalatinsk as district attorney and sought out Dostoevsky, bringing letters from Mikhail and other friends in Petersburg. The ex-convict had only recently arrived and was isolated and lonely while the twenty-one–year–old Wrangel was himself a homesick boy (Their first meeting ended with his crying on the older Dostoevsky's shoulder). They were both hungry for friendship, for a companion with whom to share ideas, and a solid connection was soon established that lasted many years. Dostoevsky always had the capacity for close relationships with brother figures, Wrangel became another in the series. His "Reminiscences" provide important information about this period and help us see what an attractive person Dostoevsky could be; an attraction compounded of emotional sensitivity, expressiveness, and a powerful intellect. He aroused Wrangel's interest in many topics, but especially in literature. They spent many late nights indulging in tea, cigarettes, and endless discussion. And Dostoevsky could be almost manic at times, reciting Pushkin from memory and spinning out the plot of whatever novel he was working on.

On his side, Wrangel was very helpful. He introduced Dostoevsky to the military governor and secured his acceptance into local society. Of greater importance, he was able to extricate his friend from his position as an exiled army private. Wrangel came from a well-connected family and he soon began pressing his relatives and others to exert themselves on his friend's behalf. Early in 1855 a new tsar, Alexander II, ascended to the throne, raising the hopes of all political exiles for more liberal policies. Dostoevsky himself wrote patriotic poems and sent them to the tsar in the hope of gaining favor. He had Wrangel deliver a letter to the national hero, General Edward Totleben, brother of a former classmate at the academy of engineering, seeking his assistance (See Dostoevsky, *Letters* 1961 90–96.) The letter is a fine example of flattery, confession, and pleading; Totleben did contact the tsar and the minister of war and urged Dostoevsky's promotion to ensign, the lowest officer rank, and requested that he be allowed to publish. Through his own efforts, and those of his friend, Dostoevsky was first promoted in the army, then granted permission to publish, and, eventually, discharged and allowed to leave Siberia, though all this took five years to accomplish.

Prison, Exile, the Second Maria

What did he write during the time in Semipalatinsk? His most significant work is the documentary account of his years in prison, *Memoirs from the House of the Dead*. He began this shortly after his arrival but did not publish it until he was safely returned to Petersburg in 1861–62. He also wrote two novels, *Uncle's Dream* and *The Village of Stepanchikova* (also translated as *The Friend of the Family*). These light pieces are far from his best work but we must not forget the realities of the Russian police state: Dostoevsky was a convicted political criminal under surveillance, and, if he was ever to achieve his goal of publishing again, he had to be exceedingly inoffensive. This accounts for his patriotic poems, his self-abasing confessions—in the letter to General Totleben, for instance —and the light and nonpolitical nature of these two novels.

A close reading of *The Village of Stepanchikova* reveals an interesting second level in which Dostoevsky refuses to bow to authority. He wrote *The Village* with an eye on the government censor—his chief concern was to be published—and the novel appears to be a harmless farce. Yet it has an underside in which he mocks the authorities who sent him to prison along with the very censors whose approval he was courting. He does this with literary allusions that attack Gogol, particularly the reactionary Gogol of *Selected Passages of My correspondence with My Friends*. *The Village* is set in a country estate out of *Dead Souls*; it is filled with the same foolish types who populate Gogol's famous novel. At its core stands the obnoxious Foma Fomich whose very name echoes Gogol's penchant for double first names, such as Akaki Akakievich, hero of *The Overcoat*. Foma, one of Dostoevsky's true creations of this period, is a horrible sycophant who maintains power by inducing guilt in everyone. In this, he both draws on Dostoevsky's father and is a satirized version of the Gogol of *Selected Passages;* Foma even quotes lines from this work. Recall that Dostoevsky was sent to prison for a public reading of Belinsky's attack on *Selected Passages.* So, in *The Village,* while presenting what appears to be an inoffensive farce, he repeats the very crime—attacking Gogol—that led to his imprisonment. (One is reminded of Freud's response in a related situation; forced to flee his home in Vienna by the Nazis in 1938, he was required to sign a statement that they had treated him with "respect" and "consideration" and that he had "not the slightest reason for any complaint." He signed and added: "I can heartily recommend the Gestapo to anyone.")

During the four years of imprisonment, Dostoevsky had no one to share the rich flow of ideas and plans that coursed through his mind. In addition, he was not able to channel this flow into writing. Now, in Semipalatinsk, both of these areas were alive again; he had a friend and communicant in Wrangel, and he was writing. But a full rebirth demanded something more: a loving relationship with a woman. This could prove the most powerful means of restoring his sense of life and countering his destructive rage. It is worth recalling that, up to this point in his life, he had not even approached a serious or complete relationship with a woman outside his family. There were contacts with prostitutes in his twenties, before his arrest, and the largely imaginary infatuation with Madame Panaeva during this same period. His imprisonment intervened, and now he found himself in an isolated Siberian town in his thirties with strong emotional needs, active fantasies, and almost no real experience. It is no wonder that his first great romance would turn out disastrously, overburdened with idealizations at the expense of realistic perceptions.

Among the few cultured souls in Semipalatinsk were an impoverished schoolteacher, Alexander Isaev, and his wife, Maria. He was an inadequate, failed man who had turned to drink. His inability to hold a job threatened his wife and nine-year-old son with poverty. She was sensitive, high-strung, and struggling with her difficult situation. Dostoevsky became friends with them both and spent many evenings at their home. He was drawn to her on several counts, some conscious and some less so. She was well educated and pretty in a frail way; he could talk with her about his ideas, which was always crucial for him. He also felt the familiar sympathetic pull to her victimized plight; here was another noble heart, beaten down by the unfair circumstances of life, in need of a saviour. Less conscious was the fact that she was married to someone else, a friend. Winning the woman from a rival was an added attraction and there were many later versions of this pattern when he returned to Petersburg, with his mistress Suslova and with the wife of his old friend Dr. Yanovsky, for example. She also showed the early signs of consumption—a fatal similarity to his mother—that was, I believe, an indispensible unconscious component of his attraction to her. As his friend Wrangel later remembered: "Even then one often saw a hectic flush on her cheeks; some years later she died of consumption." All of this came together and he found himself helplessly in love, wanting to win her for himself and desperately trying to "help" the very rivals who stood between them.

There followed a two-year courtship filled with difficulties, torture, and suffering, in other words, exactly what one would expect from Dostoevsky. She did not return his love at first—or showed him a mixed response—which aroused him all the more. Then a real difficulty intervened: Isaev was offered a job in Kuznetzk, four hundred miles distant, and the couple was forced to move. Dostoevsky pursued the romance by letter, immediately after her departure writing, "If you only knew how orphaned I feel!" He goes on to describe the emotions she arouses in him:

The mere fact that a woman should treat me in so friendly a way was a great event in my life. For even the best man is often, if I may say so, a block. Woman's heart, woman's compassion, woman's sympathy, the endless kindness of which we have no clear perception, and which, in our obtuseness, we often do not even notice—these are irreplaceable. All that I found in you; even apart from my many failings, a sister could not have been kinder and more tactful to me than you were. If we did go through some violent upheavals, it was always because I was ungrateful, and you were ill, exacerbated and wounded.

There follow more protestations of how much she means to him and then he sends greetings to her husband, whom he describes in terms that fit Marmeladov: an alcoholic who consorts with a dirty, drunken crew.

Isaev died shortly after the move to Kuznetzk, and now the young widow was available. Dostoevsky began to court her in earnest by letter. There were real obstacles; he was still a private in the army and did not earn enough to support a wife and stepchild. But he had prospects; Wrangel was doing all he could, and a promotion was possible, and there remained his strongest hope, to be published again—even anonymously—and earn money with his pen. Her response was ambivalent and, in some ways, sadistic. First, she aroused his jealousy by writing of an older suitor and then confessed that this was an invention to test his interest in her. Then, a real rival appeared on the scene, a young schoolteacher named Vergunov; she wrote that she was seriously considering his proposal. Dostoevsky's actions in this situation are revealing. He was driven to win her for himself and wrote passionately, pleading his case and depreciating the younger man whom he described as poor, ill educated, and lacking experience. Eventually, he traveled to Kuznetzk, persuaded Vergunov to withdraw, and brought Maria around.

His feelings for the defeated rival are colored by his own projections. First, he sees him as the victim in need of assistance. As Grossman says, " 'On my knees,' he [Dostoevsky] emplored Wrangel to do something for the unfortunate schoolteacher. 'He is dearer to me now than a brother.' " Then, after the wedding, at which Vergunov was one of the best men, Dostoevsky became afraid that the defeated rival would kill Maria: "What if he brings her to death?" he wrote to Wrangel. Whatever the real Vergunov's reactions were, these suppositions and fears seem to come from sources within Dostoevsky; they are projections of the two extremes of his own reactions when he lost his mother to rivals; he identifies with the abandoned child, in need of assistance, and he feels like killing the faithless woman. As usual, one finds additional support for this interpretation in his fiction. The theme of a love-hate rivalry for a woman between brother figures, recurs in the novels. In *The Idiot* it is Myshkin and Rogoshin in competition for Nastasia, with Rogoshin eventually murdering her. *The Brothers Karamazov* contains several permutations of the theme: Dimitri and his father in relation to Grushenka, Dimitri and his brother Ivan in relation to Katerina, and others. In all of these cases, as in the real Dostoevsky-Vergunov-Maria triangle, one finds the same unstable mixture of possessive love, murderous jealousy, and restitutive self-sacrifice.

Underlying the interplay of these conscious and unconscious concerns was the deep wish to be reborn in a loving relationship. As he wrote to Wrangel shortly before his marriage: "My relations with Maria have obsessed me for the last *two years*. At least I've *lived;* I may have suffered but I have lived."

Dostoevsky was promoted to ensign toward the end of 1856 and married Maria, in Kuznetzk, at the beginning of the next year. After the ceremony, they immediately set off for Semipalatinsk and, on this trip, he suffered a violent epileptic seizure. This seizure was, in my view, part of the pattern of motives being played out in the relationship with her. The epilepsy is discussed in detail in the Appendix; here let me just note its meaning in the new marriage.

In the late 1840s—before his arrest and at the time of his nervous illness—there were seizurelike states that, while not full-blown attacks, were the forerunners of those that came later. By his own report, the attacks grew worse in prison, occurring approximately once a month, mainly at night. Wrangel reports that there was one about every three months during the time he knew Dostoevsky in Semipalatinsk though he never witnessed an actual seizure. They came on most often during sleep, though Wrangel was typically summoned afterwards and was familiar with their psychological concomitants: "He [Dostoevsky] told me that he could always feel a fit coming on, and always experienced beforehand an indescribable sense of well-being. After each attack he presented a woefully dejected aspect." Up to this time, the seizures had not been officially diagnosed as epilepsy, and Dostoevsky's own view, insightful as always, was that they, "resembled epilepsy and yet were not epilepsy."

The violent seizure that occurred right after the marriage to Maria was unusual in two ways. First, it happened when he was awake and, second, it was displayed in front of another person. This was not just *any other person*, of course; it was the idealized woman whom he had only recently won away from a rival. These facts support the interpretation of the epileptic seizures as part of an unconscious ritual. First, the seizure was a punishment for his crime of defeating a rival and winning the woman for himself. His guilt in relation to Vergunov was obvious, as in his attempts to further the latter's career and his professed love for him "like a brother." While this was one meaning of the attack, I don't think it was the principal meaning, nor does this sort of guilty self-punishment account for the seizures more generally. Their principal meaning is to be found in the symbolic part they played in Dostoevsky's struggle with his inner rage and the threat it posed to a life-sustaining love.

It is clear that Dostoevsky's love for Maria, during the period of courtship, was idealized, a process that was aided by his inexperience with women and the four hundred miles that separated them. In his mind, she became the loving, understanding woman that he needed and he contrived to overlook her faults and the conflicts between them. The first letter to her after her departure from Semipalatinsk, quoted earlier, is filled with protestations of love and hymns to her wonderful qualities yet, interestingly enough, it mentions "violent upheavals" between them, which he then explains away as due to his "failings" and her "illness" and hardships. His idealization of her was a wishful attempt to create a loving union from which all bad qualities are split off. He overlooks or forgets her cruel taunting of him with a fictitious rival and imagines it is Vegunov, not he, who feels like killing her. Such an idealized image cannot be sustained in a real relationship, of course; the split-off emotions will be heard from. Along with this, is the deep wish for a complete rebirth; a relationship with a woman who loves and accepts *all* of him, his outwardly loving side along with the jealous, hateful self within.

The marriage secured the outward connection to her and, almost immediately, the rageful self appears on the scene, in the form of a violent epileptic seizure, which endangers the marriage. The blissful aura —the "indescribable sense of well-being"—symbolizes the wished-for "birth" into a perfect merger, a union from which all hate is banished. Rage and violence then make their appearance, in the form of the murderous epileptic attack, throwing him into a deathlike coma. Finally, there is rebirth, an awakening into a depressing, nonidealized reality. In addition to these meanings, the seizures were a communication to his loved one; this was their "transference function" if you will. They "say" to her, in an unconscious language of bodily act and emotion, "you profess to love and accept me but will you really, now that you see this other, violent side of my nature?" In this way, the seizures were a test of the love object, a test that Maria was not able to pass: "either [she] had not suspected the nature of her husband's attacks or had never been present at one. In any event, she was horribly frightened and also took sick."

So much for idealized love. They reached Semipalatinsk and set up house but Dostoevsky's comments show that, from this time on, he had lost his feeling for her. In addition to her inability to care for him in the face of his epilepsy, it seems she did not really appreciate his genius as an author. He had, in his imagination, married a woman who could love all of him, accept his good and bad qualities, and appreciate his unique talent. The real Maria—a moody, insecure woman with the beginning symptoms of tuberculosis—was not much like this. How different was the response of Anna, his second wife, to his unique gifts as a writer and to his seizures; whereas other women were frightened and became sick, she held and nursed him. Maria was not a bad woman, but the marriage was doomed from the beginning because of the immense gulf between Dostoevsky's fantasized image of her and the real person she was.

Official decisions moved slowly in imperial Russia, especially when they involved a convicted political criminal. Alexander II had taken power in 1855, Wrangel, Totleben, and others had been arguing Dostoevsky's case with some success—witness his promotions—but it was not until 1859 that he was finally discharged and allowed to publish his work. His epilepsy, now officially confirmed by an army doctor, served as an additional reason for his discharge. Before this occurred, Maria and he were forced to spend two desultory years in Semipalatinsk and, even after the discharge, he was compelled to live for close to a year in Tver, a provincial town located between Moscow and the capital. It was not until 1860 that he was finally allowed to return to Petersburg and resume the career that had been broken off by his arrest and banishment over ten years earlier.

CHAPTER 10

Return to Petersburg:
Journalism, Women, Gambling

He suggested that we travel to Italy together, while remaining like brother and sister. When I told him that, most probably, he would be writing his novel, he answered: "Who do you take me for! Do you think that all this is going to pass without leaving any impression!" — *Polina Suslova's Diary* (1863)

Apollinaria (Polina) Suslova, the young woman with whom Dostoevsky carried on a tempestuous love affair during the early 1860s, sensed that his real commitment was to his writing, however much he seemed to be involved with her. She may even have been aware that their whole affair, intertwined with wild bouts at the roulette tables and the usual Dostoevskian mixture of love and torment, was unconsciously constructed to provide material for a novel. It eventually did: *The Gambler*, written in 1866. Ironically, she was up to the same thing, recording their ups and downs in her diary and using this material for a short story.

Dostoevsky returned to Petersburg in 1860 after ten years of imprisonment and exile. Finally, he was back in the literary world he had dreamed of during his years of banishment; he threw himself into it with enormous energy. Russia at this time was in the midst of a social and artistic renaissance. The new tsar, Alexander II, freed the serfs in 1861 and began other long-needed reforms. Debate over a wide range of social, moral, and political questions was carried on in the journals that flourished during this period, journals that also carried stories, poems, critical essays, and monthly installments of novels by Tolstoy, Turgenev, Dostoevsky, and many others. The years leading up to the publication of *Notes from Underground* (1864)—which is widely regarded as the first of the great novels of the mature years—were ones of immense activity. Feodor and Mikhail began their own journal and the younger brother solicited manuscripts, edited, and wrote political-topical articles, along with fiction, memoirs, and travel notes. He made his first trips to Europe, was romantically involved with several women, and got caught up in compulsive gambling. There were friendships, old and new, the lurking presence of his progressively ill wife, epileptic attacks, and the usual money worries. Dostoevsky flung himself into all this in his own excited way, making up for the years when he was not fully alive. He was "living life" and transforming this life into literature.

Maria was rarely seen by his friends, nor much mentioned in his correspondence. It wasn't long before she left Petersburg, ostensibly for reasons of health, eventually settling in Moscow. He continued to support her and her son, but he was free to live the life of a bachelor, to direct his energies into other channels.

Journalism

In 1861, Mikhail received permission to begin publication of the journal *Time (Vremya)*. Since Feodor was an ex-convict, still under political surveillance, Mikhail was the nominal head of the journal; in reality, he served as agent and business manager, the younger brother was editor and chief contributor. *Memoirs from the House of the Dead* first appeared in another journal but was then brought out in *Time*. It was a great success, the most acclaimed work, critically and popularly, of these years. The first long novel of the new Petersburg period, *The Insulted and Injured*, was also serialized in *Time*. While it is not one of his better works, one can see him working his way toward the themes that would shortly emerge in the major novels. He resumed his old habit of writing through the night and sleeping until the next afternoon; then he would get together with his friends and fellow writers.

Dostoevsky was a talented editor and an engaging journalist, and *Time* quickly became a popular success, doubling its subscriptions by the second year of publication. In large part this was due to his ability to draw together a creative group of writers and critics. When he first returned to Petersburg, he began attending the "literary Tuesdays" held at his old friend Milyukov's place. Mikhail, Dr. Stepan Yanovsky, and those soon to work on *Time* were all there. The group set up editorial offices at Mikhail's apartment, where they met regularly to argue, plan, discuss, and put the journal together. There was Mikhail himself, a married man with children but still a poet and romantic; he supported a mistress and child and ran the journal. There was their old friend Apollon Maikov, poet, contributor to the journal, and a peripheral member of the group. More central were the poet-critic Apollon Grigoryev, whose quasi-mystical views played an important role in the journal's evolving political-philosophical position, and the essayist-philosopher Nikolay Strakhov, who was soon to become a leading figure in Russian literary criticism. The group was like a new band of brothers and Feodor became their intellectual leader. Strakhov tells how their novelist-editor would begin discussing some topic in his hoarse whisper, and then his voice would soar to the heights as emotion and ideas carried him away.

Petersburg intellectuals were passionately involved with the great issues of the day and debated them endlessly over tea, vodka and in the pages of their journals. Each journal had its "tendency," each took a position that defined its special identity. The Dostoevsky brothers and their collaborators Grigoryev and Strakhov developed what came to be called the "native soil" movement. It is worth a brief exploration of their ideas to dispel the popular misconception that Dostoevsky was some sort of naive conservative or political reactionary. In fact, *Time* fell between the radical and conservative journals of the period; it had both links with and important differences from each side. The radicals—Chernyshevsky and other contributors to *The Contemporary*—blended French utopian socialism and English utilitarianism. They looked to the West— to Europe—for ideas and models for society, Russia being seen as a backward, if not feudal, country; they placed great stress on the need for material progress. The conservatives were Russian nationalists, "Slavophiles," identified with the monarchy and the orthodox church. The "men of the soil," as the contributors to *Time* came to be called, sided with the radicals on a number of major points. They were sympathetic to the new laws freeing the serfs, advocated the emancipation of women, favored hospital and prison reform, full rights for the Jews, and the abolition of corporal punishment. All of this shows that sympathy for and wish to help the downtrodden and oppressed that was always an important side of Dostoevsky's beliefs. While the men of the soil saw the Slavophiles as hopelessly reactionary on social issues, they shared their belief in the unique nature of the Russian soul. They did not question the monarchy or the church, nor favor any sort of revolutionary change.

The major tenets of their program can be summarized as antirationalism, individualism, and gradualism (see Dowler 1982). The radicals derived their theories of human perfection from utilitarianism and positivism; the Slavophiles drew on Hegel. The men of the soil, on the contrary, argued that life should be defined as it is lived and not in terms of utilitarian principles or Hegelian categories. Dostoevsky always felt a powerful antipathy to attempts to force people into constraints, including the constraints of philosophy and political theory. He came to see positivist programs for the "perfection" of man as new ways in which leaders could impose themselves on others, in this case "for their own good." Hence the opposition to programs founded on rational categories. His views were soon to find their most forceful expression in *Notes from Underground*. There, one sees the Underground Man's rebellion against the constraints of "reason" as well as the conflict that arises when he tries to live his real life according to abstract ideas. Dostoevsky's message here is psychoanalytic; his attack is not on reason and rationality themselves, but on a definition of man as a wholly conscious being, a definition that overlooks his unconscious and emotional sides.

The commitment to individualism was related to antirationalism. Each person is unique and should be allowed to develop in his own way. In discussing educational reform, Dostoevsky applauded Tolstoy's ideas for free schools, institutions where a natural love of learning would replace rules and requirements—how different from the coercive education that he received at his father's hands and in the engineering academy! The belief in uniqueness was extended to nations; persons were defined by their histories, and so were countries; what worked for one did not necessarily fit another; programs applicable to France and England were not suitable for Russia. This idea of cultural and national individuality was where *Time* linked up with the Slavophiles. Grigoryev, who played the guitar, sang ballads, drank too much, and called himself "the last of the romantics," deeply believed in the value of traditional Russian culture, of native speech, and indigenous poetry. He shared with the Dostoevsky brothers a great love of Pushkin, of drama that portrayed contemporary themes, and of art, folklore and music. These artistic and literary values—more than any political beliefs—comprised the "native soil" of their program. Their ideas were then carried to romantic excess in the notion of Russian "panhumanism." Russians, alone among all peoples, could unite classes—gentry and peasants, merchants and workers—into a harmonious whole. It was here, I believe, that Dostoevsky's otherwise perceptive political and social analysis gave way to his wish for a mergerlike state of love and harmony.

The third aspect of the native-soil movement was gradualism. Dostoevsky had a deep fear of the violence that could be released if existing social constraints and laws were overthrown or changed too rapidly. He was personally in touch with the well-springs of hatred and destructiveness in people long subject to unfairness and abuse, as his creation of Raskolnikov and many other violent characters demonstrates. *Time* favored political reforms but believed these had to be carried out within the structure of the existing government. The men of the soil, Dostoevsky especially, were continually attempting to forge links with the radicals on one side and Slavophiles on the other. The goal was harmony and unity within a vaguely defined sense of Russianness.

Much of the native-soil program derived from the romantic movement in nineteenth-century literature, including the valuation of emotion over abstract theory, of personal uniqueness and individuality, and the opposition to rules and constraints, especially as these applied to art. While the writers for *Time* were concerned with political issues, they were more interested in poetry and fiction, with the place of the artist in society. One issue on which Dostoevsky never waivered from the 1840s to the end of his life was the need for artistic freedom: his most vitriolic thrusts at the radicals were aimed at their belief that art should serve political goals.

In 1862 he published a story in *Time,* "A Disgraceful Affair" (also translated as "A Nasty Tale") that expressed his political views in a more felicitous literary form. A young general, head of one of Peters-

burg's many bureaucracies, a man of "modern," and "liberal" sentiments, decides to drop in on the wedding party of one of the poor clerks
in his department. His fantasies of magnanimity are satirically contrasted with the havoc caused by his visit; his presence makes all the
poor guests uncomfortable, they buy him champagne they can ill afford,
he gets drunk, passes out, and usurps the wedding bed for the night.
While directed as satire at the programs of the liberals and radicals, as is
typical in his fiction, Dostoevsky moves beyond his own political arguments. "A Disgraceful Affair" captures the reality of Russian class relations, a reality that contrasts sharply with the fantasies of all the political
factions, including the men of the soil.

Travel

While the ideology of *Time* stressed unity, peace, and harmony, the
journal also contained criticism and attacks on its ideological opponents.
Along with Dostoevsky's capacity to love, there was always a good deal
of hostility. In the journalism, this was primarily directed at an assort-
ment of "others" who, in one way or another, fell outside the definition
of a harmoniously unified Russia. These others included the advocates
of westernization, Nihilists—a vague term encompassing those on the
Left from violent revolutionaries to college students with bad manners
—and a variety of foreigners. The more distant a group, and the less
real contact Dostoevsky had with them, the easier it was for them to
become the objects of his projected dissatisfaction and anger. In this
regard, his first trip to western Europe, and the writing inspired by it—
Winter Notes on Summer Impressions, serialized in *Time* in 1863—is
important.

As an imaginative young boy who lived mainly in books, Dostoevsky
was very taken with the literary Europe he knew from his reading. The
Gothic novels of Ann Radcliffe set in Italy or the Italy of *Romeo and
Juliet,* Schiller's romantic landscapes and Walter Scott's, the works of
George Sand, all these had the greatest appeal to the young Fedya. When
the forty-one-year-old novelist made a real trip to Europe with these
romantic images as background, he was certain to be profoundly disappointed.

Winter Notes is a fascinating book: travel notes as written by the Underground Man. It is clear that what Dostoevsky describes is the Europe of his mind and not a place that anyone else ever encountered. Strakhov, who later traveled with him, reports that he disdained the usual tourist attractions, preferring to study the people, that is, to look at them and imagine their lives. For more than a third of *Winter Notes* —in chapters entitled "In Place of a Foreword," "On the Train," and "Chapter III Which is Completely Superfluous"—he can't quite get out of Russia, or out of the literary arguments in his head. The book is half over before he finally sets foot in France, yet even then he is more preoccupied with mental comparisons between the French and Russians than with actual observations. For the rest, *Winter Notes,* is mainly filled with stereotypes and projections. The materialistic values of Paris offend him:

The Parisian absolutely adores being a tradesman, but it seems in trading and fleecing you like a sheep in his shop, he does not fleece you merely for profit, as he used to, but out of virtue, as a sacred duty. To accumulate a fortune and possess as much as possible has become the principal moral code and catechism of the Parisian.

He spends a day in Berlin and finds it depressingly like Petersburg:

I was annoyed even by the linden trees, but the Berliner, you know, would sacrifice all that is dearest to him, even, perhaps, his constitution, for their preservation; and what is dearer to a Berliner than his constitution? Besides, the Berliners themselves, every last one of them, looked so German that I, without even having attempted to see the frescoes of Kaulbach (how shameful of me!), slipped quickly away to Dresden, carrying in my soul the deepest conviction that it required special pains to accustom oneself to Germans, and that, unless one were used to them, it would be extremely difficult to stand them in large masses.

Then there is:

the smug and entirely mechanical curiosity of the English tourists, who look more at their guidebooks than at the points of interest, who expect nothing novel or surprising, and desire only to verify the information given in the guidebook and find out how much the object weighs or how high it is.

The cities do not fare much better than their inhabitants under his critical gaze. London, while big and exciting, is filled with poverty, abused children, and young prostitutes. The World Exposition of 1862 with its huge glass building, a monument to the triumphs of industry and science, would shortly become "The Crystal Palace" in *Notes from Underground,* symbol of the rationality and progress that organizes people at the expense of their personal autonomy. Dostoevsky travels through Italy—Florence, Milan, Venice—yet hardly mentions his reactions to the land of his childhood fantasies.

What makes *Winter Notes* fascinating is its self-awareness. Again and again, as he indulges his prejudices, Dostoevsky tells the reader that he is doing so, that it is unfair to the Europeans involved, that it just arises from the strain of traveling, his bad liver, or hypersensitivity. Still, for all the self-awareness, the prejudices persists. What are we to make of these views? Why should someone of his intelligence and sympathy for the mistreated—someone who had just suffered the immense cruelty of ten years' imprisonment and exhile—glorify and worship the very country that had done this to him? How can we understand such contradictions as his fervent plea for peace and unity side-by-side with his scorn for foreigners? It makes sense if we see it all as a struggle with the emotions at the core of his being: the wish for love and his powerful rage. His feelings about Russia and Europe represent a defensive resolution of the conflict between these emotions, a resolutions compounded of idealization and splitting. Russia is idealized—he conveniently forgets his considerable unpleasant experiences with real Russians of all classes —and the images—"unity," "harmony," "wholeness"—express his longing for merger. The forces that oppose the gratification of this wish are split off and projected outside; rage can then be safely directed at these "others" who are, by definition, foreigners with no real place in the unified, loving state he longs for.

While there is much that is of interest in Dostoevsky's journalism and travel notes, they are marred by his xenophobia and idealized nationalism. Fortunately, this was always a minor side of his work; even at the height of *Time*'s popularity, he devoted more care and energy to his fiction. As we know from his letters and notebooks, the novels often started out along the same lines as the journalism. That is, they often began with idealized plans, whether to present Christlike figures (for example, Myshkin) totally evil creatures (such as Svidrigailov and Stavrogin) or to attack his political enemies (as in *The Possessed*). But as he wrote and rewrote in the late night hours, working toward self-imposed standards of artistic truth, a new form of insight emerged that far transcended his prejudices.

Women

As with so much else in his life, Dostoevsky lived the many sides of his feelings for women to the fullest. He was married to Maria—the idealized-love-turned-disastrous-disappointment—felt guilt, sent money, and stayed as far away from her as possible. At the same time, he was open to love affairs, both casual and prolonged. While his own discretion prevents us from knowing all the details, a picture emerges from several reliable sources. When Dostoevsky met Wrangel in 1865, his friend and companion from earlier Siberian days reminisced about "our love affairs. We spoke much of his first wife Maria Dmityrevna [Wrangel could never figure out what Feodor saw in her], and of the fair Marina, of whom she had been so terribly jealous." This Marina was a seventeen-year-old—a "blooming, pretty creature"—whom Dostoevsky tutored in Semipalitinsk and with whom there was, at the least, a flirtation. There was also his landlady's daughter: "She took care of Feodor Mikhailovich lovingly, I think, worked for him and was inseparable from him." Back in Petersburg, Strakhov, an inveterate bachelor and something of a prude, was offended that Feodor moved in a crowd that tolerated "all kinds of physical excesses and abnormalities" and where, though "spiritual vileness was judged strictly and subtly, carnal vileness did not count at all." Clearly, Dostoevsky partook of the sexual freedom characteristic of an age of artistic efflorescence and social upheaval. There may have been other affairs that were not recorded, we know of at least one later encounter with a woman named Martha Brown, in 1864.

When his romantic relationships became more than casual, they would encompass the usual cast of characters from his inner scenarios. Jealous rivalry with another man and the attachment to a pair of sisters—one sexual and the other a close friend and confidante—recur. He seems to have sent more letters to Maria's sister Varvara Constant than to his tubercular wife herself. And, of course, there was that unique mixture of love, torture, suffering, and atonement that is such a dominant life theme.

Several sides of Dostoevsky's unconscious pattern can be seen in his flirtation with the wife of his old friend Stepan Yanovsky. In the years just before his arrest and imprisonment, one of his closest attachments was to Dr. Yanovsky. In the grip of his painful nervous illness, he saw the doctor daily for almost three years. Despite all the sickness and symptoms of his later life, Dostoevsky never again put himself into the hands of a doctor the way he did in the late 1840s. (A complete account of Dostoevsky's medical history and treatment can be found in Rice 1985.) Yanovsky—who also loaned him money during the difficult early years—was very helpful; it is clear that a good deal of what we would today understand as transference developed between them.

Returning to Petersburg ten years later, Dostoevsky found Yanovsky among the group of sympathetic friends and intellectuals at Milyukov's. The doctor was now married to the talented actress Alexandra Schubert, but the marriage was in difficulty. She wished to pursue her career on the stage and moved from Petersburg to Moscow for that purpose. Yanovsky, a conventional fellow, felt the marriage should come before her art. Enter Feodor: he placed himself between them, established a friendship with her, visited her in Moscow, and developed a correspondence. They confided their mutual marital woes—always a good way to establish intimacy—and he took her side, urging her to pursue her career even if it offended her husband. He described the doctor as jealous, vain, and egotistical. To her he declared,

I tell you frankly: I love you very dearly and warmly, so much that I was able to tell you I was not in love with you, because I prized your just opinion. . . . It makes it possible for me to be ever more devoted to you, without fearing for my heart. I shall know that mine is disinterested devotion.

Not so disinterested as to stop Yanovsky from becoming very suspicious and jealous. I would guess that, in addition to the conscious pleasures of this attractive woman's confidences, there was an old unconscious need: Dostoevsky was driven to win the woman away from this father-brother figure, the former doctor-therapist on whom he had been so dependent. In his correspondence with Alexandra Schubert, he continually compares himself with her husband: Yanovsky—now a successful civil servant—is dull, conventional, jealous, and an impediment to her freedom; he, on the other hand, shares her artistic sensibility and view of life. Nothing more came of their relationship as far as we know.

Dostoevsky's more casual involvements and his flirtation with Yanovsky's wife served as prologue to his grand affair with Polina Suslova. This was a relationship that put all his unconscious dynamics on display: the wish for the young, healthy, and giving woman; his need both to take from her and for revenge; and the resultant guilt and need to suffer and seek forgiveness. There was even a younger sister on the sidelines in whom he could confide, thus facilitating the split. Her name was Nadezhda Suslova. Intelligent and more sexually restrained than Polina, she became the first woman doctor in Russia. All this was played out over a period of several years, intertwined with the gambling compulsion which gave expression to the same unconscious conflicts.[1]

Dostoevsky and Polina became lovers sometime around 1862. She was an aspiring writer of twenty-one or twenty-two; most likely they met when he published one of her stories in *Time*. His time and energy were heavily committed to writing and editorial duties, and he treated the affair, at first, as a casual liaison. He was certainly very concerned to keep it a secret from Maria. While casual, it was still imbued with his fantasy of what a woman could do for him:

Your love descended to me like a gift from heaven, unawaited and unsuspected, after fatigue and despair. Your young life near me promised so much and has already given so much. It revived my faith and what little was left of my former energies.

He was twenty years older than she was.

Polina was a radical young woman of the 1860s, a rebel against conventional mores. She was an aspiring writer, a romantic, drawn to the forty-year-old writer whose past as a political martyr and fame as a novelist must have looked heroic in her young eyes. She gave him her heart and her body. This was her first love and she idealized him: "I gave myself to him in love, without asking and without expecting anything in return." She later spoke of her initial love for him as "beautiful, even grandiose."

But it was not long before this idealized love was shattered. She came to sense that he was just using her to satisfy his sexual needs, that he did not share her feelings of exclusivity and devotion. She later wrote,

You behaved like a serious, busy man who understood his obligations after his own fashion, but would not miss his pleasures either; on the contrary, perhaps even found it necessary to have some pleasure, on the grounds that some great doctor or philosopher once said that it was necessary to get drunk every month.

Clearly, she resented the time and attention given to other sides of his life. She also resented the clandestine nature of their affair and his inability to break with Maria. Twenty years later, her second husband reported her answer to the question of why she and Dostoevsky became estranged.

"Because he did not wish to divorce his wife, who was tubercular and dying."
"You say she was dying. . . . "
"Yes, she was dying. She died six months later. But I was no longer in love with Feodor."
"Why did you stop loving him?"
"Because he would not get a divorce. . . . I gave myself to him, out of love, without asking anything. He should have behaved in the same way! He behaved otherwise and I left him."

In 1864 she wrote in her diary,

People talk to me about Feodor Mikhailovich. I hate him. He made me suffer so much while there was no need to suffer.

I now feel and see clearly that I cannot love, that I cannot find happiness in the pleasures of love, because men's caresses will remind me of insults and suffering.

In Polina Suslova, Dostoevsky had found a worthy adversary, someone who shared his capacity for idealized love and the anger brought forth by its frustration and disappointment. She was, like him, a person of emotional extremes, capable of loving and hating, of tenderness and coldness, of giving and tormenting. Their time together in Europe in 1863 — documented in her diary and in his short work *The Gambler* — is the lived version of one of his novels.

In May 1863 *Time* was suppressed because an article, written by Strakhov, was incorrectly viewed by the censor as critical of the government. Dostoevsky used the occasion to plan a liaison with Polina in Paris. She went ahead with him to follow; now they would be able to consummate their love, free from the distractions of his work and marriage, in the European capital famous for grand passions. But Dostoevsky was months in following her. One cannot be certain why it took him so long to leave Russia, the biographers, who often try to exonerate him for the conflicts in the affair, find various plausible reasons. But even they are struck by the fact that after finally leaving Petersburg and going to meet the love of his life, he could not help stopping four days at Wiesbaden for a fling at roulette. This was probably the real beginning of his gambling compulsion (to be discussed in the next section). The effect of his long delay was to do to Polina what he had done with her all along: arouse her hopes for his exclusive attention and then frustrate these hopes. It is no surprise that when he finally got to Paris in August, she was sick of waiting and turned the tables on him.

Polina's first words to him when they were finally together:

"I thought you were not going to come, because I wrote you a letter."
"What letter?"
"So you wouldn't come."
"Why not?"
"Because it is too late."
He hung his head
"I must know everything, let's go somewhere, and tell me, or I'll die."

She told him. Tired of waiting, she had fallen in love and given herself to another man, Salvador, a young Spaniard. It also became clear that Salvador was in the process of getting rid of her. Dostoevsky's reaction:

He fell at my feet, and, putting his arms around my knees, clasping them and sobbing, he exclaimed between sobs: "I have lost you, I knew it!" Then having regained his composure he began to ask me about the other man. "Perhaps he is handsome, young and glib. But you will never find a heart such as mine."

Dostoevsky displayed a variety of reactions: he was rejected, hurt, and sad—he felt the full impact of these emotions—yet he "knew it": that is, he had unconsciously contrived to bring about the very rejection that he suffered. There was, at the same time, a curious objectivity: he pressed her to tell him everything and, at various points, was quite the impartial therapist with her, interpreting her feelings and actions. The structure of the whole affair was a repetition of the central theme of his life: the loss of the loved woman to another man, anger, the wish to win her back, and the need to be punished. He had played it out earlier with Maria and Vergunov in Siberia, and, in a minor key, with Yanovsky and his wife.

Out of this whirlwind of emotion and unconscious repetition came Dostoevsky's proposal that they embark on the trip to Italy that they had planned earlier, but now traveling "as brother and sister." How significant, in view of the role that Dostoevsky's younger sisters—and the sister figures of his adult years—played as representatives of the desired woman.

Suslova documents their two-month journey in great detail. She is fairly clear on her own motives: Salvador had enraged her with his rejection: "I would not like to kill him . . . but I would like to torture him for a very long time," she told Feodor. Since Salvador was not at hand—indeed in some ways he seems a convenient fantasy—Dostoevsky, who had treated her in the same way, became the object of her revenge. It took the form of tantalizing him with her body and the possibility of love and then frustrating his aroused desire. There were nights in hotel rooms with her naked under the bedcovers as they held hands and talked, with him finally sent off to his room in humiliation. As she says quite directly in her diary,

While we were en route here he told me that he had some hope, though he had earlier insisted he had none. I did not say anything to this, but I knew that it was not going to happen . . . .[I] refused to be drawn into a discussion of the subject, so that he could neither cherish hope nor be quite without it.

Her punishment of him was exquisitely designed to fit his earlier crimes against her.

Dostoevsky was not the innocent recipient of all this mistreatment; he played his part in the drama, submitted to her torment, arguing, attempting to make her feel guilty, and indirectly attacking her. This he mainly did by rejecting her for the greater allure of the gaming tables where he fantasied a magical gratification of his desires with money. Mikhail wrote to him, "I don't understand how its possible to gamble while traveling with a woman whom you love." The humiliation of his inevitable losses was passed on to her as he depleted their resources and pressed her for loans.

They encountered his old rival Turgenev on their wanderings through Baden-Baden, and Dostoevsky took the occasion to subject his brother writer—and himself—to a small version of the unconscious drama he was enacting with Polina. He humiliated himself by borrowing money from his fellow novelist—hating him for it—and took his revenge in a way that he must have known would be most painful. Turgenev gave him his latest piece *(Phantoms)* to read and possibly publish, and Dostoevsky returned it unread—ostensibly because he was too caught up in roulette. What greater insult to a writer than to return his manuscript unread? Dostoevsky let the unpaid debt to Turgenev rankle between them for years afterward.

The majority of the biographers stress Polina's cruelty to Dostoevsky during this phase of their affair: they see her as the model for the tempestuous heroines of the later novels, "Polina" in *The Gambler,* of course, and also Nastasya Filippovna in *The Idiot,* Liza in *The Possessed,* and Grushenka in *The Brothers Karamazov.* She was certainly a woman of power in her own right, but I would stress Dostoevsky's greater control over what happened between them. This is not always obvious since his control was exercised indirectly. We must remember that he was older, with a great deal more life experience, an established writer, her editor and publisher; he set up the whole enactment and stayed with her throughout, playing his part as the victim. A striking glimpse of Dostoevsky's inner scenario is revealed in a fantasy that came to him on this trip. One evening, she became tender with him and they drew close. Later,

he said, looking at a little girl who was taking her lessons: "Well imagine, there you have a little girl like her with an old man, and suddenly some Napoleon says 'I want this city destroyed.' It has always been that way in this world."

Here we see a version of his rage at women—especially innocent young girls—that will soon find its expression in *Crime and Punishment.*

Dostoevsky's travels with Polina ended, fittingly, with her return to Paris and his taking a final fling at roulette in Homburg. He lost his money and wrote to her in desperation; she was forced to pawn her watch and chain to send him funds. Rejected and broke, but with his health restored—there were very few epileptic seizures during this whole affair—he returned to Petersburg. The connection with Polina was not finished though it never again reached this intensity. They remained in contact by letter for a few more years. In 1865 he wrote her sister Nadezda, attempting to answer Polina's charges that he "liked to feast on the suffering and tears of others." He tries to shift the blame to her:

Apollinaria is a great egotist. Her egotism and self-esteem are colossal. She demands everything of people, perfection in every respect, she won't forgive a single imperfection. . . . To this day she keeps reproaching me, saying that I was unworthy of her love, complaining to me, and upbraiding me incessantly.

He then attempts to establish Nadezhda as the ideal woman who will relieve him of his guilt: "Don't you, at least, blame me. I have high regard for you; you are a real human being among all whom I have met in my life, and I do not want to lose your affection." He ends with the image that always kept his faith alive: "You are dear to me, as you stand for what's young, and new, besides that I love you as one would love one's favorite sister."

Gambling

The early signs of Dostoevsky's peculiar relations with money can be found in his adolescence. The miserly Dr. Dostoevsky never let his children have any money of their own; it was not until Feodor was away at school that he finally came into possession of some cash. He never had enough, and whatever he managed to lay his hands on did not remain with him for long. The letters between him and his father are filled with pleas for money and the mutual induction of guilt. On his own, as a young man in Petersburg in the 1840s, he was always in debt, always borrowing from friends and relatives. At one point he came into possession of a thousand rubles as part of his inheritance and lost it in a single day playing billiards. In the months before his arrest in 1849 he was, as usual, borrowing from everyone, Dr. Yanovsky, Mikhail, other friends, and Speshnev, whom he called his Mephistopheles because of the five hundred rubles he owed him. There was an unconscious purpose to all this; he was an artist, a free spirit, a bohemian, and not one of those careful Germans or crooked French shopkeepers that he mocks in *Winter Notes*. His way with money reveals a deep and persistent theme: others are greedy, they horde and exploit the needy innocents of the world; he gives freely, so freely as to be always in the position of a poor innocent himself. Of course, there is a good deal of indirect hostility to the whole business; his borrowing is a form of aggression against those who have; the borrowing itself is irritating, he tries to make them feel guilty for what they possess, and his own rage is always close to the surface. He comes to the comfortable Turgenev for a loan and says he hates himself for having to ask for money and then storms off saying he hates Turgenev even more. The gambling compulsion is a specific symptomatic or ritualized expression of the emotions and conflicts long apparent in this more general pattern with money.

First, it should be clear that Dostoevsky's passion for roulette is a species of compulsive gambling. That is, while the conscious motive was to win, he was driven to lose, and he always did, over and over in the stereotyped manner so characteristic of unconscious repetition.[2]

In common with other neurotic symptoms and character styles, Dostoevsky's gambling compulsion gave symbolic expression to the various sides of the conflict that drove it: wish-impulse, guilt, punishment, and restitution. It was a self-contained system that, as long as it remained unconscious, was not modified by reality. In addition, because it was a ritual that played out the whole conflict on a symbolic stage, it was relatively safe. That is, while he caused a good deal of trouble and discomfort for himself and others with his gambling—he was always "ruined," always in the most dire financial straits—nobody was ever hurt in any serious way. At bottom, it was all a game. Finally, we must keep in mind the crucial way that he differed from most other gamblers; in the end, it was all material for writing. While it took a few years, he worked his way out of this compulsion, aided by the insights gained from transforming the conflicts into novels, not so much with *The Gambler*—which was dictated in haste—but with *Crime and Punishment,* written at the same time.

When Dostoevsky left for Europe in 1863 he had several reasons to feel guilty. *Time* had just been closed down by the censor, and his brother had the arduous job of getting it started again. Mikhail, who had a wife and children to support, had invested his own money in the journal and was left to struggle with financial as well as publishing troubles. Feodor writes to him from Italy with characteristic insight and irony: "To seek happiness in leaving everything, even in that in which I might have been useful, is egoism, and this thought now poisons my happiness—if there is such a thing as happiness at all."

A more important source of guilt was his wife, whose health continued to deteriorate. He had mainly avoided Maria since returning from

Siberia; now he was taking their money and running off to Paris in pursuit of his young mistress. The core of Dostoevsky's guilt arose from his anger at the woman who disappointed his hopes for love; he certainly felt this in relation to Maria and he was to play it out again with Polina. These were the circumstances under which his gambling erupted with full force. The real answer to Mikhail's question of how it was "possible to gamble while traveling with a woman you love" was that it was better than killing her: the symbolic expression of anger via gambling was the safer course.

Dostoevsky's own description of his psychological state when gambling is, as usual, revealing of his unconscious dynamics. His play at roulette was based on a "system" that was really no system at all. Here, he describes it in a letter to his wife's sister Varvara Constant:

The fact is, darling Varvara Dmitrievna, that I have a certain small request to make of you. You see, on the way here I spent three or four days in Wiesbaden and of course I played roulette. And what do you think? I didn't lose, I won; although I didn't win as much as I should have liked, not 100,000, all the same I did win just a little bit. . . .

Please don't think I am so pleased with myself for not losing that I am showing off when I say that I know the secret of how not to lose but to win. I really do know the secret; it is terribly silly and simple, and consists of keeping one's head the whole time, whatever the state of the game, and not getting excited. That is all, and it makes losing simply impossible and winning a certainty. But that is not the point; the point is whether, having grasped the secret, a man knows how to make use of it and is fit to do so. A man can be as wise as Solomon and have an iron character, and still be carried away. Even the philosopher Strakhov would be carried away. Therefore blessed are they who do not play and regard the roulette-wheel with loathing as the greatest of stupidities.

Of course he could neither stay away from the roulette tables nor stick to his system. A week later he writes to his sister-in-law again:

Dear friend and sister, Varvara Dmitrievna, I write you only a few lines to inform you of something and make a request. I am travelling today, in an hour's time or even sooner, and so have not a minute. The whole point is that here in Baden I have lost everything at roulette, absolutely and completely everything. I have lost more than three thousand francs. I have now only 250 francs in my pocket.

There follows some scheming as to how she is to get some money to Mikhail without Maria's knowledge so that Mikhail may send it on to him in Europe.

The pattern revealed in these letters was to be repeated over and over: with Maria, Mikhail, Polina and, later, with his second wife, Anna. His curious "system," in which he must "keep his head," "not get excited," and not be "carried away" symbolizes the control of impulses of a wider sort. It is a version of the larger conflict between control-reason and freedom-emotion that runs through his life and fiction. The gambling "system" requires him to be a good boy, one without greed and anger. Being Dostoevsky, he is always carried off on a tide of passion, then punished for giving in to his impulses and, finally, reduced to the position of penitent seeking forgiveness and love.

Like certain forms of sadomasochistic alcoholism—such as that Dostoevsky masterfully pictures in the relationship between Marmeladov and his wife—the gambling was always played out with a loved one. In 1863 he was doing it with Polina as they traveled together through Europe. She was not particularly forgiving of him and they parted. By 1865–66 he was in the process of transforming the underlying conflicts into fiction: *Crime and Punishment* gives the most profound insight into this issue. Raskolnikov, like Dostoevsky the gambler, has a "rational" plan to obtain riches quickly, if only he can remain calm and in control of himself. It is not gambling but murder—pointing to the aggression underlying the pattern—and the novel shows how his plan is overtaken by emotion and ruined by guilt. This is followed by the need to seek forgiveness from the loving women, embodied in Sonia.

As Dostoevsky was finishing *Crime and Punishment* he dictated his short novel *The Gambler* to a young woman stenographer who, shortly thereafter, became his second wife. Anna, much more than Maria or Polina, was able to fill the role of his Sonia: a healthy young woman who would accept him, gambling, epilepsy, murderous impulses, and all. This didn't happen immediately, he needed to put her acceptance to repeated tests, and one way was with gambling. Shortly after the marriage they fled their creditors for Europe. Once again, he could not resist the lure of roulette and Anna was caught in the drama. Here, he writes to her from Homburg in 1867:

Forgive me, my angel, for going into some details concerning my enterprise, concerning this game, so it will be clear to you what this is all about. Already some twenty times or so I have gone to the gaming tables and had the experience that if I play with sangfroid, calmly, and calculating, there is *absolutely no chance of losing!* I swear it to you, there is no such chance! There's blind chance, while I have a calculation on my side, consequently, the odds favor me. But what has usually happened? I have usually started play with *forty gulden,* took them from my pocket, sat down, and placed them, one or two gulden at a time. In a quarter of an hour, I have usually—always—won double. That would be the time to stop and go away, at least until the evening, so as to give my excited nerves a chance to calm down—besides, I have made the observation—most certainly correct—that I can be calm and composed for *no longer than half an hour at a time,* when I am gambling. But I would walk away just to smoke a cigarette, and then return to the gaming table immediately. Why did I do that, knowing almost for certain that I would not contain myself, i.e., go on to lose? That's because every day, upon getting up in the morning, I told myself that this would be my last day in Homburg, that I would be leaving the next day, so that, consequently, I could not play a waiting game at roulette. I tried hurriedly, with all my strength, to win as much as possible, right away, that very day—for I was to leave on the following day—lost my sangfroid, my nerves got excited, I started taking chances, I got angry, proceeded to place my bets without any calculation, having lost the thread of it, and eventually lost—because anybody who plays without calculating, helter-skelter, is a madman. My whole mistake was to have parted with you, rather than taking you with me. Yes, yes, this is so. And here we are, I am yearning to see you, and you, nearly dying without me. My angel, I repeat, I am not reproaching you for that, and I love you even more for your yearning to see me. . . .

I was so overjoyed, and had such a terrible, almost *mad* desire to finish off everything right there, *that very day,* to win perhaps twice that amount and then leave immediately, that I threw myself at the roulette table, without having given myself a chance to rest up and collect myself, took to betting gold pieces, and lost *everything everything,* to the last kopeck, i.e., all I had left were *two* gulden for tobacco. Ania, my dear joy! You must understand that I have debts to pay, that I'll be called a scoundrel unless I pay them.

Two days later, another letter:

Ania dear, my dearest, my wife, forgive me, don't call me a scoundrel! I am guilty of a criminal act, I lost everything that you sent me, everything, everything to the last kreutzer, I received it yesterday, and lost it yesterday. Ania, how am I going to face you now, what are you going to say about me after this! One *and only one* thing horrifies me: what will *you* say, what are you going to think of me? It is your judgement alone that I fear! Can you, will you respect me now! And what is love, even, without respect! Why, this has shaken the very foundation of our marriage. Oh, my dear, don't condemn me altogether! I hate gambling, not only now, but even yesterday, the day before yesterday, even then I was cursing it.

There is more of this, mixed in with pleas that she send money, and then:

P. S. My angel, don't worry about me! I repeat, if I were all by myself, I'd just laugh and forget about it. You, your judgment, that's the one thing that is torturing me! That's what pains me, and nothing else. Meanwhile I have tortured you to death! Au revoir.

Oh, if only I could be with you sooner, if only we could be together, we would come up with something for sure, wouldn't we.

These letters show the unconscious scenario in clear form: "I got angry," a "mad desire to finish off everything right there," "I have tortured you to death," and "*only one* thing horrifies me: what will *you* say, what are you going to think of me? It is your judgement alone that I fear!" While still not fully conscious, Dostoevsky—both in his writing and in communications with Anna—was becoming aware of the meaning of his gambling.

Anna, who had her own reasons for idealizing her much older husband, was a woman of great patience and acceptance. She also came to have some understanding of the whole pattern, including the role that he cast her in; she came to realize that love and forgiveness was what he required. Out of this combination of the insight achieved through writing and the real love and acceptance of his wife, the gambling was finally overcome. Just a few years after these letters were written, he gave it up. It never recurred.

CHAPTER 11

The Death of Maria:
Notes from Underground

> In my impatience I thumped the cabby on the back of the neck. What's that for, why are you knocking me about?' cried my wretched peasant, but he whipped up his miserable nag, so that it began to lash out with its hoofs.

Notes from Underground stands at the threshold of a new sensibility: published in 1864, it anticipates the modern novel in form and content. Its hero—or antihero—who is never named, argues with imagined opponents and aims a monologue at the reader, displaying a tortured and darkly humorous self-awareness. The work is also pivotal in Dostoevsky's own literary development; almost all the biographers and critics see it as the prelude to the great novels of his mature years. It is also a crucial point in the self-exploration; it initiates the plunge inward that reaches its deepest level in the next novel, *Crime and Punishment*.

As a model for interpreting the different levels of *Notes from Underground* I will treat it the way a psychoanalyst works with a dream, moving from conscious concerns and current life events to associated personal emotional issues. Closest to the present is the running argument that Dostoevsky and his journalist collaborators were carrying on with the radicals (especially Chernyshevsky, but also Pisarev and Dobrolyubov). In the *Notes,* references to these arguments are clear in the Underground Man's attack on utopian schemes for social reform, in his mockery of rationality, and his espousal of individuality and will. I propose that we treat Dostoevsky's preoccupation with these issues as the day residues that go into the composition of the novel as "dream."[1] That is, they were emotionally central events and make up one level of the novel's content. Another source of material—another kind of residue—is his personal life. Most central here was his wife's death; much of the novel was composed in an apartment as Maria lay dying of tuberculosis in an adjoining room. A long and revealing mediation on her death and the meaning of their relationship is found in the private *Notebooks,* interspersed with arguments with Chernyshevsky, and an early idea for *Crime and Punishment.* (See *The Notebooks,* edited by Proffer, Dostoevsky 1973–76, 1:38-55.)

In this chapter I will attempt to trace all these residues in *Notes from Underground* and follow the way they are transformed into the final form of the novel. We will see that most of the commentators focus their analyses on one level of the work—a meaningful level, to be sure—but one that does not tell the whole story.[2] They only follow things back a short distance to the novelist's conscious preoccupations. The psychoanalytic reader is more alert to personal events and, given Dostoevsky's powerful ambivalence toward women, we would suspect that Maria's death had a great impact on him, that it aroused a life and death conflict between his inner selves. With this in mind, one is immediately struck by the obvious: *Notes from Underground* is a cry from the grave. Its hero describes himself as a man who is no longer a part of life, yet he is not dead; in the face of his isolated existence in a "dark corner" or "cellar," he insists on thrusting forth his living self in all its guilty obnoxiousness.[3] He will not be done in by guilt and this assertion of the will to live is the point at which personal concerns and social-political ideas come together. But, I am getting ahead of the story.

In my analysis of the different levels of meaning in *Notes from Underground* I will attempt to steer a course between the extremes defined by early psychoanalytic-literary studies—which overemphasized infantile determinants—and those critics and biographers who write as if the unconscious had never been discovered. The most meaningful approach, in my view, is one that begins with current life events and works carefully with them to discern unconscious patterns. I will not take Dostoevsky's political-social views at face value, as do a number of the biographers and critics, nor will I discard them as indifferent material in a rush to discover "deeper" childhood determinants. The day residues of Dostoevsky's life—his journalism and conscious preoccupations as revealed in *The Notebooks* and correspondence—are worthy of careful analysis, both in their own right and as they relate to underlying patterns and themes. The interpretation of these themes—the latent or unconscious meaning of the material—will be aided by what Dostoevsky does as he transforms them into fiction; writing was the ground on which his self-analysis took place, it was where he explored and brought forth the wider meaning of his conscious preoccupations. Thus, in our attempt at a psychoanalytic interpretation, we have Dostoevsky the novelist as our co-analyst.

The Day Residues

In the early 1860s, debate over a wide range of social, moral, and political questions was carried on in journals that espoused different points of view. As we have seen, the Dostoevsky brothers and their collaborators were associated, first in *Time* and then *The Epoch,* with native-soil conservatism. The men of the soil stood somewhere between the Slavophiles and the radicals.

Chernyshevsky, the best known of the radicals, blended French utopian socialism and English utilitarianism into a vision of a future world of love and moral perfection. His philosophy, as expounded in articles and the extremely popular novel *What Is to be Done?* (published in 1863), presented a version of ideas current in Europe at the time. He espoused the "unity of nature," the belief that man has no special nature, that free will is an illusion, and that a common set of scientific laws govern rocks, trees, and people. There is a great faith in science and reason in all this, a widespread nineteenth century phenomenon, a faith that remains very much alive today. Chernyshevsky assumes that there are laws of human life, of the same form as the laws of physical science and, if we have not discovered them yet, we soon will and can govern ourselves accordingly. This general faith in science and reason was taken to mean that all human conduct is—or could be—directed by rational self-interest. People do what is necessary for self-preservation—there is no inherent good or evil—and, since they are presumed to be rational, education will lead to a society that runs smoothly along planned lines; everyone will live harmoniously, satisfying themselves and helping others. A related aspect of this set of beliefs was materialism. A concern to better the material lot of the vast understratum of Russian society was taken to an extreme; man was seen as entirely a creature of material needs; satisfy these and you eliminate human problems and conflicts. In the writings of Pisarev, for example, this took an antiart form, and various examples were given of how farmers and workers contributed more than artists and writers.

Dostoevsky thought all this was nonsense; his observations of society and human life, and his insight into himself, had led to a very different —a much more complex—view of man. He was inflamed by the certainty and self-satisfied tone of the radicals and discerned the hostility beneath their professed desire to help others and perfect society. Chernyshevsky's views not only clashed with the native soil program, but they also offended his deepest personal sympathies. He was nothing if not an individualist, and his novels—both before and after this period —are filled with characters who struggle to assert their uniqueness. He was also a man who lived in his imagination; the center of his existence, from adolescence on, was built on literature and an identification with great writers. In the creation of literature he expressed his individuality and revealed truths about human nature that had only partly to do with "reason"—they came more from imagination, dream, and emotion. Man's urge for freedom was as important as—and often more important than—his material needs; literature should never be conscripted to serve political ends. He had disagreed with Belinsky on this issue in the 1840s and he felt just as strongly about it in the 1860s. His private *Notebooks* are filled with scoffing references to the utilitarian ideas of the radicals of which the following is typical: "[the radicals strive] to prove that there is nothing beyond what the belly contains. Let them dare to deny it. They admit *with pride:* boots are better than Shakespeare." He was also very antagonistic to what he saw as their attempt to force life into theory; there are many references to Chernyshevsky's ignorance of real life.

Dostoevsky's sensitivity to hostility made him very aware of its presence, in thin disguise, within the radical's rhetoric. One of his strongest convictions was that we need beliefs and ideals to counter our anger and selfishness. A good deal of his journalism was devoted to the search for unity and reconciliation—between radicals and conservatives, Slavophiles and westernizers—and his own quest for Christian belief—never a certainty with him, always a search—was the principle area in which he sought a unifying ideal. The radicals believed that if restraints were removed and people allowed to pursue self-interest, a reasonable and harmonious system would evolve. Dostoevsky felt, and attempted to demonstrate in his novels, that this would simply give license to the most amoral, self-willed destructiveness. This brings us to the consideration of how his arguments were transformed into fiction.

The opening monologue of *Notes from Underground* contains a fairly direct satire of Chernyshevsky's views. Dostoevsky shows how a reasonable, "perfected' society would be an intolerable constraint on one's freedom. Confronted with such a society, his protagonist chooses to assert his individuality in whatever way he can. But the novelist demonstrates this—and here is the crucial point—not with argument or a political tract like *What Is to Be Done?* but by creating a great literary character—the Underground Man—who takes on a life of his own. As this happens, the novel moves into realms far beyond the argument with Chernyshevsky, realms that are more personal and, at the same time, of broader significance. This can be clearly seen in the principle way in which Dostoevsky attacks the idea of "rational self-interest." In *The Insulted and Injured*, written before the *Notes*, he contrasted the writer-hero—an embodiment of the dreamer or imaginative-romantic side of his own personality—with Prince Valcovsky, one of his first attempts at the self-willed type that assumes such a prominant place in the later novels. Valcovsky spouts various of Chernyshevsky's lines about science and reason.

Things become much more complicated in the succeeding novels. By the time of *Crime and Punishment*, the positivist ideology is divided up among at least three characters. Luzhin is a direct representation of rational self-interest and several of his speeches could have appeared in the pages of the radical journals. But, compared to Raskolnikov and Svidrigailov—who embody these ideas in more complex ways—he is a stereotype who doesn't come alive as a character. They do, as does their immediate predecessor, the Underground Man. In creating these three, Dostoevsky moved beyond political argument and drew on his own experience and imagination. What would it be like to live in Chernyshevsky's perfected society? Indeed, how did he feel when confronted with these ideas? All his life he had struggled against constraints on his individuality; he knew, from early on, that his very sense of life depended on the freedom to express what was within him. In a related way, he could not stand the idea of slavishly following someone else's theory. These commitments produced a powerful opposition to the radical's program. In other words, he found within himself the emotional reactions that he gives to the Underground Man, Raskolnikov, and Svidrigailov.

To come at the point from a different direction, we might ask why, in his argument with Chernyshevsky, Dostoevsky creates types like Svidrigailov and Stavrogin. They are not radicals. Indeed, they are not at all concerned with politics. In both of these characters, as well as in the Underground Man, self-will and amorality reach their extreme form in sexual attacks on women and young girls. This comes directly from a personal source, stimulated by his wife's death, a source that is only tangentially related to political arguments. In other words, the ideological debates were one residue for *Notes from Underground,* Maria's death was another; in the working out of what both these situations aroused in him, he discovered a latent source of much larger importance than the time-bound political issues.

Dostoevsky saw the radicals as men who were so entranced with their own theories that they failed to see real life. In *Notes from Underground* this conflict between theory and life is taken in a much different direction. While the initial stimulus was the political debate, most of what Dostoevsky projects through the Underground Man is a personal conflict between the romantic idealism of his early years and the far-from-ideal reality he had come to know. *At the core of the Underground Man's de-idealized view of life is an acute awareness of his own fear, insecurity, humiliation, and need to hurt others.* Dostoevsky's stark awareness of these feelings was brought out by Maria's death, for their relationship was one that began on an idealized, romantic plane and degenerated to sordid depths. As he put it in a letter to his friend Wrangel:

The Death of Maria: *Notes from Underground*

She loved me boundlessly, and I, too, loved her immeasurably, but our life together was not happy. Although we were positively unhappy together—because of her passionate, over-sensitive and morbidly imaginative nature—we could not stop loving each other. In fact, the unhappier we were, the more attached we became to each other.

The truth was that he lived apart from her after the return to Petersburg, carried on affairs with other women—he was off gambling in Europe with Polina Suslova just before Maria's final days—and almost never mentioned her in his correspondence. When he returned from Europe he found her dying:

Maria Dmitriyevna has death constantly on her mind; she is melancholy and beginning to despair. Such moments are very difficult for her. Her nerves are extremely frayed. Her chest is bad and she has withered away like a matchstick. Horror! It's painful and dreadful to see.

And, in a letter to his brother Mikhail:

My wife is dying, *literally*. Each day there is a moment when we expect her death. Her sufferings are terrible and are reflected on me. . . . Then writing is not a mechanical work and nonetheless I am writing and writing. . . . Sometimes I fancy that it will be rubbish, but still I write with passion; I don't know what will emerge. . . . Here is something more: I'm afraid that my wife's death will be soon, and then *necessarily* there'll be an interruption in my work. If it were not for this interruption, then, of course, I would finish.

This passage is extremely significant. First, it shows how *Notes from Underground* poured forth in the context of the death of the formerly idealized woman. This parallels the way the initial burst of work on *Crime and Punishment* erupted out of debt and destitution. Second, it shows a certain callousness; the writing seems to matter more to him than the death of his wife, for all its horror. To put this in different terms, we see how his primary identity as writer protected him; how it facilitated mastery of the tragedies in his life. He is both involved with her death and, at the same time, outside it, transforming it into literature. And, finally, his remarks to Mikhail show that he was no more aware of the specific connections between her death and *Notes from Underground* than the later commentators. Insight is a result of the writing, it comes later.

The private *Notebooks* contain a long meditation prompted by Maria's death. Interestingly, this material gives one of the clearest statements of Dostoevsky's unique religious views. In a related way, it can be read as a discussion of the theme, so central in the novels, of the disparity between the individual with all his earthly needs and faults and the idealized self, symbolized by Christ.

April 16. Maria is lying on the table. Will I ever see Maria again? To love another as one does oneself, as Christ's teachings require, is an impossibility. The law of the individual on earth prevents it. *Ego* is the obstacle. Christ alone was able to do this, but Christ was eternal, an eternal ideal toward which man strives and should by the laws of nature strive.

He is clear here; the relation with Maria was very un-christlike. It was dominated by antagonism, infidelity, and absorption in his work: his "Ego" and selfishness. But this self-centered way must be balanced by hope and ideals, lest he follow the path of a Svidrigailov or Stavrogin.

Meanwhile, after the appearance of Christ, as the *idea of man incarnate,* it became as clear as day that the highest, final development of the individual should attain precisely the point—at the very end of his development, at the very point of reaching the goal—where man might find, recognize and with all the strength of his nature be convinced that the highest use which he can make of his individuality, of the full development of his Ego, is to seemingly annihilate that Ego, to give it wholly to each and every one wholeheartedly and selflessly. And this is the greatest happiness. In this way the law of the Ego merges with the law of humanism, and in the merging both, both Ego and the *all*—in appearance two extreme opposites—mutually annihilate each other, at that same time each apart attains the highest goal of his individual development. This is indeed the paradise of Christ. All history whether of humanity or in part of each man separately is only development, struggle, striving and attainment of that goal.

But if that is the final goal of humanity—and having attained it, it would no longer be necessary to develop, that is, to attain, to struggle, to glimpse the ideal through all one's falls and eternally strive towards it—consequently it would not be necessary to live—then it follows that man attaining it would also end his earthly existence. Thus on earth man is only a developing creature, consequently one not completed but transitional.

Here, Dostoevsky outlines a religious way of life that is far from the Judeo-Christian mainstream. The core image, in which the self, or "Ego," disappears in a merger with the "all," is more Eastern (Buddhist or Hindu) than Western. It is linked to that minor voice in Christianity that goes back to the Gnostics and that reappeared in the nineteenth-century Romantic movement. While one can connect it to various sources such as these, I believe Dostoevsky worked it out for himself. In addition to the image of merger, this vision stresses process or being; it contrasts with the more familiar Christian doctrine, which defines earthly life as a means to a higher end. Significantly absent from Dostoevsky's view is the image of a judgmental, patriarchal God. There is little stress on compliance with rules or renunciation in this life for rewards in the next. In psychoanalytic terms, this is a maternal religion with the core image loss of self in a blissful merger, a return to mother-infant, preseparation, preambivalent oneness. It fits with what Freud, in *Civilization and Its Discontents*, calls the "oceanic feeling," and contrasts sharply with his own image of religion: childlike man struggling to obey a punitive father-God.

The passage in *The Notebooks* concludes with a reference to Dostoevsky's own marriage:

And so, on earth man strives for an ideal that is contrary to his nature. When he finds he cannot achieve the ideal, that is, if he has not sacrificed his Ego to love of people or of another being—Maria and I—he suffers, and he calls this condition sin. And so a man must suffer constantly; this suffering is counterweighed by the heavenly pleasure of striving to carry out the behest, that is, of sacrificing. This is what earthly equilibrium is, otherwise the earth would be meaningless.

One source of these ideas was the awareness of the contrast between the real relationship with his wife and the sacrifice—that he was unable to make—of his "Ego to love of another being." Behind the disappointment of the marriage lay the feelings stimulated by his mother's death. And behind this loss—what made it such a profound event—were the ways he had lost his mother and nurses as an infant and young child. The first Maria died when Feodor was fifteen, a time when he was very wrapped up in romantic fantasies derived from literature. It was then that he was confronted by the very unromantic events of this period, events memorialized in the horse and courier emblem. All this was reenacted in the marriage. His initial love for Maria Isaeva was an attempt to regain the lost paradise; the real relationship, her tuberculosis, and death—and especially his angry and selfish treatment of her— were a repetition of the unromantic, un-christlike side of his being. What emerges—as the final passage makes clear—is a recognition of *both* sides of human nature: the "sinful" and the ideal. He espouses a view of life as an active process, a "striving," a meaningful "equilibrium" of conflicting forces.

Levels of Memory

Dostoevsky's political arguments of the 1860s and the death of his wife comprise the day residues for *Notes from Underground* viewed as a dream. Connected to these residues are memories from earlier periods. This model of interpretation is supported by the structure of the novel, which bears a resemblance to the regression that one can observe in psychoanalytic treatment: it begins with material from the "present," associates back to memories from earlier periods, and eventually focuses on a core emotional conflict. The first part—about one-third—is a monologue delivered by the forty-year-old Underground Man from the dark cellar where he has withdrawn from life. The second part—the remaining two-thirds—details events from his twenties. The contrast between these two periods can be understood in several ways. As many critics note, the novel's structure counterposes the beliefs of the Russian intelligentsia during the 1840s with related beliefs in the 1860s. The first was a period of idealistic or romantic social reform and the second the time of the radicals and Nihilists whose ideas so agitated Dostoevsky. Some critics describe this in terms of the conflict between the values of fathers and sons, as in Turgenev's novel of that name, a novel responsi- ble for the very label *Nihilist*. Dostoevsky later elaborated this genera- tional conflict in *The Possessed* (written in 1871–72), where it appears as the contrast between Stepan Verkhovensky, a liberal dreamer from the forties, and his son Peter, a malicious revolutionary of the sixties. *Notes from Underground* criticizes both positions: in the first part—the monologue of the forty-year-old Underground Man—the radical beliefs of the 1860s are exposed and attacked, while in the second—the flash- back to his twenties—he reveals the ridiculous nature of his earlier romantic aspirations.

The commentators are correct in their interpretation of the two periods of the novel in political terms; this was part of Dostoevsky's conscious intention. At the same time, this contrast between the 1840s and 1860s has a more personal meaning, a meaning that is connected to, and deepens, the political interpretation. In this view, we can hear Dostoevsky speaking more directly about his own disillusion, the way in which he began as a dreamer and romantic idealist and how this side of him came to grief on the hard shores of reality. Again, some critics interpret the *Notes* along these lines, contrasting the dreamer figure from such early novels as *The Landlady* with the murderers and self-willed types that emerge in the later books. While there is, again, some truth in this interpretation it needs to be qualified: none of Dostoevsky's novels are simply romantic or idealistic. It is possible that the early dramas *Maria Stuart* and *Boris Godunov* (written in his last years as a student in the engineering academy and apparently discarded) were pure romance, but his first published novel, *Poor Folk,* is structured around the collision of romantic beliefs with selfishness, power seeking, and other grimy aspects of real life. This conflict remains central to all the later novels. What this means, I think, is that the clash between romantic ideals and reality is a core issue for Dostoevsky, but that its origin is to be found in a still-earlier period of his life.

The memory of the horse and courier scene points the way back to the time of his mother's death and the complex of feelings, internalizations, and conflicts that were aroused then and memorialized in that emblem. My guess is that the idealized relationship with her underlay his romantic image of women and that this was elaborated in his imagination with themes and identifications from his reading—Pushkin, Schiller's *The Robbers,* the novels of Walter Scott, Eugene Sue, and George Sand. Her death and the rage, guilt, and sickness that he found within himself contrasted starkly with these fantasies. His disillusion found ample support from the life he observed in the military academy, with its corruption, hazing of young students, and other cruelties.

The years following his mother's death saw the passing of his identification with the fictional heros that had meant so much to him as a youth. In many ways, he went through the typical struggles of late adolescence, made more intense by the deaths of his parents, his isolation, and his powerful imagination. Out of these struggles, his identity as a writer took form and, significantly, became invested with the same heroism and grandiosity that formerly belonged to his identification with literary heroes. That is, while he no longer imagined himself a Manfred or a Hamlet, he did aspire to be a Pushkin or a Shakespeare: a grand ambition for a boy in his teens, yet one that he eventually achieved.

When Dostoevsky began his career in Petersburg in the late 1840s, his identity as an author was firmly in place. As we have seen, his first novel, *Poor Folk,* met with instant acclaim. This initial success unleashed his private ambitions and fantasies, both for literary fame and for the love of a beautiful woman. He became infatuated with Madame Panaeva, though she had no idea of this, an infatuation that left images that lingered over the years. It is possible that her beauty and aspects of her personality were given to Dunia Raskolnikov, who shares her first name, and, in *The Idiot,* to Nastasya Filippovna, whose description matches hers. And what happened, in reality, with this early love? She became the mistress of his friend and publisher Nekrasov, the same young poet who so loved *Poor Folk.* While it is not clear what role Nekrasov played in the conflicts at the Panaev's, Dostoevsky's loss of her to a brother figure must have been an additional defeat for his romantic dreams. Like the attacks of his literary rivals, the disappointment of his love was a wound to his narcissism, a blow to his newly emerging self. What is more, it echoed the loss of his first love—his mother—to the many rivals that were born after him, a series of losses culminating in the most painful and difficult one: her death.

In sum, Dostoevsky's early success unleashed his private ambitions and fantasies. As in everything, he went to the limit, with little heed for the reactions of others. His style in life was the same as in writing; he would be taken over by inner selves, dreams, and plots. To use his own words, after an adolescence of introversion and isolation, he came "alive"— began to experience "living life"—in the Petersburg literary world. His fantasies came to wreck on the rocks of realtiy—criticisms, attacks, and disappointments—and this precipitated a nervous crisis or illness in which he was symbolically visited by death. The anxiety and deathlike states were the vivid way he experienced the attack on his newly emerged self or identity. As we will see, this entire theme of the clash of romantic ideals with real others and the struggle of the humiliated self to survive and "live" is central to *Notes from Underground.*

The Death of Maria: *Notes from Underground*

All the events and feelings of what Dostoevsky later referred to as his "literary quarrels" find their way, with varying degrees of directness, into the *Notes*. In both content and style, he alludes to his early novels. Many of the Underground Man's "adventures" are commentaries on the way in which real life contrasts with the romance found in books. The theme of disappointment in love is given its clearest expression in the novel's final section, the scenes between the Underground Man and the prostitute Liza. Nekrasov himself even makes an appearance: his poem about the redemption of a fallen woman is cited, and the Underground Man plays out a satirized version of it with Liza. It is as if Dostoevsky were saying to his old friend, "You were a fool to believe in such romantic nonsense, but I believed it too—in my love for Madame Panaeva—and was equally a fool."

The imaginary romance with Madame Panaeva was a memory from almost twenty years earlier; Dostoevsky wrote *Notes from Underground* in 1864, at the time of Maria's death. The connection between these two loves is the emotional configuration common to both: they began on an idealized plane and then degenerated into loss and death. Furthermore, each relationship—his imaginary one with Madame Panaeva in his twenties and his marriage to Maria in his thirties—was an attempt to recapture the life-sustaining relationship with his mother, an ideal that ended in her death and the incorporation of her illness into himself. *Notes from Underground* traces this theme back in time; it begins with the disillusioned forty-year-old man, holding forth from his gravelike setting and then moves to an account of the disappointments of his twenties. Then, in the novel's final scenes, those between the Underground Man and Liza, the need for a woman's love and the urge for revenge are directly portrayed amid images of tuberculosis and death.

Notes from Underground: *Peeling the Onion*

I am a sick man. . . . I am an angry man. I am an unattractive man. I think there is something wrong with my liver. . . . I am not having any treatment for it, and never have had, although I have a great respect for medicine and for doctors. . . . I refuse treatment out of spite. That is something you will probably not understand. Well, I understand it. I can't of course explain who my spite is directed against in this matter; I know perfectly well that I can't 'score off' the doctors in any way by not consulting them; I know better than anybody that I am harming nobody but myself. All the same, if I don't have treatment, it is out of spite. Is my liver out of order?—let it get worse!

So begins the monologue of the Underground Man: attacking himself, yet defiant; engaging the reader and arguing with him; making a virtue, a strength, out of his "illness."

Dostoevsky's style, from the very beginning of this complex novel, involves a movement between various points of view; one hears the many voices of his inner selves. The paragraph that prefaces the entire work begins: "The author of these *Notes* and the *Notes* themselves, are both, of course, imaginary." It is signed "Feodor Dostoevsky." Then we have, "I am a sick man. . . . I am an angry man" as the Underground Man establishes himself as the "author" of his confession and reminiscences. And, through the course of the book, he carries on a dialogue with "the reader"—both his imagined audience and the actual reader—*and* steps outside himself and is acutely aware of how he appears in the eyes of others.

These multiple points of view give expression to a central concern of the author (Underground Man/Dostoevsky): who *is* he? Or, more precisely, how can he establish a viable, a *living,* identity. In the second paragraph, the struggle to establish a sense of self is introduced. The Underground Man remembers how he was nasty and rude in his days as a civil servant. But then:

I was lying when I said just now that I was a bad civil servant. I was lying out of spite. I was simply playing a game with the officer and my other callers; in reality I never could make myself malevolent. I was always conscious of many elements showing the directly opposite tendency. I felt them positively swarming inside me, these elements. I knew they had swarmed there all my life, asking to be let out, but I wouldn't let them out, I wouldn't, I wouldn't. They tormented me shamefully; they drove me into convulsions and—in the end they bored me, oh, how they bored me!

What are these "elements" that were "swarming inside" and that "tormented" him "shamefully?" As is so often the case with Dostoevsky, he tells us here, directly, the dilemma posed by his inner selves. Behind the outwardly cynical self is the dreamer who longs for acceptance and love; but to expose that is to run the risk of rejection and humiliation;

along with a superior self-image—"I have always thought myself cleverer than anybody I knew"—is a part of him that condemns this superiority. And there are other self-attacking "elements," some so powerful that they threaten the very sense of life, though he tries to turn this threat aside with humor:

Not only couldn't I make myself malevolent, I couldn't make myself anything: neither good nor bad, neither a scoundrel nor a honest man, neither a hero nor an insect. Now I go on living in my corner and irritating myself with the spiteful and worthless consolation that a wise man can't seriously make himself anything, only a fool makes himself anything.

To be a "hero" or an "insect": the very opposition reveals the humiliation when the imaginary heroic identity is tested in reality. It is the same dilemma that Raskolnikov struggles with, of course—is he a Napoleon or a louse?—and, in *Crime and Punishment* the life and death nature of the struggle is more clearly revealed.

The Underground Man next launches an attack on intellectuality and false ideals that works on two levels; it is a critique of utopian beliefs and an attack on the romantic fantasies of his—and Dostoevsky's— own youth. He speaks of himself as infected with the disease of thinking too much and then:

Why is it that in those moments, when I was most capable of recognizing all the subtle beauties of "the highest and the best," as we used to say, I could not only fail to recognize them, but could actually do such ugly, repulsive things as . . . well, such things, in short, as perhaps everybody does, but which always happened to me, as if on purpose, when I was most conscious that I ought not to do them? The more aware I was of beauty and of "the highest and the best," the deeper I sank into my slime, and the more capable I became of immersing myself completely in it. . . . I didn't believe the same thing could happen to other people, and so I have kept the secret to myself my whole life. I was ashamed—perhaps I am ashamed even now—I got to the point where I felt an abnormal, mean, secret stirring of pleasure in going back home to my corner from some debauched St.Petersburg night, conscious in the highest degree that I had once again done something vile and that what was done could never by undone. And secretly, in my heart, I would gnaw and nibble and probe and suck away at myself until the bitter taste turned at last into a kind of shameful, devilish sweetness and, finally, downright definite pleasure. Yes, pleasure! pleasure! I stand by that.

How is "thinking too much" a disease? On one level this is a criticism of utopian dreamers for whom thinking and talk were substitutes for real life. But the references to himself as an insect reveal a more personal difficulty with "thinking"; this is the kind of thinking that envelopes Raskolnikov in his coffinlike room: obsessive rumination in which one struggles with guilt, inner attackers, and critics. The quoted passage also indicates what the guilt is about; he longs for "the highest and best"—for the idealized woman, for romantic love—but is involved with prostitutes, slime, and debauchery. Worse yet, he recognizes that there is a kind of sexual pleasure in his own vileness, in his very attack on the romantic ideal.

There follows an insightful exploration of what we would today call masochistic pleasure. With a variety of devices, the Underground Man struggles to extract a living identity from his self-abasement. He takes pleasure in his own degradation and would have welcomed a "slap in the face": "despair can hold the most intense sorts of pleasure when one is strongly conscious of the hopelessness of one's position. And here, with the slap in the face, it is forced in upon you what filth you are smeared with." This hyperconscious, masochistic mode of being is then contrasted with "the man of action." Using the example of being slapped in the face and desiring revenge, he contrasts himself with those who would directly deal with life's "slaps" while he is a "mouse":

A highly conscious mouse, but all the same a mouse, while the other is a man, and consequently . . . and so on . . . at last comes the act itself, the revenge. The wretched mouse has by this time accumulated, in addition to the original nastiness, so many other nastinesses in the shape of questions and doubts, and so many other unresolved problems in addition to the original problem, that it has involuntarily collected round itself a fatal morass, a stinking bog, consisting of its own doubts and agitation, and finally of the spittle rained on it by all the spontaneous men of action standing portentously round as judges and referees and howling with laughter.

The self-attack is extreme and the final line—the image of "judges and referees howling with laughter"—conveys the near-annihilating sense of guilt. But the Underground Man will not be annihilated; throughout his self attack we already sense an indirect attack on the other, so characteristic of masochism. Men of action are portrayed as stupid, after all and, for all his humiliation, the Underground Man is intelligent and sensitive. In fact, it is these very qualities that foreclose a simpler identity. Now, he begins to turn the tables on his imagined enemies. Having identified men of action with "the laws of nature" he launches the well-known attack on these "laws" and the novel moves toward the criticism of materialistic utopias:

These gentlemen, although they roar full-throatedly like bulls, . . . calm down at once when they are faced with an impossibility. Impossibility is a stone wall. What do I mean by a stone wall? Well, of course, the laws of nature or the conclusions of the natural sciences or of mathematics. When it is proved, for example, that you are descended from an ape, it's no use scowling about it—accept it as a fact. Or if it is demonstrated that half an ounce of your own fat ought essentially to be dearer to you than a hundred thousand of your fellow-creatures and that this demonstration finally disposes of all so-called good deeds, duties, and other lunacies and prejudices, simply accept it; there's nothing to be done about it, because twice two is mathematics. Just try to argue.

"Half an ounce of your own fat ought essentially to be dearer to you than a hundred thousand of your fellow-creatures" is, of course, a scathing reference to the utilitarian doctrine of rational self-interest. The Underground Man elaborates his opposition to "the laws of nature," an image, or metaphor, that operates in several ways. In one direction, there is the picture of the man of action who, in obedience to these laws, charges through life like a stupid bull. In another, is the attack on the doctrine of rational self-interest, which is revealed to be nothing but an excuse for greed and selfishness. There is also an exposure of the myth of rationality; again and again the Underground Man shows how little of human action is accounted for by reason. All of this is demonstrated both by argument, on the one hand, and the example of his own consciousness and life, on the other. The ultimate law of nature, of course, is that which dictates our mortality. So behind the various political arguments there is, again, the struggle to *live*.

In the midst of his longing and self-criticism in relation to these "rational" types, he exalts his superiority; he is more sensitive, and more intelligent, and struggles with more complicated issues. This is one solution to the difficulty of defining a living identity: to make the very guilt and masochism that weaken the self into a virtue. As he pursues his attack on the laws of nature he further undoes his guilt and solidifies his sense of self. He does so by showing that, far from being an isolated case, he is an exaggerated version of everyone. Put in other words, he shows how the feelings and conflicts that he discovers within himself are those of all intelligent men of the nineteenth century: for who really governs his personal life by reason or the laws of nature? If the things the Underground Man feels—opposition to those laws, a drive to assert his will, pleasure in hurting others, enjoyment of his own pain—are universal, then he need not feel so guilty, he has, in effect, resolved his alienation by defining himself as part of a larger group.

As the monologue progresses there is a marked shift in tone. In the beginning the sense of inferiority and self-attack predominate, but, as the Underground Man goes on, he more and more takes the offensive. In the later passages "they"—the advocates of reason, self-interest, and a planned society—have been made to look foolish. Their view of man has been mocked, their plans would turn society into an anthill: they would turn life into a mechanical, deathlike existence. In contrast, the Underground Man has shown that his personal qualities, at first quirky and shameful, are, in fact, aspects of universal human nature. The whole line of discussion in part 1 is both a criticism of materialistic utopias and the building of a personal identity that counters guilt and alienation. As he draws to the close of the monologue he has accomplished both these goals at the level of general—political, social—argument.

But guilt returns, he will have to run through the whole process again at the level of personal memory. This is analogous to the working through that occurs in psychoanalysis: no one interpretation or insight is sufficient to overcome a conflict such as this.

Part 1 ends with:

In every man's remembrances there are things he will not reveal to everybody. ... There are some things that a man is afraid to reveal to himself, and any honest man accumulates a pretty fair number of such things. ... Now, when I am not only remembering, but have decided to write them down, now I want to test whether it is possible to be completely open with oneself and not be afraid of the whole truth. ... for example, I am particularly oppressed by one ancient memory. It sprang clearly into my mind the other day, and since then has remained with me like a tiresome tune that keeps on nagging at one. And yet one must get rid of it. I have hundreds of memories like it; but from time to time one out of the hundreds becomes prominent and oppresses me. For some reason I believe that if I write it down I shall get rid of it. Why not try?

This is the introduction to the novel's second part, the reminiscences from his twenties. The "oppressive memory"—the sharpest focus of his guilt—only emerges at the end of these reminiscences. It involves, as is so often the case with Dostoevsky, the cruel treatment of an innocent young woman. The monologue in part 1 has run through one version of the struggle with inferiority, guilt, and self-attack. He has won out over rivals and brother figures—Chernyshevsky, the men of action—and established a home for his willfulness and aggression. He is possessed of these unsavory characteristics but so is everyone: man is like that. But how far can one assert such qualities? Kicking over the Crystal Palace is one thing, torturing innocent women another. As the final quotations from part 1 indicate, he is now ready to explore this personal source of guilt.

Part 2 is subtitled "A Story of the Falling Sleet," a reference to the Nekrasov poem about the redemption of a prostitute. It consists of three sections: the first is the account of his mock romantic attempts to challenge an officer who he fancies has insulted him. The second section has him humiliating himself with a group of acquaintances as he crashes their party. And the final section—the confession of his "oppressive ancient memory"—shows him passing hurt and humiliation down the line: the attack on the loving woman.

He begins by describing himself as he was at twenty-four, "gloomy, untidy and barbarously solitary." He hates the way he looks; he feels both superior and inferior in relation to his fellow civil servants.

In his isolation he lives, primarily, in books:

I did a lot of reading. I wanted to stifle all that was smouldering inside me with external impressions and reading was for me the only possible source of external impressions. Reading, of course, helped me a great deal—it excited, delighted and tormented me.

Reading fills him with grand ambitions and romantic fantasies and he is painfully conscious of the gulf between these and the meager actions he is able to take in the world:

I would suddenly plunge into dark, subterranean, nasty—not so much vices as vicelets. My measly little passions were keen and fiery from my constant morbid irritability. . . . My debauches were solitary, nocturnal, secret, frightened, dirty, and full of shame that did not leave me at the most abandoned moments, and indeed at those moments reached such a pitch that I called down curses on my own head. Even then I already carried the underground in my soul.

199

There follows the wildly funny—yet sad—account of his attempt to stand up to an "officer" who he feels has treated him as an "insect." It is clear—and he himself is painfully aware—that the whole affair exists in his imagination; the officer is not aware of his existence. Still, he cannot stop planning duels, writing letters that are never mailed, and, finally, spending months screwing up his courage not to move aside when he encounters his enemy on the boulevard. After a great deal of humiliation, he carries his plan into action:

Suddenly, three paces away from my adversary, I unexpectedly made up my mind, scowled fiercely, and . . . our shoulders came squarely into collision! I did not yield an inch, but walked past on an exactly equal footing! He did not even glance around, and pretended he had not noticed; but he was only pretending, I am certain of that. I am certain of it to this day! Of course I was the greatest sufferer, since he was the stronger, but that was not the point. The point was that I had attained my object, upheld my dignity, not yielded an inch, and publicly placed myself on an equal social footing with him. I returned home completely vindicated. I was delighted. I sang triumphant arias from the Italian operas. . . . The officer was later transferred elsewhere; it is fourteen years since I last saw him. Where is he now, my darling officer? Whom is he trampling down now?

As was the case with the monologue in part 1, this episode can be understood on several levels. There is a scene in *What Is to Be Done?* in which one of the heros—a man of action with none of the inner divisions of the Underground Man—grabs a dignitary who collides with him on the street and sticks his head in the gutter. Dostoevsky's version shows how much more complicated things are in reality. In this sense, Chernyshevsky is the one who knows only books, not life. In a more important way, the incident is a commentary on the gap between romantic fantasy and life in the real world. The twenty-four–year–old Underground Man represents Dostoevsky at the time of his literary quarrels: thinking of himself as cleverer than everyone else, living primarily in writing and books, and coming to grief when he tries to realize his dreamy ambitions in the world. But the ironic, satirical treatment of the whole episode puts these events into perspective. It very much has the feeling—not entirely free from pain—of someone looking back from middle age at the foibles of his youth. "It is fourteen years since I last saw him. Where is he now, my darling officer? Whom is he trampling down now?" shows that the officer has been elevated to the level of a symbol; he is a creation of the writer's imagination; Dostoevsky controls him and has gained a good deal of insight into the events and emotions that so troubled him in the 1840's.

The next section of part 2 takes up the theme of fantasy and reality directly. Here, there is little connection with political arguments; Dostoevsky, through the reminiscences of his Underground Man, describes his own predicament:

> But I had one resource that reconciled all these contradictions—escaping into "all that is best and highest," in my dreams, of course. I dreamed endlessly. I dreamed for three months, crouching in my corner, and you may rest assured that during those moments I was not in the least like that humble and chicken-hearted gentleman who sewed an imitation beaver collar on his overcoat. I had turned into a hero. My six-foot lieutenant wouldn't even have been allowed to call on me. . . . Particularly sweet and powerful were the dreams that came to me after a bout of dissipation, accompanied by repentence and tears, curses and raptures. There were moments of such positive ecstasy, such happiness, that I swear I felt not the slightest stirring of derision deep inside me. . . . How much love, oh lord, how much love I used to experience in those dreams of mine, those escapes into "all that is best and highest" although it was mere fantasy, that love, not applied in reality to any actual human object; but there was so much abundance of it that later I never really felt the need of any object to project it on to: that would have been a superfluous luxury. Everything always ended happily, however, with a lazy and entrancing transition to art; that is, to beautiful ready-made images of life, forcibly wrenched from poets and novelists and adapted to every possible kind of service and requirement.

In his twenties, Dostoevsky's only relations with women were with prostitutes. It seems likely that these passages in the *Notes* are a direct account of the way he enlived his sexual pleasure with romantic dreams.

Private fantasies can only go on so long: "When my dreams were so happy I absolutely must embrace somebody, indeed all mankind; and for this I must have available at least one real living person."

The Underground Man goes to the apartment of Simonov, an old school fellow, where he encounters two other acquaintants from his school days; they are planning a farewell dinner for their friend Zverkov, an army officer who is leaving to take up a new post. Despite the fact—or because of it—that he feels they all hate him and look on him as "something in the nature of a very ordinary fly," he invites himself along to their party. He will both attempt contact with some "real living persons" and get even with everyone by humiliating himself. Zverkov is

another man of action, another "officer" like the lieutenant in the preceding episode, but, unlike that figure, the Underground Man knows
him from school and cannot help seeing that he is not really such a bad
fellow. In other words, it is harder to force him into an invented image.

Let me again turn to the model of the novel as a self-exploration in
which Dostoevsky regresses back through the levels of his memory. The
episode with the officer blended together political arguments from the
1860s with memories from the 1840s, when Dostoevsky made his debut
as a writer. The Zverkov episode mixes together memories from the
1840s with those from the preceeding period: his years in the academy
of engineering. He describes the "oppressive memories" and "wretched
bondage" of his schooldays, recalling how he felt isolated and rejected.
The Zverkov episode then plays out a version of the school years,
exaggerated to comic heights. At its core is the clear *disillusion* when his
dreamy bookish pretentions clash with reality.

At the party, he insults Zverkov, there is talk of a duel, but mainly
the action takes place in his mind: the most he can do to "get even" with
them is to pace up and down:

Smiling scornfully, I paced backwards and forwards on the side of the room. . . .
I was trying with all my might to show that I could do without them; meanwhile
I purposely made a clatter with my boots, coming down hard on the heels. . . . I
continued to pace from the table to the stove and back. "Oh, if only you know
what thoughts and emotions I am capable of, and how enlightened I am!" I
thought sometimes, turning in imagination to the sofa where my enemies sat.
But my enemies acted as though I wasn't even in the room.

The others finish their dinner and head off for a brothel; he follows
and the novel moves to its final scene: the encounter with the prostitute
Liza.

"So here it is, it has come at last, my encounter with reality," I muttered, rushing
down the stairs. "This isn't a case of the Pope leaving Rome and travelling to
Brazil; this is no ball on Lake Como!"

The reality that he will encounter in this final episode consists of a
relationship that is—finally—unliterary: a potentially loving connection
with a woman that is fouled by his own need to turn humiliation into
revenge. This encounter is surrounded with symbols and images that tie
it to the real women in Dostoevsky's life: images that contrast hope with
disillusion, youth and love with tuberculosis and death.

The Death of Maria: *Notes from Underground*

He arrives at the brothel, Zverkov and the others are gone, and he goes off with a young prostitute. After sex he awakens in the room with her.

Anger and misery seethed up in me again, seeking an outlet. Suddenly, beside me, I saw two eyes open, regarding me with curiosity and fixed attention.

A resentful feeling arose in my mind and swept through my body with something like the unpleasant sensation of going into a damp and musty cellar. . . . I remembered, too, that for two whole hours I had not spoken a single word to this being, or considered there was any need to do so; until a few moments before I had even felt pleased about it.

He engages her in conversation, learns she is called Liza, is twenty, and only recently arrived in the city, apparently estranged from her family. She seems, in other words, to be a lonely soul like himself. And what comes out of him next?

"They were carrying a coffin out this morning and very nearly dropped it, " I burst out suddenly. I had had no intention of starting a conversation; it had simply slipped out.

"A coffin?"

"Yes, in the Haymarket; it was being carried out of a cellar."

"A cellar?" . . .

"It's a nasty day for a funeral!" I began again, for something to say. Here . . . it's impossible to dig a dry grave."

"Why?"

"Why? Because it's such a wet place. There's marsh everywhere here. So they just plant them in the water. I've seen it myself . . . lots of times." I had never seen it, indeed had never been to Volkovo Cemetery—I had only heard people talking about it.

"Does it really make no difference to you, dying?"

"Why should I die?"

"Some day you will and you'll die exactly like that woman I saw. She was a girl like you. . . . She died of consumption."

His interactions with Liza in the brothel vacillate between this sort of sadistic talk and efforts to arouse her hopes for love and a good life, following the same pattern as Dostoevsky's relations both with Maria and Polina Suslova. He confronts her with the specter of tuberculosis and death, predicting her descent into degradation, illness, and death. Liza is not, at least initially, responsive to this, so he launches a long speech about the warmth and love to be found in families, the beauty of love between fathers and daughters, and husbands and wives, ending with:

It is heavenly bliss! Do you like children, Liza? I do, terribly. You know—a rosy little baby sucking at your breast, and any husband's heart will turn towards his wife when he sees her sitting with his baby in her arms! A rosy, chubby little child, stretching and sunning itself; plump little legs and arms, transparent little nails, so tiny that you laugh to see them, and little eyes that seem to understand everything already.

While this began as a game he has gotten carried away with real feeling:

"Pictures, you have to go on painting that sort of pretty picture!" I thought to myself, although I swear I had spoken with real feeling; and then suddenly I blushed. "What if she bursts out laughing, what shall I do with myself then?"

His game has become real and he is terribly concerned with her response:

"Somehow, you . . ." she began, and then stopped.
But I had understood: a different note had quavered in her voice, not the old harsh, brutal, defiant tone, but something gentle and shy, so shy that somehow I felt ashamed and guilty.
"What?" I asked, with indulgent curiosity.
"Well, you . . ."
"What?"
"Somehow you . . . it sounds just like a book" she said, and again there was a note of mockery in her voice.
The remark stung me painfully. That was not what what I had expected.

This is somewhere between his hope that she will respond with love and his fear of rejection. In fact, she does sense the reality of his longing but is also aware of the literary pretentions that obscure its expression. In his extremely sensitive state—the "rosy little baby sucking at her breast" is an image that reflects his own desire—he is angered by her response. He goes back on the attack, pulling out all the stops as he pictures her degraded life and tragic end. He tells her if she were living a different kind of life he might fall in love with her but, as it is, she will

die soon of consumption somewhere in a corner, in a cellar, like that girl I told you about just now. . . . Consumption is a special kind of illness; it's not a fever. With it, a person can hope till the last minute, and say she's well. She can reassure herself. . . . When you're really dying, you'll be pushed into a stinking corner of the cellar, in the darkness and the damp; what will you think about then, lying there alone? . . . They'll buy a box and carry you out as they did that poor girl today, and hold your wake in the pub. There'll be wet snow, and slush and slime in the grave, and they're not likely to stand on ceremony with the likes of you. . . . You can knock as much as you like on the coffin lid at night, when the dead awaken: "Let me out, good people, to live in the world. When I was alive I saw nothing of life, my life ran away down the drain."

The specific form of this attack on her is telling; he causes pain by doing to her what has been done to him. That is, he arouses her wishes for love, family, and happiness and then shatters these hopes with images of sexual degradation, consumption, and death. Note, too, that the end that he predicts for her—living death in a "corner of a cellar" or locked in a coffin crying to get out and "live in the world"—is precisely the way he pictures his own life at age forty. This life—the underground existence to which he feels condemned—is the punishment in kind for his attack on the innocent loving woman. It is the version in this novel of what happened to Dostoevsky at age fifteen when his mother died and what he was struggling with as he wrote *Notes from Underground* —to not be destroyed by guilt as his wife died.

The Underground Man's attack on Liza proves successful:

Never, never had I witnessed such despair! She was lying face downwards, with her head buried in the pillow and her arms strained tightly round it. Her heart was bursting. Her whole young body shook as if she had a fever. Stifling sobs crowded into her breast until they forced their way out as wails and cries; at those moments she would press her face deeper into the pillow, for fear that any living soul in that place should know of her tears and agony.

Her pain and tears arouse his sympathy:

"Liza, my dear I didn't mean . . . forgive me" I began, but she pressed my hand in hers with such force that I realized I was saying the wrong thing.
    "Here is my address, Liza; come to me."
    "And now I am going: good-bye . . . au revoir."

He awakens the next morning troubled by his "sentimentality" with Liza. The Zverkov affair bothers him less: he borrows money from someone else to pay Simonov back and writes a letter explaining away his behavior at the party. But he can't dispense with Liza so easily:

The thought that Liza might come never ceased to torment me. It was especially, almost separately, oppressive. By the evening I had succeeded in forgetting all the rest, I had shrugged my shoulders over them, and I remained completely satisfied with my letter to Simonov. But this was something I could no longer be complacent about. The thought of Liza still nagged at me.

He made himself out a "hero" to her but if she comes she will see his real life: his poor and shabby apartment, dirty clothes, and petty quarrels with his servant. As he runs over his thoughts, the core of his guilt is revealed:

One moment out of all those I had lived through the day before kept presenting itself to me with especial clarity; that was the moment when I struck a match and saw her pale distorted face with its expression of martyrdom. How pitiful, how unnatural, how twisted her smile had been at that instant! I did not know then that even after fifteen years I should still go on seeing Liza in my imagination with the same pitiful, twisted useless smile on her lips as she had worn at that moment.

He attempts to deal with this by turning to fantasies drawn from literature. He imagines "saving her"—an image drawn from Nekrasov's poem about the redemption of a prostitute—and then makes fun of his own fantasy as "a lot of European George-Sandish ineffably noble and subtle nonsense."

And then, reality: Liza comes to his apartment when he is in the midst of a squabble with his servant. The chapter in which she appears is, ironically, introduced with the line from the Nekrasov poem:

> Enter now then, bold and free,
> Be mistress of my house and me!

Her actual presence calls forth wild swings of feeling on his part: he is ashamed, apologetic, then enraged, then he bursts into tears, and then the anger returns. He launches an attack on her, saying he was only playing with her feelings to get revenge for the humiliation he suffered with Zverkov and the others. His attack succeeds: "She went as white as a sheet and tried, with painfully distorted lips, to say something, but only dropped back on her chair as though she had been felled with an ax."

(The image of the ax anticipates the attack on the old pawnbroker and Lizaveta—Liza's namesake—in *Crime and Punishment,* of course.)

"Save you?" I went on, jumping up from my chair and almost running backwards and forwards in front of her. "Save you from what? ... It was power,

power, I wanted then, the fascination of the game; I wanted to get your tears, your humiliation, your hysterics—that's what I wanted then!"

Then, as he goes on, his attack turns into a confession:

For the last three days I've been shaking with fear that you would come. And do you know what worried me particularly all those three days? That I'd made myself out to be such a hero to you and now all at once you would see me in this ragged dressing-gown, poverty-striken, repulsive. I said just now that I was not ashamed of being poor; let me tell you that I am ashamed of it, more ashamed than of anything else. . . . The saviour, the hero, flying at his servant like a mangy, neglected mongrel, while the servant laughs at him! And the tears that I could no more hold back just now than some old woman who's been put to shame, I will never forgive you those! And I shall never forgive you for what I am confessing now, at this moment. Yes, you and you alone will have to answer for everything because you turned up, because I am a cad, because I am the nastiest most ridiculous, pettiest, stupidest, most envious of all the worms on this earth. . . .

But at this point something exceedingly strange happened.

I was so used to thinking and imagining everything like a book, and seeing everything in the guise in which I had previously created it in my dreams, that at first I didn't even understand this strange circumstance. But this is what happened: Liza, whom I had so abused and humiliated, understood a great deal more than I imagined. She understood that part of it that a woman always understands first, if she sincerely loves, and that was that I myself was unhappy. The terrified and outraged feeling in her face changed first of all into sorrowful bewilderment. But when I began to call myself a cad and a scoundrel, and my tears began to flow again—I uttered the whole tirade to the accompaniment of tears—her whole face underwent a kind of convulsion. She tried to rise to her feet, and to stop me somehow; when I finished, however, she paid no attention to my cries of "Why are you here! Why don't you go away?" but only to the fact that it must be very difficult for me to say all this, and she was so cowed, poor thing; she considered herself so infinitely beneath me; why should she be resentful or offended? On some sort of irresistible impulse she sprang up from her chair, and straining towards me but still timid and not daring to move from the spot, held out her arms to me. . . . Now my heart too turned over. Then she rushed towards me, flung her arms round my neck, and burst into tears. I also was unable to control myself, and sobbed as I never had before. . . .

"They gave no . . . I'm incapable of being . . good!" I cried, hardly able to get the words out, then I went over to the sofa, fell face downwards on it and sobbed for a quarter of an hour in real hysterics. She pressed herself against me, embraced me, and remained motionless.

This whole scene directly parallels Raskolnikov's initial interviews with Sonia in *Crime and Punishment*. Recall how he first attacks her and how she senses his pain and unhappiness and, rather than attacking back, offers him sympathy and love. The specific image of the out-stretched arms and loving embrace is even the same. The Underground Man has found real love, in contrast to his bookish dreams and, at least briefly, he accepts it.

But only briefly. He becomes ashamed of crying in front of her, his need for power and revenge well up once again:

A different feeling was kindled in my heart and flared up all at once . . . a feeling of mastery and ownership. My eyes glittered with passion and I squeezed her hands hard. How I hated her and how strongly I was attracted to her at that moment! One feeling reinforced the other. It was almost like revenge . . . !

She tries to love him but he cannot accept this real human contact; he drives her away with further insults, even attempting to give her money —which she throws back—and sinks into the underground where he has remained ever since.

In the final passages there is an awareness that the recounting of the incident with Liza is a kind of self-analytic confession:

Even now, after so many years, all this comes back to me as very nasty. There are many things that I remember as bad, but . . . ought I not to end my "Notes" here? I think I made a mistake in beginning to write them at all. At least, I have felt ashamed all the time I have been writing this *Story of Falling Sleet:* therefore it is no longer literature, but penal correction.

Exposing his most disgraceful secret to public view is one way of trying to come to terms with it. Another is to call attention to the universal nature of his guilty acts:

We have all got out of the habit of living, we are all in a greater or lesser degree crippled. We are so unused to living that we often feel something like loathing for "real life" and so cannot bear to be reminded of it. We have really gone so far as to think of "real life" as toil, almost as servitude, and we are all agreed, for our part, that it is better in books . . . after all I have only carried to a logical conclusion in my life what you yourselves didn't dare take more than half-way; and you supposed your cowardice was common sense, and comforted yourselves with the self-deception. So perhaps I turn out to be more alive than you.

In the end, Dostoevsky as author comes back on the scene: "This is not the end, however, of the 'Notes' of this paradoxical writer. He could not help going on. But to us too it seems that this will be a good place to stop. 1864."

The struggle to live, to construct a viable identity in the face of a murderous guilt and inner attack continued, of course, both in Dostoevsky's life and in the writing of his next novel, *Crime and Punishment*.

CHAPTER 12

Death and Rebirth

In spite of everything I have lost, I love life ardently, I love life for
life's sake, and seriously, I am still planning to *begin* my life. I will
be fifty soon, yet I cannot make out whether I am ending my life or
only beginning it. This is a principal attribute of my character and,
perhaps my work.

Maria's death and the composition of *Notes from Underground* brings
us back to our starting point: Dostoevsky on the verge of writing *Crime
and Punishment*. Her death, as well as Mikhail's, activated an enormous,
potentially self-annihilating guilt. Yet he had developed means of overcoming this threat through the years: he was, in different symbolic ways,
always dying and being reborn. There were the ritualized enactments of
the epileptic seizures, as well as the financial ruin and recovery of the
compulsive gambling cycle; these expressed the complex of merger-
attack-death-rebirth in manageable forms. Of greater value was the way
he overcame this threat by transforming it into literature. The detailed
analysis of *Notes from Underground* has shown how the writing of that
novel kept him alive in his gravelike setting following the death of his
wife and brother. *Crime and Punishment,* as we saw earlier, carried the
self-exploration further and deeper. With this writing in process, and
free from the burden of the first marriage, he was ready for that most
powerful form of rebirth, a real Sonia who would restore him with her

acceptance and love. He was to find this with Anna Snitkina, the woman who became his second wife at the time *Crime and Punishment* was completed. It remains, in this final chapter, to discuss the marriage and follow out his life and career for the last fifteen years, years that saw the composition of the great novels that followed *Notes from Underground* and *Crime and Punishment*.

Anna

Maria was dead and the affair with Suslova over, though correspondence with her continued for a few years; Dostoevsky began to court a series of young, healthy women. He was more or less in love with his niece Sonia—daughter of his favorite sister Vera—whose name he gave to Sonia Marmeladov and, later, to his first child. Since he could not consummate this incestuous attraction, he proposed marriage to one of her friends, though it is not clear how serious this was. He next paid court, quite seriously, to Anna Korvin-Krukovskaya, an intelligent and accomplished young woman who had published a story in *The Epoch*. She considered his proposal of marriage but turned him down, correctly sensing that he needed someone who would submerge her personality in his; she knew she was too strong and independent for this.[1]

The story of Dostoevsky's meeting with Anna Snitkina has been told many times. With no money and in debt as usual, he took an advance from a publisher named Stellovsky; the contract promised a new book by a certain date. If the required manuscript was not delivered, Stellovsky would get the rights to all Dostoevsky's past work plus everything he would write for the next nine years. This was surely playing roulette with his career! He was deeply immersed in *Crime and Punishment*— under contract to his regular publisher Katkov—when the dreaded deadline approached; little more than a month away. What to do? His friends suggested that he try dictating the new novel to a stenographer and, with this in mind, he hired Anna. She was a serious and practical young woman, still mourning the recent death of her father. They quickly arrived at a working arrangement: she came to his apartment every morning and he would dictate for a few hours, interspersed with tea and conversation. As was typical, he was very open with her, describing the tragedies of his life: his seizures, imprisonment, and financial woes. Following the day's dictation she would go home and transcribe her notes into longhand and then return the next day. With her competent help and reassurance the short novel *The Gambler* was finished, at the very last minute, of course, and Dostoevsky rescued once more from a financial disaster of his own making. He proposed, she accepted, and they were married shortly thereafter.

Dostoevsky was in a particularly receptive state when he met Anna in 1866. The initial shape of their relationship placed her in a therapist-like position; she was the calm and patient recipient of his feverish literary and personal outpourings; she then helped put this material in order. She was also instrumental in rescuing him from the contractual mess with Stellovsky. She, too, was in a specially receptive state, and this had a great deal to do with the success of their marriage. Anna came from a relatively stable and happy middle-class family. Just five months before meeting Dostoevsky she suffered the first major loss of her life, the death of her father. She was going to college when she realized that:

My father's illness was not responding to treatment, and he had not long to live. It was then that I, not wishing to leave my beloved invalid alone for days at a time, decided to drop out of school for a while. Papa suffered so from insomnia that I used to read to him from the novels of Dickens for hours on end, and I was very content when he was able to doze off for a bit to the sound of my monotonous reading.

Shortly thereafter:

My father died. . . . It was the first real sorrow I experienced in my life, and my grief was stormy. I wept a great deal, spent whole days . . . at his grave and could not come to terms with this terrible loss. My mother was made distraught by my depressed state and begged me to settle down to some kind of work.

Before his death her father had encouraged her to study stenography. She received special attention during the period of her grief from her "kindly Professor Olkhin" who then sent her out on her first assignment. When she learned that the job was with the writer Dostoevsky, she

was quick to agree. The name of Dostoevsky had been known to me since I was a child. He was my father's favorite author. I myself had been enraptured with his works and had wept over *Notes from the House of the Dead*. The very idea, not only of meeting this gifted writer, but also of helping him in his work, filled me with excitement and elation.

Death and Rebirth

It is more than clear from all this that Anna was prepared for an instant transference love. She was in awe of the much-older author—he was forty-four, she twenty—as well as drawn to his pain and suffering. She idealized him and he replaced the father she had lost. Her grief was assuaged and whatever guilt she felt over her father's death was channeled into the help and self-sacrifice she offered to this new man. Her own words put it best:

My love was entirely cerebral, it was an idea existing in my head. It was more like adoration and reverence for a man of such talent and such noble qualities of spirit. It was a searing pity for a man who had suffered so much without ever knowing joy and happiness, and who was so neglected by all his near ones, whose duty it should have been to repay him with love and concern for everything he did for them all his life.

The dream of becoming his life's companion, of sharing his labors and lightening his existence, of giving him happiness—this was what took hold of my imagination; and Fyodor Mikhailovich became my god, my idol. And I, it seemed, was prepared to spend the rest of my life on my knees to him.

They were a match made in heaven, or, perhaps one should say, in each other's unconscious. He needed a young woman to idealize him and she an older man to idolize. This special fit stood at the core of their relationship; it saw them through the many difficult years ahead.

There were other ways in which they complemented each other. While Anna was a reasonably intelligent and educated woman, she was not a deep thinker; she made no pretense at understanding the more complex aspects of her husband's work. There was something quite ordinary about her; she had none of his hypersensitivity to slights nor his special need for acceptance—none of the fragile narcissism—she was quite a contrast to his first wife in this regard. Where he was hypochondriacal and epileptic she was strong and healthy—again in contrast to both the tubercular Marias. And, finally, where he lived in literature and his imagination, she was content to spend her time amidst life's small practicalities.

Shortly after their marriage, he dictated the final two parts of *Crime and Punishment* to her, the parts of the novel in which Raskolnikov finally allows Sonia's love and acceptance to penetrate his isolation. By no means did all go smoothly after the marriage; in fact Anna's love was to be tested—as Raskolnikov tested Sonia—in small and large ways for several years. Immediately after the wedding, while they were visiting Anna's sister, the young bride had her first actual contact with her husband's epilepsy. In the midst of a lively conversation he broke off, turned white, uttered "a horrible inhuman howl" and toppled over. The sister ran sobbing hysterically from the room and had to be cared for by her husband, but the redoubtable Anna grappled with his falling body, finally sitting on the floor with his head in her lap where she comforted him through the attack. He regained consciousness only to have another, more severe seizure an hour later. The seizures almost always occurred at night during sleep; a double seizure during the day was quite rare. While the epilepsy had multiple determinants, I think a central meaning of this unusual attack was an unconscious test of his new bride: would she be able to love and accept him, murderous fit, crazy illness, and all? Unlike his first wife—who was subjected to the same test on her wedding day—Anna passed with flying colors.

Married life in the early months proved a test of another kind. Dostoevsky's daily world was filled with numerous characters: friends who dropped in at all hours and relatives who depended on him for money. Residual guilt in relation to Maria and his brother left him an easy prey to her son, Paul, and Mikhail's widow, who were continually taking money from him. They were naturally resentful of the new wife, an intruder with claims of her own, and they seem to have made her life miserable. Dostoevsky did little to prevent this and she was driven to create a tearful scene to arouse him to action. At her insistence, they left for Europe to escape the dependent relatives—as well as the many creditors—and establish a life together.

Their trip was planned for three months but they stayed four years, years that saw additional testing as well as a growing closeness and love. The most powerful test at this time was posed by his compulsive gambling. Anna had been forewarned of this; their initial contact revolved around the dictation of The Gambler, a novel based on his experiences with roulette, and he had told her of his identification with the hero. Now she was subjected to it in reality. The gambling followed the same pattern with her as it had earlier with Suslova; he would take their money, go off to play roulette with his "system," lose all, write letters begging for more money, confess his guilt, and promise to stop, only to repeat the pattern again and again. His letters to her (quoted in chapter 10) reveal his own preoccupation with guilt over the torment he was causing her; her account shows how much real difficulty it created for the new bride, living in strange European cities with no family or friends and limited funds. Anna quickly saw through the whole business—she knew his promises were meaningless and that he would always lose— but her idealization of him led to forgiveness rather than retaliation. She felt about the gambling the same way she did about the epilepsy; it was an unfortunate "illness" with which her beloved husband was afflicted; it required acceptance rather than punishment. She also saw that his literary productivity would increase once he had reduced them to financial destitution and, of course, the bouts of torment and guilt were always followed by love and reconciliation.

The gambling was finally brought to an end with a brilliant stroke on her part: at a particularly low point she *positively encouraged* him to do it:

Fyodor Mikhailovich spoke so often of the inevitable "destruction" of his talent, tormented himself so with the problem of how he was going to feed his beloved and ever growing family, that I sometimes felt desperate as I listened to him. In order to soothe his anxiety and dispel the somber thoughts which prevented him from concentrating on his work, I resorted to the device which always amused and distracted him. In view of the fact that we had some money on hand . . . I brought the conversation around to roulette and asked him if he didn't want to try his luck again—he had won a few times, after all, why not hope that this time luck would be on his side, and so forth.

Of course I did not believe for a moment that he would win, and I very much regretted the hundred thalers which would have to be sacrificed. But I knew from my experience of his previous visits to the roulette table that after undergoing some intense emotions and satisfying his craving for risks, for gambling, he would return assuaged. And, having convinced himself of the futility of his hope of winning, he would settle down to his novel with new energy and make up for all the lost time and work in two or three weeks.

My suggestion about roulette was only too close to my husband's heart, and he did not raise any objections. Taking with him one hundred and twenty thalers with the agreement that in the event of loss I would send him the fare home, he left for Wiesbaden, where he stayed for a week.

The roulette playing had lamentable results, exactly as I had surmised. [He lost] . . . a very considerable sum for us at that time. But the cruel torments he went through in the course of that week, when he kept upbraiding himself for taking the money away from his family, from me, and his child, weighed so heavily on him that he resolved that he would never again in his life play roulette.

This is what he wrote to me on the 28th of April, 1871:

A momentous thing has happened to me: the disappearance of the base fantasy that *tormented* me for almost ten years—or, rather, since my brother's death, when I was suddenly overwhelmed by debt—I used to dream perpetually of winning; I dreamed passionately, in earnest. But all that is over and done with! This was really the *last* time. Can you believe it, Anna, that my hands are untied now? I was shackled to gambling, body and soul; henceforth I will think about my work and not dream for nights on end about gambling, as I used to.

He never played again. She had passed the test; her very encouragement was final proof that she accepted the impulsive side of him expressed through this enactment. His own comments make clear that the onset of the gambling occurred at the time of Mikhail's death when he "was suddenly overwhelmed by debt." This was also the time of Maria's final illness: "debt" was the concrete manifestation of the guilt brought about by both deaths and, with Anna's steadfast acceptance, he was finally able to move beyond the attack–self-punishment–rebirth that constituted the compulsive gambling.

Dostoevsky's epilepsy and gambling were the large tests that confronted Anna in the early years of the marriage, but there were smaller, though psychologically significant, ones as well. She reports how he would sometimes talk:

For hours on end in the words and thoughts of one of his characters, the elderly prince of *Uncle's Dream*, . . . in the tone of voice of an old man no longer good for anything but trying to make himself younger than he was.

This elderly prince is a decrepit lecher; Dostoevsky was here playing with one of the underlying meanings of his attraction to young girls, satirizing the great difference in age between them. Anna "was very ill-at-ease" at this and would "change the subject to something else."

He was, as we might expect, prone to rather violent outbursts of jealousy. If she so much as looked at another man, especially a younger man, he would be overtaken by rage and accuse her of betraying him. These outbursts would be followed by periods of tender reconciliation. As with so much else, Anna adapted herself to this, dressed modestly in sombre tones, and was careful how she spoke to other men.

In all the most important ways, Anna loved, idealized, and accepted her husband. She was the Sonia he required but, lest I present too one-sided a picture, it should be stressed that she was not so passive, not so totally giving, so unreal, as her prototype in *Crime and Punishment*. She was an emotional Russian woman after all, not an American puritan or a Victorian English woman; she was capable of fighting back and of giving way to intense feeling with him; there seem to have been many scenes of mutual tears, whether of grief, despair, or joy, as well as bouts of hilarity. And, while she wrote in her *Reminiscences* of the "cerebral " nature of her love, it had its carnal side as well. Dostoevsky was not one to inhibit his impulses, including his sexuality. In 1879, quite late in the marriage, he was in Germany, taking a water cure and wrote that she was constantly in his thoughts: "I kiss *you all over in a way that you can't even imagine*," he says, and dreams about her "in a seductive form," a vision that occasioned "nocturnal consequences." [2]

For four years, Dostoevsky and Anna lived in Europe: in Dresden, Milan, Florence, Geneva, Vevey and other cities. Their life fell into a pattern: they took walks together, visited museums, sought out fellow Russians when this was possible, but were largely thrown in on each other. His literary production continued, of course; he wrote *The Idiot*, *The Eternal Husband*, and the first half of *The Possessed*. Anna was pregnant the first year and gave birth to a girl whom they fittingly named Sonia. She died, apparently of an infectious disease, at three months of age, and they both gave way fully to their grief. A year later a second daughter, Liubov, was born. Anna's account reveals her husband's intense emotional involvement with his children. He was much more the modern father, in this respect, than a typical European or Russian professional man of the nineteenth century, who had with little contact with his children. Dostoevsky was a direct participant, caring for the babies, holding and playing with them on the many journeys, and grieving powerfully at Sonia's death.

The four years in Europe were of great importance in cementing the marriage. Dostoevsky experienced the love and acceptance of a woman that he so much required, and Anna grew strong dealing with the many difficulties she faced: life in strange cities, their always-precarious finances, the birth of two children, the death of one of them, and her husband's seizures, gambling, and moods. All of these trials might have destroyed a weaker woman but she became tempered and grew under their impact. He, too, changed during this period. The time away allowed for greater concentration on his writing, but, of greater significance, was the *internalization of her love*. Anna sums up this period as follows:

Despite numberless cares, constant financial embarrassments, and sometimes oppressive boredom, so protracted a life of solitude had a fruitful effect on the appearance and development in my husband of the Christian ideas and feelings which had always been present in him. All the friends and acquaintances who met us again after our return from abroad told me that they did not recognize Fyodor Mikhailovich, so strikingly had his character improved, so much milder, kinder, and more tolerant to others had he grown. His customary obstinacy and impatience had almost entirely disappeared.

Strakhov, who knew him both before and after the time in Europe, noted that "he would constantly bring the conversation around to religious themes. Not only that: his manner changed, acquired greater mildness sometimes verging on utter gentleness."

They returned to Petersburg in 1871 and their son Feodor was born, just after their arrival. As the years progressed, Anna increasingly took charge of their practical affairs, leaving him free to concentrate on his writing and related intellectual matters. She dealt with the creditors and, eventually, got all the old debts paid off. Tired of the poor return received from publishers, she gradually took over the printing and distribution of his novels. All this in addition to raising two children and managing the affairs of the household. In 1875 a second son, Alyosha, was born only to die three years later of what appeared to be convulsions. Again, there was profound grief, openly expressed, at the loss of this lovely young boy.

Her love, idealization, and commitment to her husband continued long after his death in 1881. She dedicated the rest of her life—she lived on until 1918—to preserving his memory and perpetuating his work. She founded the Dostoevsky Museum, commissioned the first biography, brought out numerous editions of the novels, categorized notes, correspondence, and indexes, defended him against critics, and wrote her *Reminiscences* of their life together.

The Novels

Dostoevsky had long been a prolific writer, but, from the time of his second marriage in 1867 until his death fourteen years later, he was astonishingly more productive than ever. *Crime and Punishment* was followed by *The Idiot, The Eternal Husband, The Possessed, A Raw Youth,* and *The Brothers Karamazov.* There were, in addition, short stories, editorial work, journalism, and his own special journal, *The Diary of a Writer.* I have no intention of attempting an analysis of all these works here; to do so would double the length of this book. I wish, rather, to offer some brief comments on the later novels, comments that will place them in the scheme of Dostoevsky's development. There is a great deal more than this development in each of these masterpieces, and I do not mean to suggest, by the brevity of my comments, that they can be reduced to the particular psychological themes that I will describe.

As we have seen, *Crime and Punishment* was the deepest point in the self-exploration that Dostoevsky carried out through his writing. In it he penetrates to the emotional world of the deprived infant and the needed-hated mother. It is, at its core, a dyadic world, one without much awareness of others. Emotionally, there are no fathers in the novel, only Mother, who brings forth love and hate, splitting and projection.

With *Crime and Punishment* completed—it was both a critical and a popular success—and the marriage to Anna secured, Dostoevsky was ready to move on to progressively higher levels of development. This does not happen all at once; the theme of maternal ambivalence—and the murder of women—continues; but one sees more rivalry amongst siblings and the increasing prominence of fathers and themes dealing with paternal authority. Dyads fade and triads arise; splitting diminishes and rivalries become more salient; by the time of *The Brothers Karamazov,* we have a novel as strongly focused on the paternal world as *Crime and Punishment* is on the maternal.

The Idiot was the next novel after *Crime and Punishment.* In Europe with his new wife, Dostoevsky conceived a plan to write about a "positively good man." He would try to portray a modern Christ; give literary form to the "good boy" side of his fantasy; an all-loving son of Maria. The realization of this attempt took place during the early years of the marriage, with all the testing to which he subjected Anna. In the marriage he tried to be good, to achieve a loving union not fouled with hate, an attempt, during these initial years, that had mixed results. His realization of a fictional "good man" in *The Idiot* was also a mixed one. Prince Myshkin—to whom he significantly gives his own epilepsy—is the idiot of the title, an ironic name for a Christ figure. He is "good" on the surface—naive, kind, loving, unworldly—in contrast to almost all the other male characters that surround him. Yet he has another, unconscious side: this is revealed in his seizures; the "accidents" he brings about—the famous vase-breaking incident—and the chaos he causes with his naiveté and passivity. As an example of this last, when slapped in the face he turns the other cheek, but the effect of this Christlike act is to make his attacker suffer with guilt. Perhaps most revealing of Myshkin's unconscious side is his "other," or double, the worldly and violent Rogozhin. We know, from early drafts in *The Notebooks for "The Idiot,"* that these two began as one character; the epileptic prince was also violent. It was only in later revisions that Dostoevsky split them into two characters. Like Svidrigailov and Raskolnikov, they function in the novel as two sides of a single self. In the end, Rogozhin murders Nastasya, the woman they are both involved with. He lies crying by her corpse and Myshkin, comforting him, is so close that his tears run down Rogozhin's cheeks. The two halves of the self are rejoined in this remarkable scene.

In what sense can *The Idiot* be said to show psychological development beyond *Crime and Punishment?* There are several ways. None of the women in the novel are imbued with the emotions from infancy. No one is as hateful as the old pawnbroker—certainly not Madame-Epanchin, the novel's main mother figure. The heroines, Nastasya—who was drawn from Suslova and, perhaps, Madame Panaeva—and Aglaya and the other Epanchin girls—drawn from his sister Vera's household—are mature, sexual women, and not unreal, one-sided figures like Sonia Marmeladov. They relate to Myshkin and other men with a range of emotions: Nastasya is seductive and giving, yet vengeful; Aglaya, sweet and loving, yet teasing and willful. In all these ways, the feel of the relationships is less oral, more genital; the women are romantic, sexual objects and not giving-depriving maternal beings.

Dostoevsky had a great deal of difficulty writing *The Idiot;* he went through at least eight drafts before settling on its final form. While it contains many wonderful scenes and a number of fully realized characters, it is flawed structurally; it lacks the focus and coherence of *Crime and Punishment.*

The next work, the short novel *The Eternal Husband,* presents the rivalry of two men for the same women. Velchaninov, a somewhat tempered Svidrigailov type, has seduced the wife of Trusotsky—the cuckolded eternal husband of the title—and sired a girl by her some years earlier. At the time of the novel's action the wife has died and Trusotsky appears to haunt Velchaninov; he is as a symbol of guilt for Velchaninov's crime. The daughter, Liza, another mistreated young girl, is passed between her two fathers, who alternately abuse and rescue her. The crime, interestingly, is one that stands midway between those of *Crime and Punishment* and *The Brothers Karamazov;* that is, it has elements of an attack on the mother-innocent girl and a rivalry between men. Sometimes neglected amidst the longer novels of this period, *The Eternal Husband* is a small gem.

The Possessed, like *Crime and Punishment* and *The Brothers Karamazov,* is one of Dostoevsky's greatest creations. All of these long novels are rich and multilayered books. The novelist's concern with revolutionary politics was the initial stimulus for *The Possessed,* particularly the activities of one Nechaev, who incited the members of his revolutionary cell to murder a student whom he saw as a political rival. These events, which Dostoevsky followed in the Russian newspapers available in Europe, were the day residues for the novel-as-dream. That is, they provided the current stimuli, which then opened into several underlying themes. The Nechaev murder is an example of aggressive rivalry among a band of brothers, a theme connected with Dostoevsky's childhood and manifested throughout his adult life in the many literary-ideological battles he waged with other journalists and writers. These battles also connect with the theme of conflict between generations—relations between fathers and sons—which makes up an even more important strand of *The Possessed.*

Finally, it must be said that the novel does not focus entirely on generational conflicts. Like *The Eternal Husband,* it has elements of both preoedipal and oedipal themes. Dostoevsky was still preoccupied with his Great Sinner configuration and his creation of Stavrogin is the last major attempt at the realization of this fantasy: the man who can commit the most heinous crimes—the rape and destruction of innocent young girls—without guilt. As we saw in the analysis of Stavrogin in chapter 8, Dostoevsky shows, as he did earlier with Svidrigailov, that this way of life lends to emptiness, alienation, and self-destruction.

The theme of rivalry between brothers is brought forth in Peter Verkovensky, the character inspired by the student revolutionary Nechaev. Peter incites his group to kill one of their members, Shatov, and, in other ways, is portrayed as an immoral troublemaker. Those portions of the novel centered on him contain a number of scenes that portray rivalry and competition.

The theme of fathers and sons is the novel's most potent. It is played out both in terms of characters and value conflicts: the romantic-vision-ary schemes of the 1840s—Dostoevsky's own generation—contrasted to the more violent, antiauthority beliefs of the 1860s. All of this comes together in the character of "old" Mr. Verkovensky—Stepan Trofimovich—who is the actual father of the revolutionary Peter and a father figure in relation to Stavrogin (He was his tutor; Stavrogin's father is absent). Mr. Verkovensky was apparently inspired by the liberal philosopher Granov-sky and by Dostoevsky's old friend Dr. Stepan Yanovsky, who had been a kindly father-figure doctor to him at the time of his nervous crisis. Dostoevsky blends these two together with a central component of his own personality: the romantic dreamer. At the time he wrote *The Pos-sessed* he was nearing fifty and was, after many years, finally a father himself. His own paternal position, like the ideological conflicts, served as further day residue for an exploration of the images, models, and identifications involved with fatherhood. In the scheme of his own devel-opment, he was ready to take up these themes.

Mr. Verkovensky begins as a caricature of the dreamy romantic; he lives in a world of books and imagined past glories. It is not only the beliefs of the 1840s that Dostoevsky represents here but his own earlier self; the dreamer who flounders in the real world: Golyadkin and the Underground Man. While Mr. Verkovensky is initially painted with exaggerated strokes, his character develops over the course of the novel, revealing greater depth. When tested he shows courage and the integrity of his beliefs. In the end he emerges as a humane and lovable man, and, at his death, his relationship with Madame Stravrogin reflects a mature tenderness. Dostoevsky could not consistently mock the side of his own nature that Mr. Verkovensky embodied; it was too close to the core of his identity as a man of the imagination, a writer.

Mr. Verkovensky's unworldly romantic character leaves him very flawed as a father, however. He lives off the wealthy Madame Stavrogin in a state of childlike dependence, only working part-time as a tutor. While he imagines himself an intellectual and entertains fantasies of the effects of his ideas, he never manages to publish anything. Thus, he cannot serve as an adequate male or career model to either of his "sons," Peter or Stavrogin. The vacuum he leaves in their lives is filled with revolutionary ideas, violence, and amorality.

One can think of the creation of Mr. Verkovensky as an experiment with one type of fatherhood: it is as if Dostoevsky were saying, "What if I ran this model out to its extreme and observed the results?" He is very much the opposite from Dostoevsky's own materialistic, petty tyrant of a father, of course, that model was clearly unappealing. But the way of the completely unworldly romantic, although preferable to tyrants, revolutionaries and amoral types, has its flaws. Mr. Verkovensky does not have the strength, independence, or discipline to serve as a model to his sons. This exploration of paternal types and values will continue in the novels that follow.

The Possessed was begun in Europe and completed after Dostoevsky, Anna, and their two young children were settled in Petersburg. He next took up the editorship of the conservative weekly *The Citizen*. His unique *Diary of a Writer* was first developed here. In *The Diary*, Dostoevsky carried on a dialogue with his readers—who sent him their questions, problems, and opinions—and aired his views on a wide range of topics. The articles are much less worked over than the fiction; they present a more immediate expression of ideas and feelings. It is here that one finds the narrow nationalism and petty prejudices that are singularly absent in the novels. *The Diary* also contains a great deal of interesting material, Dostoevsky's unique views on a variety of topics, as well as literary vignettes: both *The Peasant Marey* and "The Horse and Courier" appeared there.

Dostoevsky's next long work was *A Raw Youth* (also translated as *The Adolescent*); it is widely regarded as the weakest novel of these years. It is of interest in terms of the scheme of development, however.

The hero, Arkady Dolgoruky, is a "raw youth," an unpolished young man attempting to find his way in the world. A major theme is the adolescent's search for a viable identity; Arkady is looking for a father who can serve as a model, a theme which allows Dostoevsky to continue the exploration of paternal authority begun in *The Possessed*. He does so with his central literary device, the creation of two selves that exemplify the possibilities of different modes of life. Arkady has two fathers: the saintly Makar Dolgoruky, his biological father, and his stepfather, the worldly, if somewhat immoral, Versilov. The playing out of these issues in *A Raw Youth* may be passed over since the theme is worked through in superior form in the next and final work: *The Brothers Karamazov*.

Dostoevsky began writing the novel that many critics consider his greatest at the age of fifty-seven. He worked at it steadily for three years. Almost all the themes, issues and character types from his previous work find expression in *The Brothers Karamazov,* yet compared to these earlier novels there is greater calmness and maturity. Dostoevsky had taken up the themes of fatherhood and paternal authority after *The Idiot* and explicitly worked them over in *The Possessed* and *A Raw Youth*. In his correspondence at the time be began *The Brothers* he refers to the as-yet-untitled novel as "my fathers and children" and "fathers and sons." As preparation he visited schools, wrote to friends for information on children ages seven to sixteen, and collected newspaper stories about the cruelties inflicted on innocent children (used by Ivan Karamazov, in his argument against accepting God's world). While the novel as a whole deals with "fathers and sons," the initial concern with younger children is relegated to the subplot centered on Kolya Krasotkin and the band of young boys.

At the time he began *The Brothers* Dostoevsky had himself fathered four children. The last child, apparently a very lovable boy, died of convulsions at age three just before his father began his final novel. Dostoevsky was then confronted, not only with the grievous loss of a beloved child, but with a death brought about by what must have seemed his own illness. This was further stimulus to guilt that could be worked over in the writing of *The Brothers*. He gave the name of this child to the youngest Karamazov brother, the innocent Alyosha.

The grief brought on by his son's death prompted a pilgrimage to

Death and Rebirth

Optina Pustyn, a well-known monastery, where Dostoevsky sought the blessing and advice of certain monks, or "elders." The image of the monastery was later used in the novel as an alternative way of life to that of the sensual, materialistic Karamazov world, the elders as alternative fathers to Feodor Karamazov. The figure of Father Zosima in the novel was apparently constructed from aspects of two of the elders at Optina Pustyn, along with features of the eighteenth-century monk Tikon Zadonsky, whose writings were familiar to Dostoevsky.

Dostoevsky made another trip at the time he was formulating *The Brothers*. This was to Darovoe, his parent's country estate where he had spent summers as a child. He had not been back to the estate since his early teens, the years before his mother's death and the breakup of the family; he walked around his old haunts, saw the peasants, some of whom still remembered him as a young boy, and visited the nearby wood—Chermashnya—where he used to play. Clearly, many memories from the childhood years were brought back by this visit, including the memory of his father's murder. The name Chermashnya is used in the novel for the wood associated with the murder of the Karamazov father.

The Brothers Karamazov, as rich and multifaceted as any novel ever written, has been discussed from a great many points of view (see Terras 1981 for a compendium). Here, let me focus on what it demonstrates about Dostoevsky's psychological development. Viewed in this way, the novel is an exploration of male identify formation. How is one to be a man in the world? With whom is one to identify? What father, or father figure, can serve as an acceptable model? How, as a man, is one to relate to women? And, on a broader scale, what beliefs and values are to guide one's life? In *The Brothers,* these questions are explored on both the personal and ideological levels. The novel depicts the relations between sons and their father (Dmitri, Ivan, Alyosha, and the half-brother Smerdyakov with Feodor Karamazov), what they inherit from him and how they are, each in their own way, alike and different from him. The Elder Zosima presents a very different paternal model. And the subplot involving the band of young boys portrays another variant in the relationship between the humiliated Captain Snegirov and his son Ilyusha. These all show the personal versions of father-son relations. The search for identity is also explored on an ideological level in the various debates that pit rationalism against religious faith, man against God, the Russian way against that of the West. These arguments were in the forefront of Dostoevsky's consciousness, but it is the intertwining of the ideological and the personal—and the opening up of the subterranean personal, emotional world—that gives the novel its great power and universal appeal.

The issue of absent or ineffective fathers and the lack of what was called a "positive hero" in Russian literature was well known to Dostoevsky, as his Pushkin speech of 1880 testifies (see *The Diary of a Writer*, 967–80). Literary heroes from Pushkin's Eugene Onegin and Lermontov's Pechorin, through the characters in Goncharov, Tolstoy, Turgenev, and Dostoevsky himself, so often lack a meaningful and integrated male identity (see Mathewson 1975). This stems from the actual family experience of many writers who, like most of the nobility, were raised by servants, nannies, and tutors; they frequently had little or no contact with their actual fathers. This was true for both Tolstoy and Turgenev, for example. Dostoevsky's own family situation was atypical; he saw a good deal of his father, but this contact inspired a powerful *disidentification*. If anything, he was more identified with his artistic mother, which left him with his own special version of the struggle to define himself as a man. As I have attempted to show in my earlier analysis, *Notes from Underground* and *Crime and Punishment* are focused on conflicts within the maternal sphere. Problems of male identify are present but they are overwhelmed by the force of maternal ambivalence. Thus Raskolnikov—whose dead father is but a shadowy and ineffective memory—seeks a model in Napoleon, much as Dostoevsky did in his adolescent identification with the heroes of Schiller and Walter Scott. The action that flows from this heroic identification—the murder of the pawnbroker and her sister—is motivated by hatred of the depriving mother, however, and it is only after this conflict is worked through that fathers and male identity can be more directly explored. The movement to this theme can be traced in both Dostoevsky's life and the novels he wrote after *Crime and Punishment*.

The marriage to Anna provided a relationship where the ambivalent feelings toward women were worked through to a relatively integrated solution. Over a period of years Dostoevsky gave up other women and compulsive gambling and became a father himself. He internalized Anna's love and the need to test women waned. As he stopped playing at being a Great Sinner in his life, so did this figure gradually fade as a preoccupation in the fiction. And, concurrently, the novels more and more portray relations between sons and fathers. *The Idiot,* while representing some movement beyond *Crime and Punishment,* still provides no fathers for its heroes. Myshkin arrives in Russia from Switzerland where he had been under the care of a doctor, a distant and insubstantial model. Rogozhin lives in a house with his mother, his father long dead. In *The Possessed,* as we saw earlier, Stepan Verkovensky is the actual father of the revolutionary Peter and tutor to Stavrogin. Yet he has abandoned Peter as a boy and is relatively useless as a model for both of them. It is only in *A Raw Youth* and *The Brothers* that father-son relations come to occupy the center of the stage.

How does Dostoevsky deal with the issue of male identity in *The Brothers?* As was typical of his approach—and as can be seen in his correspondence and journalism—he begins with the wish for a simple, idealized, or ideologically pure solution. The novel was to be a paean to Christ and the unique Russian soul, a vindication of his "conservative" position. Yet once involved with the writing itself, his demanding standards of artistic truth took command. As almost always happened, the expression of issues in the fiction emerged in a most complex and profound form. Attempts at idealized characters appear in the novel—like Myshkin, Alyosha was initially meant to be a Christlike innocent, for example—but the evolution of the characters repeatedly demonstrates the limitations of idealized identities. Again and again, Dostoevsky brings out the many sides of each brother and father. To put this in different words, the various male figures start out as pure types: Father Karamazov, the incarnation of sensuality; Zosima, pure Christian love; and the three brothers, the different extremes of a single personality: Dmitri, emotionality; Ivan, cynical intellectuality; and Alyosha, innocence and love. Yet, as they unfold in the novel, they become much more than these pure types; each reveals the contradictions and other sides of himself; they become, in other words, full human beings who struggle with their ideas, emotions, and counterselves.

As a specific example of the complexity that Dostoevsky introduces consider the contrast between the two poles of fatherhood represented by Feodor Karamazov and the elder Zosima. Father Karamazov is the embodiment of sensuality, greed, and those self-serving business tricks that always enflamed Dostoevsky. He is incapable of putting his son's needs—or anyone else's—on a par with his own. He is not a Great Sinner, not a man of powerful amorality—he is too much the buffoon and coward for that—but more an undisciplined baby, in continual pursuit of his own pleasures. In his sensuality he contrasts sharply with Zosima, who has withdrawn from this world to a life of contemplative peace and Christian compassion.

But the conflict between sensuality and spirituality cannot be settled so simply. All the brothers have the Karamazov "beast" in them. Man is a creature of appetite and sensuality, Dostoevsky says here. And, in Dmitri, this appears as emotional directness and lust for life, qualities that the novelist always prized. Dmitri has poetry in his soul, he is capable of real love, he acts from the heart and not the head. And he is honorable: he might kill you in a fit of temper—and almost does kill both his father and the old servant Grigory, who was a like loving father to him in his early years—but he would never lie, cheat or steal! These are important distinctions. Sensuality, emotion, even rage that assumes murderous proportions, are not, by themselves, man's great faults—we all have these urges within us, they both give life its power and create conflict. One can come to terms with them if they are openly and honestly faced. This is Dostoevsky's message regarding confession and the need to take responsibility for one's crimes. He does not value punishment and suffering for their own sake, but only as they lead to emotional honesty and responsibility. The life of falseness, social pretense, hostility indirectly expressed, and coercion by guilt leads to the truly immoral life.

Early in the novel Zosima, responding to the Karamazov father's question as to what he should do to "gain eternal life" tells him to "stop indulging in drunkenness and incontinence of speech" and not to "give way to sensual lust and particularly your passion for money. . . . And, above all, stop lying." He goes on:

The important thing is to stop lying to yourself. A man who lies to himself, and believes his own lies, becomes unable to recognize truth, either in himself or in anyone else, and he ends up losing respect for himself as well as for others. When he has no respect for anyone, he can no longer love and, in order to divert himself, having no love in him, he yields to his impulses, indulges in the lowest forms of pleasure, and behaves in the end like an animal, in satisfying his vices. And it all comes from lying—lying to others and to yourself.

Zosima here gives voice to Dostoevsky's deep antipathy to hypocrisy and falseness, for the father is a consummate dissembler, a man so steeped in role playing that he is incapable of real emotional connection.

Zosima's message is not directed at sensuality per se, not just at the father's ravenous appetites; the elder is not an apostle of asceticism. In fact, the monastery—which is not an idealized house of God without personal conflicts—does contain a real religious ascetic, Zosima's enemy, Father Ferapont. He is a frightful man, filled with an insane "moral" rage. Ferapont, an extreme example of self-denial, contrasts sharply with Zosima whose Christianity, like Dostoevsky's, is mystical and individualized. The elder preaches love, forgiveness, and compassion; he recognizes that men must live real and full lives, express all that is within them, and, out of this process—rather than by ascetic renunciation—come to terms with their appetites. He tells his disciple Alyosha to leave the monastery; the path to virtue must take the young man through the fully lived life. In all these ways the novelist's exploration has taken him far from the simple views of his orthodox and conservative compatriots.

Let us turn to another example of the way in which Dostoevsky transcends simple types—idealized identities—as his initial plans are realized in the novel. In the years leading up to *Notes from Underground,* he was engaged in a debate with the radical critics and westernizers, with those who argued for a "scientific" society founded on man's capacity for reason. The dimensions of this debate shifted around for him; sometimes it was phrased in terms of Russian values versus those of western Europe, at others rationalism versus religious faith. A persistent strand was materialism versus the life of feeling and imagination. He was convinced that the radicals and socialists were dangerously deluded in their belief that society could be governed by force of reason alone. Their faith in "rational self-interest" neglected man's unconscious, unreasoning side; it gave too little place to passion and impulse; it would serve as a cover for violence and self-willed chaos. "Rational self-interest" in practice would become "all is permitted," which is Raskolnikov's justification for crime and the reasoning of Ivan Karamazov that gives Smerdyakov permission to murder their father.

In *The Brothers,* Ivan is the spokesman for this position, he is the cynical intellectual, the man without deep ties to his motherland or religious faith. As is typical in transforming this issue into fiction, however, Dostoevsky does not oversimplify, he does not make Ivan a one-sided radical or westernizer. The novel does contain two such caricatures —the liberal landowner Muisov and the careerist seminarian Rakitin— but they are minor voices compared to Ivan who is presented as a brilliant, troubled, and appealing young man; his arguments against God's world are intellectually powerful and emotionally convincing. Ivan does not spout radical cant. Dostoevsky is inside him; the character gives voice to the novelist's own deep divisions and religious doubts. In his private *Notebooks* he says:

Ivan Fedorovich is profound, not one of your contemporary atheists, demonstrating in his disbelief merely the narrowness of his conception of the world and the obtuseness of his own stupid abilities. . . . These thickheads did not dream of such a powerful negation of God as that put in the "Grand Inquisitor" and in the preceding chapter, to which the *whole novel* serves as an answer. I do not believe in God like a fool [a fanatic]. And they wished to teach me, and laughed over my backwardness! but their stupid natures did not dream of such a powerful negation as I have lived through.

He later adds "Even in Europe there have never been atheistic expressions of such power. Consequently, I do not believe in Christ and His confession as a child, but my hosanna has come through a great *furnace of doubt.*"

The centerpiece of Ivan's argument is his account of the atrocities visited upon innocent children: real incidents that Dostoevsky culled from the newspapers. If God can permit such horrors, Ivan does not want to be part of his world. He then recounts his "poem," *The Grand Inquisitor,* a stinging indictment of man's inability to live with his own freedom, his need to be dominated by a church that seduces him with "miracle, mystery, and authority." I won't rehearse all of these arguments or *The Grand Inquisitor* here for they are well known. Dostoevsky, who was himself an "abused child"—and adult—who waged a continual struggle with the temptation to pass his insults and injuries on to those beneath him, knew all these feelings intimately. That is to say, the same capacity for empathy and the unique way he could absorb other selves into his own being, left him terribly open to the suffering of children. It was this direct experience of the abused child's pain, along with the attendant urge for revenge, that made this whole area the crucial test of faith. In the novel, Ivan recounts a particularly gruesome incident to Alyosha: a wealthy general, angry at a peasant boy over a minor infraction, sets his hounds on the unfortunate child. They tear him limb from limb before the eyes of his helpless mother, who is herself done in by the horror. Alyosha agrees with Ivan: men like the general should be killed. Even the most loving and virtuous of the brothers can wish the death of this cruel "father."

In his correspondence and notebooks, Dostoevsky says he is deliberately making the radical position, as espoused by Ivan, a strong one so that its later refutation by Zosima—and "the whole novel"—will be all the more convincing. The end result, however, is ambiguous: many readers—Freud and D. H. Lawrence among them—were persuaded to Ivan's position. While Ivan's argument contains much truth, it is a mistake, in my view, to see the issue as it was initially framed: as a debate between atheism and Christianity or the radicals and conservatives. These categories capture but a small piece of the truth. Ivan finds himself in an unbearable position, he professes to like and get along with his father yet, like Svidrigailov and Stavrogin, he has hallucinations, is terribly isolated, and contemplates suicide. His need for faith is an aspect of the broader need for a meaningful identity, one that will encompass all of him, including his repressed hatred, which is finding displaced, intellectual expression in his attack on God. He needs to know and accept his own emotions if he is to escape the hell of his constricting intellect. Without such awareness, his rational philosophy is a rationalization, as he eventually discovers when he recognizes that it was he who gave Smerdyakov license to kill their father. As he confesses in the end, "all men desire their father's death." He and Smerdyakov have unconsciously conspired to do it; Dmitri would have killed in a blind rage out of rivalry for a woman and his long-term grievances; and even the saintly Alyosha reveals his capacity for revenge. "Why does a man like that deserve to live?" cries Dmitri. All the brothers are shown, ultimately, to harbor the same murderous wish and the reader is made to feel the same way; the world would be better off without a greedy selfish creature who brings so much pain to his own children. It is the same plaint that Raskonikov raised against the old pawnbroker. Dostoevsky's genius here lies in drawing us into this state of feeling, in showing how we are all capable of primal violence. We must have ideals and beliefs to counter our capacity for cruelty; a way of life or identity must be defined that has room for the Karamazov in man and for his capacity for love and faith.

The whole novel does provide such an answer but not in a simple way. The most meaningful, the most viable identity is an achievement, not a fixed essence. It is what one lives and not something that one is. It must be reached via struggle—passing through the "great furnace of doubt"—and not taken as given. The novel makes this point not with debate on argument, but by its process, by revealing how the lives of the characters unfold. There are positive and negative heroes, good and bad brothers, fathers and models: the major difference between them is their capacity for self-awareness and their ability to change. The Karamazov father, in addition to his many obnoxious qualities, will never know himself; he believes his own lies and is comfortable in the world of his rationalized greed. So, in their own ways, are Muisov, Rakitin, Father Ferapont, and Smerdyakov. The positive characters are all evolving, open to change. Ivan has the farthest to go, but his cynical intellectual stance has brought him to a crisis, and, by the novel's end, he has recognized his parricidal wishes and suffered an emotional breakdown from which new growth may emerge.

Dmitri, more than any of the others, has plumbed his own emotional depths in the realms of love and hate. Although I have not discussed it so far, relations with women and the possibilities of love are also explored in the novel. Dmitri is at first involved with Katerina who, beneath a surface of beauty and pride, organizes her relations with men around guilt. She is the end of a line of Dostoevsky women stretching back to Katerina Marmeladov. In case there is any doubt about her use of guilt as a weapon, she testifies against Dmitri at his trial, thus sealing his conviction for the murder of which he is innocent. As the most developed of the brothers, Dmitri early recognizes the sickness between him and Katerina; he leaves her for Grushenka, a more mature, riper, and openly sexual Sonia. She is not without her own need to torment, but, like Dmitri himself, she is open about her emotions. She is also capable of real love. Ivan, less far down the road than his older brother, is drawn to Katerina. Both the heroines, like the three brothers, also show the ability to change, to become more aware of themselves. As the novel draws to its close Grushenka undergoes a "moral regeneration" and commits herself to Dmitri.

Dmitri's openness and emotionality also include violence and hatred. Of all the brothers he is most aware of his murderous urges. His growth in this sphere is not a matter of becoming conscious of the violence within him but of acquiring empathy for others, of recognizing the effects of his acts. He needs to appreciate the damage he causes, and, eventually he moves in this direction. His decision to accept punishment for his father's murder, even though he is technically innocent, is based on the recognition that his violence has caused pain to others and that—with Grushenka's love secured—he is ready to take up a less vengeful, more compassionate life.

Alyosha is pictured as a man on the threshold of life. His time in the monastery with Zosima was a moratorium. Zosima sends him out into the world, and we see him beginning to experience sexual attraction and anger. In other words, he begins his struggle with adult life. Significantly, Dostoevsky had plans for another novel—never written—that would follow Aloyasha through a life of sin to his ultimate redemption.

Even Father Zosima was not born a saint. Dostoevsky gives him a past as a heedless young Army officer who undergoes a conversion experience. His Christian love and compassion are, thus, not gifts but the outcome of his own life's struggle.

The later portions of the novel describe a band of young boys and their leader, Kolya Krasotkin. They begin by tormenting the unfortunate Ilyusha Snegirov—whose father, in turn, had been attacked and humiliated by Dmitri—and then, under Alyosha's guidance, make amends to their victim. This episode contains, in miniature, the same message regarding openness to change. Children are not innocent; one sees the capacity for cruelty quite early. It must be openly recognized and actively opposed, and reparations must be made. Alyosha's message to these young boys stresses the need for belief and ideals. One good memory from childhood, he tells them, can get you through the hardest of times, can counter doubt, cynicism, and hatred. His own early memory, significantly, is of the loving mother of his infancy. One must learn to love and work at putting it into practice with the people in one's life.

The love between the young boys has its parallel in the love between the three Karamazov brothers themselves. While, at different times, they are rivals for Katerina and Grushenka, the more powerful bond between them is one of mutual concern and support. The father is such an infantile competitor for maternal love—as represented by his efforts to cheat Dmitri out of the inheritance from his dead mother and the more direct rivalry over Grushenka—that the brothers can easily unite in opposition to him. Much of this echoes Dostoevsky's own family experience: the jealous, infantile father and the sustaining relations between siblings. The closeness with his brother Mikhail—and a later series of brother figures—was a powerful loving force in his life.

Returning to the theme of identity formation we can say that, lacking a father to serve as an adequate model, young men have a special difficulty in working out meaningful and integrated adult selves. In their search, they turn to outside ideals—such as Zosima and Christ—as well as to each other. In a sense, young men without "fathers" must find ideals and models in each other; must invent and work through their own identities. And this brings us back to Dostoevsky himself. *The Brothers Karamazov* can be viewed as the final stage in his personal evolution, the brothers as a reworking of three central aspects of his own identity. Dmitri gives clear expression to his labile emotional self, his passion, lust for life, ability to love and give, as well as his hatreds, jealousy, and cruelty. The "Ivan" in him—his own rational, doubting, and cynical side—is given a thorough airing. And Alyosha gives expression to his Christlike innocence, Maria's loving young son. Dostoevsky's mystical, ecstatic experience—the way he felt a blissful oneness with the universe in his epileptic aura—gave a concrete reality to his faith and love. In the novel this is seen when Alyosha, at a time of doubt, restores himself by falling to the ground and hugging the earth in all its goodness.

The Brothers brings ever more of the novelist's—and the reader's— human nature into the open. This makes possible awareness, acceptance, and integration. But there is no fixed end point. The novel concludes, as *Crime and Punishment* did, with the characters on the verge of further development. Dmitri and Grushenka are off to Siberia where punishment must be endured, preparatory to their new life together. Ivan's "rational" world has cracked apart, with the possibility of reconstitution. And Alyosha is embarking on a full adult life.

Dostoevsky himself was fifty-nine when he finished his last novel, yet he felt another twenty years of writing projects in him. Like his fiction, his life itself was an unending process, always replenished from his inner sources. Was *The Brothers Karamazov* a success? Had he realized his ambitious intentions? He was both certain of his genius and accomplishments and open to criticism and the reactions of readers. As the writing of this novel neared its end, he was increasingly aware that he had achieved a good measure of the recognition that his immense talent deserved. *The Brothers* was a popular success even if the critics were at first divided along ideological lines. He was invited to Moscow for the unveiling of a statue of Pushkin and was honored, feted, and recognized everywhere. His speech on the great Russian poet, who was so crucial to his own early literary inspiration, received a very enthusiastic reception.

While his imagination and writing might well have gone on for another twenty years, his body could not. Throughout the years of his great literary output the epileptic seizures had continued. More ominous was a lung condition—variously diagnosed, most likely emphysema aggravated by his heavy smoking—that steadily worsened as the years went by. The last installments of *The Brothers* were sent off in November 1880. By the new year he was back in Petersburg pursuing further writing projects, worrying about his children's future, fighting with relatives over money, conferring with his publisher, receiving friends and visitors, and basking in Anna's care and love. He began to hemorrhage from the lungs and knew the end was at hand. He gathered his wife and children around him and read to them from his most cherished possession: The Bible given him by the Decembrist women on his way to prison in Siberia more than thirty years before. He died in January 1881.

APPENDIX

Epilepsy

The height of harmony and beauty, and gives an unheard-of and till then undreamed-of feeling of wholeness, of proportion, of reconciliation, and an ecstatic and prayer-like union in the highest synthesis of life.

This, interestingly, is a description of the emotional state—the aura —just before a seizure in the words of Dostoevsky's most famous fictional epileptic, Prince Myshkin. Speaking directly of his own seizures, Dostoevsky says:

For a few moments, I experience such happiness as is impossible under ordinary conditions, and of which other people can have no notion. I feel complete harmony in myself and in the world, and this feeling is so strong and sweet that for several seconds of such bliss one would give ten years of one's life, indeed, perhaps one's whole life.

This blissful state is followed by the seizure itself and then a return to consciousness where he felt, "I was an evildoer, that I had committed a terrible crime which had gone unpunished."

Dostoevsky's epilepsy has been discussed by biographers, psychoanalysts (including Freud), neurologists, and others. How is one to understand it? How did it effect his life, and what role did it play in the production of his fiction? At one extreme are those from the world of literature who are loath to grant any role to disease in the creation of great art. Much has been written about *The Idiot* and *The Brothers*

Karamazov with no more attention to the author's epilepsy than an acknowledgement that, like his characters Myshkin and Smerdyakov, he suffered from it. At the other extreme are those with a medical-psychiatric-pathological orientation who write as if they could account for Dostoevsky's works by properly placing him as a certain "epileptic type." The truth lies elsewhere. Like the highly individual nature of his fictional characters, Dostoevsky had his own, unique version of the disease. That is to say, while there were features shared with other sufferers, these only provide the general boundaries of an explanation; it will be useful to see what they are and then examine how he elaborated his own condition within these boundaries. We will want to know from what specific form of epilepsy he suffered, what is known about this condition today, and—of greatest interest in understanding the fiction —how he experienced the disease, how it felt to him, what meanings it came to have, and how feeling and meaning were integrated into life and art.

Before turning to an account based on contemporary evidence I had best discuss Freud's well-known interpretation. Freud's essay "Dostoevsky and Parricide," published in 1928, is a landmark in the application of psychoanalysis to literature and biography. It is in many ways a brilliant and penetrating essay yet, at the same time, his interpretation of Dostoevsky—whom he confessed he did not like—is flawed.[1] This is due to three factors: the early state of psychoanalytic theory—Freud's tendency to explain much too much in terms of the father, castration anxiety, and the Oedipus complex; the incomplete, and sometimes incorrect, historical, biographical material available to him; and the inadequate state of understanding of neurology, in general, and epilepsy in particular. We are in a much better-informed position today on all three of these counts.

The greatness of Freud's essay lies in its presentation of a general explanatory model; a model that ties together childhood history, literary theme, and specific symptoms. We have become so accustomed to this Freudian way of thought that we take it for granted, but it did not exist until Freud invented it in essays such as this. It is the model that underlies all of applied psychoanalysis, including the interpretations in this book.

When he applies the general model to Dostoevsky, Freud is right about a few specifics and wrong about many others. His interpretation that Dostoevsky's compulsive gambling was a form of self-punishment, and that the burden of debt that the novelist always managed to take on was the tangible manifestation of guilt, are brilliant insights. However, Freud's interpretation of the source of this guilt reduces it to the familiar oedipal theme: rivalry with the father for mother, death wishes toward the hated, feared father—in Dostoevsky's case realized when his father was murdered by his serfs—and the turning of these emotions around on the self: "You wanted to kill your father in order to be your father yourself. Now you *are* your father, but a dead father."

In this view, the epileptic seizures are the symptomatic expression of the death-dealing attack of the inner father—the superego—on the ego. In working out this interpretation of Dostoevsky's guilt and self-punishment, Freud gives as clear an account of the origin of the punitive superego as he does anywhere in his writings; again this is valuable as a general model even though incorrect as applied to Dostoevsky. Psychoanalysis has moved a great distance from the oedipal reductionism of 1928—with some orthodox holdouts, to be sure. The whole of the present book elaborates a different interpretation of Dostoevsky's unconscious dynamics; one more in keeping with current psychoanalytic theory and clinical observations as well as more consistent with the facts of the novelist's life.

Freud supports his interpretation of the epilepsy in several ways. He argues, first, that the novelist's seizures were "hysterical," were not the product of physical disease but the expression of unconscious conflict:

It is therefore quite right to distinguish between an organic and an "affective" epilepsy. The practical significance of this is that a person who suffers from the first kind has a disease of the brain, while a person who suffers from the second kind is a neurotic. In the first case his mental life is subjected to an alien disturbance from without, in the second case the disturbance is an expression of his mental life itself.

While he is wrong about the hysterical nature of Dostoevsky's seizures, he gets himself into needless difficulties here, a point to which I will return. In support of his oedipal interpretation Freud argues that Dostevsky's first seizure occurred when he received the news of his father's death. The blissful aura is seen as the feeling of "triumph" and "liberation" on hearing the news, quickly followed by the punishing attack of the inner father. He also supports his case by assuming that the seizures vanished during the years of imprisonment in Siberia; being punished by the tsar in reality presumably obviated the need for punishment from within. Both of these assumptions turn out to be false. Dostoevsky did not have a seizure at age eighteen when he learned of his father's death, the earliest attacks appeared in his mid- to late twenties. Far from disappearing during the years of his imprisonment, the seizures became definitely established during that period, occurring about once every four weeks. (See Frank 1976, 379—91; Rice 1985. The latter presents the most detailed review of the evidence bearing on Dostoevsky's epilepsy.)

The issue of the "hysterical" versus "organic" nature of Dostoevsky's epilepsy requires some further discussion. Freud's discovery of unconscious meaning in the putative physical symptoms of his hysterical patients was the starting place of psychoanalysis. Hysteria was his orienting explanatory model: for other neuroses, for dreams, for the mistakes of everyday life, for a wide range of phenomena. It was a model that allowed him to tease out the *meaning*—the hidden desires, the unconscious conflicts—in the heretofore neutral or personally meaningless. In the early work on hysteria this meant moving from an explanation in terms of physical disease to one of psychological motive and, as part of this movement, the explanation was burdened with an either/or mode of thinking current at the time: either the patient had a "real" disease or it was all psychological. In the first case medical treatment was called for, in the second, psychoanalysis. We have come a long way from this starting point. The mind and the body are an interactive whole; a variety of psychological factors are implicated in many forms of organic disease —most clearly in psychosomatic conditions such as migraine headache, asthma, peptic ulcer and hypertension—but in others as well. And, almost any physical disease takes on important meanings in the life of the person who has it. When Freud argues that Dostoevsky's epilepsy was hysterical he is asking us to view the seizures as imbued with personal meaning. Seeing the epilepsy as hysterical is not necessary from today's perspective; we do not need the either/or split of a "disease of the brain" versus a "neurosis" to find meaning in a condition such as this. Dostoevsky had a form of epilepsy based on neural pathology but his seizures emerged in interaction with the events and stresses in his life. His "real disease" had personal meaning, served motivational ends, was used to test and punish himself and those close to him, and played a central role in his fiction. Dostoevsky himself was aware of *both* the physical and psychological aspects of his condition. For the last twenty years of his life he kept a log in his private journal, attempting to correlate the seizures with a variety of factors (Rice 1985 presents a coalition of this seizure record, 287–98). In his late entries he says, "The farther it goes, the weaker the organism in enduring attacks, and the more severe is their effect," pointing up the physical aspect yet, at the same time, speaking of the "fantastic" and "mystical" effects, the "sense of unreality" and "sense of guilt," that continued to accompany his seizures.

"Hysterical epilepsy" is a recognizable entity today; it appears in patients who mimic, or act out, seizures, almost always before an audience. It is clear that Dostoevsky did not have this particular condition; his seizures mainly occurred during sleep when he was alone. What is more, he suffered physical injuries as a result of them, something that does not occur in hysterical epilepsy. Still, someone with "real" seizures would know how to mimic an attack when it could serve his ends; Dostoevsky has Smerdyakov do just that in *The Brothers Karamazov*.

What, then, was the nature of Dostoevsky's epilepsy as we can reconstruct it today? A number of neurologists have examined all the available evidence; there is a clear consensus that Dostoevsky suffered from temporal-lobe epilepsy.[2] This is the most common form of the disease; in a majority of cases a definite structural lesion of the brain is involved. Temporal lobe epilepsy that makes its appearance in adulthood is usually not hereditary; hence the death of Dostoevsky's last child from what appeared to be seizures was not necessarily due to his father's illness.

Let me give a brief review of this condition, based on the excellent overview of Glaser 1975 and also Bear et al. 1984. There are a variety of epilepsies, all having in common disordered cerebral function. Groups of abnormally functioning neurons produce the various symptoms associated with the disease. A variety of factors can produce lesions that predispose portions of the brain to such abnormal functioning among them, birth injuries, infections, tumors, head injuries, cerebral vascular disease, and toxins. A person predisposed to such abnormal brain functioning can manifest a range of symptoms from mild, transitory lapses of consciousness ("absences") to the full-blown or grand mal seizure.

Symptoms may be triggered by a variety of factors including periodicity
—as in the sleep cycle, menstrual periods, and unpredictable body rhythms.
Seizures may be set off by physical stimuli such as flickering light and
drugs. Dostoevsky reported a great increase in seizure frequency during
a period in the army when he was forced to keep his commanding officer
company in the consumption of alcohol. It is also well established that
seizures are related to psychological factors. As Glaser puts it:

In most patients there is a direct interplay of emotional disturbances with
classical seizure activity; patients in a state of psychological turmoil have increased seizure susceptibility. . . . The achievement of psychological adjustment
often reduces seizure frequency and intensity.

The temporal lobe of the brain is intimately involved in the experience
of emotion as well as playing its role in memory and perception. Like
many temporal-lobe epileptics, Dostoevsky experienced intense fluctua-
tions of feeling, along with unusual sensory and perceptual states. These
particular psychological states probably extended back into the years
before the full-blown seizures made their appearance, before he knew
himself to be an epileptic.

Grand mal seizures are the most dramatic outward manifestation of
the disease and, in Dostoevsky's case, they followed a typical course.
There is, first, a *prodromal* phase lasting minutes or hours and characterized by emotional activation: increase in anxiety, depression, or elation.
This is followed by the *aura*, a very brief sensory experience immediately
before the seizure itself. The large majority of auras are unpleasant,
consisting of a sense of fear, dread, swelling of the throat, foul odors,
and the like. Dostoevsky's experience, "the height of harmony and
beauty . . . the ecstatic union in the highest synthesis of life," is an
example of a rare, though not unknown, pleasurable aura.[3] The *seizure*
itself often begins with a characteristic "epileptic cry," loss of consciousness, loss of voluntary motor control and convulsive movements of the
body, impaired breathing, and, sometimes, biting of the tongue and
incontinence. The excessive motor activity ceases after some minutes,
breathing becomes normal, and consciousness gradually returns. The
person has no memory of the seizure, though he may recall the prodromal phase and the aura. The *postseizure* phase is characterized by confusion, memory disturbance, headache, and other symptoms. In Dos-

toevsky's case, there was the sense of depression and guilt, that he was "an evildoer" and "had committed a terrible crime which had gone unpunished."

Anyone who has seen a grand mal seizure knows its frightening and dramatic aspect. The person is seemingly struck down from nowhere— the word *epilepsy* comes from a Greek root meaning *taking hold of* or *seizing*—with the loss of voluntary control of his mind and body. In the case of disturbances involving the temporal lobe, there are also less outwardly visible emotional and perceptual changes that constitute an internal "seizing" of the person's feelings and sensations. These too come on suddenly and are outside of voluntary control. Dostoevsky experienced these as relatively sudden shifts of mood, ranging from outbreaks of irritability to sensations of ecstasy. There is also some evidence that he experienced hallucinations at different times: the cry of "wolf" in the *Peasant Marey* episode, the sound of snoring that disturbed his sleep during his twenties; a "mystical horror" that appeared during his nervous crisis. He may also have had first-hand experience with the hallucinations he gives to various literary characters: Golyadkin's double is the autoscopic phenomenon associated with temporal-lobe epilepsy and there is Svidrigailov's hallucination of his dead wife and Ivan Karamazov's conversation with the devil. All of these are consistent with distortions of sensation and perception found in temporal-lobe epilepsy.

The literature on epilepsy contains descriptions of an "epileptic personality"; observers describe characteristics that make up a "temporal-lobe epilepsy type." These include: emotional lability, irritability, preoccupation with religious, philosophical, and metaphysical ideas, "hypergraphia" (excessive and compulsive writing), and hyposexuality (reduced sexual interest). It is interesting that Dostoevsky did share most of these traits with other temporal-lobe epileptics. His wide swings of emotion were characteristic as were his well-known anger and irritability, though he was certainly not hyposexual. He was clearly occupied with religious and philosophical ideas and I suppose we could say that one of the world's most prolific and productive writers was hypergraphic.

These last points begin to reveal the problems with this diagnostic form of explanation. Epileptics—like the rest of us—are individuals with their own backgrounds, histories, skills, and liabilities. Lumping them together as a diagnostic type does a great disservice to this individuality. They do—or may—share characteristics based on their abnormal brain functioning and seizures but even here much depends on what the individual does with this experience. The peculiar neural discharge of temporal-lobe epilepsy is often associated with certain psychological experiences: feelings that seem to come from nowhere, hallucinations, visions, and the seizures themselves. The person is then impelled to make sense of these unusual experiences; hence the preoccupation with religious and metaphysical ideas. What comes out of these attempts varies widely. The hypergraphic and religious preoccupations of most of these epileptics seem to have negligible literary or philosophical merit, though I think labeling them symptoms of a disease does a disservice to the person. It strikes me that these activities are attempts to impose order— to give meaning—to experiences that others do not share or understand. The epileptic is trying to communicate his unusual ideas and visions as well as his pain, fear, and distress.

In discussing the prevalence of psychological disturbance in many forms of epilepsy, Glaser notes that

severe emotional problems and disturbances in the patients have been found to develop most often as a reaction to restrictions, to the presence of an uncontrollable, overwhelming seizure disorder, and also, at times even more common, intrafamilial denigration. Severely neurotic, maladjusted behavior then developed into the so-called "epileptic personality," which is just a collection of secondary reactive phenomena.

Let me explore another aspect of the epilepsy. Dostoevsky suffered a number of powerful psychological experiences: intense and shifting emotions; vivid, perhaps hallucinatory, visions; glimpses of paradise; near-mystical merging with the universe; and deathlike attacks that reduced him to a state of guilty depression. He then worked these over in the process of transforming them into literature. This "epileptic source" of his fiction is one explanation for the unconsciously driven quality possessed by so many of his heros and heroines: for the way in which Raskolnikov, Dmitri Karamazov, Rogozhin, and Stavrogin are pushed about by emotional forces outside of their personal control. Their creator was in direct contact with his own epilepsy—an enhanced version of such emotionally driven experiences—and he then saturated the characters with these qualities. His readers, who are not epileptic but have their own unconscious motives, are then able to identify with characters who, in their emotional intensity, display the essence of unconsciously driven action.[4]

The developmental course of Dostoevsky's epilepsy can now be traced with some accuracy. As noted before, there were no seizures in childhood or adolescence, none—contrary to what Freud assumed—associated with the death of his father. Sensory-perceptual and emotional experiences of a peculiar kind probably antedated the actual onset of seizures though we have no way of knowing exactly what these were or how far back into childhood they extended. There is some dispute as to whether the seizures began during the years of imprisonment in Siberia or in the period two or three years immediately preceding his arrest. In later years, Dostoevsky himself promoted the idea of onset associated with his imprisonment but there are reasons to distrust this. He used the epilepsy as a reason to secure his release from the forced army service that was a condition of his sentence and, in addition, liked to emphasize the martyrdom he suffered in Siberia. For these reasons he would speak as if the attacks had begun in prison. Rice makes a convincing case for their onset during the immediately preceding years. This was the time of the severe nervous crisis (described in chapter 7) when Dostoevsky was under the daily care of Dr. Yanovsky. Drawing on Yanovsky's unpublished materials, it seems clear that Dostoevsky had a number of pre–grand mal "equivalents" during these years—states of confusion, absences, memory disturbances—as well as at least three seizures. This was the time of the "nervous crisis" with its many symptoms: dizziness, sleep disturbance, anxiety, oversensitivity, suspiciousness, and a general hypochondria, according to both his own account and Yanovsky's.[5] The seizures themselves were precipitated by specific events: one by the sight of a funeral and another by his receipt of the news of Belinsky's death. Given the ambivalent nature of Dostoevsky's relations with the great critic, this news must have been a shock of great intensity.

Following his imprisonment and exile, Dostoevsky continued to suffer epileptic attacks for his remaining years. By his own records these occurred on the average of once every four weeks, but this varied greatly with life events. Particularly stressful times produced more seizures, and periods of calmness fewer. And, this brings us, finally, to the meanings expressed by the epilepsy.

In my earlier discussion of Freud's essay I argued that the general psychoanalytic model that points to a common underlying explanation for symptom, childhood history, and literary theme provides the structure for understanding Dostoevsky's epilepsy. This is so even though Freud's interpretation in terms of oedipal conflicts is flawed. To be more precise I should say that an oedipal interpretation is not entirely wrong: there were times when Dostoevsky's seizures expressed self-punishment for guilt in relation to the father. For instance, his attack upon learning of Belinsky's death may have been one such, since Belinsky stood in a paternal relation to the young author. But such oedipal precipitants played a minor role. As it became established in his adult life the entire epileptic drama—or the physiological-psychological experience as Dostoevsky came to dramatize it—had a clear and recognizable shape: it was the enactment of a fantasy of idealized merger, rageful attack, death like punishment, guilt, and resurrection. Let me elaborate this interpretation and then examine the evidence in its support.

As they became regular events in his life in the years following his imprisonment, Dostoevsky's epileptic seizures assumed a structured form. It is doubtful if every attack took this form, but those he thought about, described to others, and worked into his fiction did. There was, first, the blissful aura, accompanied by intensely pleasurable sensations: voluptuous, sexual, and religious-ecstatic. As the evidence from both life and the novels will demonstrate, this represents a merger of the loving infant boy with the idealized mother, a capturing of the longed-for state of preambivalent, pleasurable oneness. It is what Freud, in his discussion of religious feeling in *Civilization and Its Discontents,* calls "the oceanic feeling," a feeling that he too traces to the state of mother-infant oneness. Dostoevsky's own imagery most frequently depicted this in terms of Mary and Christ, the perfectly loving mother-son pair.

The aura is followed by the seizure, which represents the attack on the mother. This violent attack is played out on the novelist's own body; it is a symbolic murder. The postseizure feeling expresses the guilt over murderous rage. Dostoevsky's epileptic seizures provided a vivid and emotionally intense setting in which this drama of gratification, crime,

Appendix

and punishment could be played out again and again. It was a drama of great compression containing, as it did, the basis of pleasure, hope, and fulfillment, on the one side, along with the venting of rage, guilt, and punishment, on the other.

We turn now to the evidence supporting this interpretation. It can be found in three sources: the description of the epileptic drama itself, the life contexts in which the seizures occurred, and the portrayal of epilepsy in the novels. Let us consider each of these in turn.

The drama of aura, attack, death, and guilty rebirth is described in language that places it in the early—preoedipal—stage of psychological development. The words *complete harmony, wholeness, union, synthesis,* and *bliss,* and the all-or-none nature of the feelings, suggest the all-loving, all-hating, life-or-death quality of emotional experience from the early years of life when the infant is just emerging from an undifferentiated oneness with the mother figure. Here I must turn to the clinical experience of psychoanalytic observers: these images and emotions are most frequently encountered in connection with memories and events from the early, maternal sphere. As we saw in chapter 5, Dostoevsky's own early experience of loss of his wet nurse, his nanny, and his mother, the last two of whom he repeatedly lost to a series of sibling replacements, provided ample cause for feelings of a pleasurable relationship suddenly disrupted in a manner likely to engender rage.

The second source of evidence for this interpretation comes from the life contexts in which the drama was played out, particularly when the attacks occurred in public. A large number of the seizures took place during sleep; they were not directly inflicted on anyone though Dostoevsky did not hesitate to talk about his disease, for example, to young women whose reactions he could test in this way. There were times, however, when he had seizures in the presence of others, and several of these occasions are of great significance. Unusual double attacks occurred on the days following both of his marriages. Returning to Semipalitensk following his marriage to Maria, he had a rare, especially for those years, attack in the daytime. Maria, who knew little of her new husband's disease, was horrified and herself required care. The marriage, in my view, degenerated from that moment onward. His second wife, Anna, describes the first seizure she witnessed, though he had told her of his condition before their marriage (see Anna Dostoevsky 1975, 79–81).

Appendix

It was shortly after the ceremony, and they were making the rounds of friends and relatives where much champagne was consumed. He almost never drank, aware of alcohol's role in precipitating seizures. He was engaged in animated conversation with Anna's sister and brother-in-law when the attack struck, to be followed by a second an hour later. The rare double seizure was attributed to the excitement and wine, which, no doubt, played their parts. More important was the marriage itself, which represented union with the longed-for idealized woman. He could not stand all this happiness, love, and acceptance without bringing his evil self on the scene. There was the deathlike punishment, reduction to a dependent state, and a test of his new wife: "You think you love me, but will you still, after you are acquainted with this other, murderous side of my nature?" As we have seen, Anna passed this test, as she did many others—such as further seizures and the compulsive gambling—that had the same meaning.

Dostoevsky's wives were not the only persons subjected to the unconscious drama embodied in his epileptic seizures. The philosopher-critic Nikolay Strakhov was his closest friend during the early 1860s, the years between the two marriages. He was the recipient of the novelist's intimate confidences, the only person to whom Dostoevsky could comfortably display his epilepsy. Like Dr. Yanovsky at an earlier time, Strakhov had unwittingly assumed the position of transference figure in Dostoevsky's unconscious enactment, which may account for why he later turned against the novelist with such vehemence. He provides the following account of a seizure. It was Easter Eve, near midnight, and the two friends were alone at Strakhov's deep in talk.

He [Dostoevsky] was saying something that was full of exaltation and joy. When I supported his thoughts with a remark, he turned to me with the face of one at the peak of ecstasy. He hesitated a moment as though seeking for a word, and had already opened his lips to pronounce it. I looked at him with keen attention, feeling that he was about to utter something extraordinary, that I would hear some revelation. Suddenly, a strange long drawn-out meaningless moan issued from his mouth, and he sank to the floor unconscious. . . . The body was rigid with convulsions and foam appeared at the corners of the mouth.

Sofya Kovalevskaya provides a similar account; she describes Dostoevsky's own version of his "first" seizure. He was in exile in Siberia, arguing the night away with an atheist friend. Again it was

Appendix

Easter Eve and, as the church bells sounded, Dostoevsky proclaimed, "There is a God—there is" and felt

that heaven had descended to earth and swallowed me. I truly attained God and was penetrated by him. . . . All you healthy people don't even begin to understand what happiness is, the happiness that we epileptics experience during the instant before an attack. Mohammed . . . saw Paradise and was in Paradise . . . I don't know whether that bliss lasts seconds or hours or months, but believe me, I wouldn't exchange all the joys life can offer for that bliss!

Ecstatic merger with the idealized woman, the close friend, God himself; the attainment of Paradise; Easter Eve (the death and resurrection of Christ)—all these images lend support to the present interpretation.

The third and most powerful source of evidence, in my view, comes from the novels. It is here that Dostoevsky gives articulate expression to the themes that were expressed unconsciously in such enactments as the compulsive gambling and the seizures. *Crime and Punishment* revolves around the theme of maternal deprivation, the expression of rage, guilt, punishment, and rebirth. There is no need to repeat the analysis of that novel here. While the theme permeates the novel—while it is drawn from this unconscious source in the author—epilepsy itself does not appear. But it does in the novel that Dostoevsky wrote next, *The Idiot*.

The Idiot was written during the first years of the marriage to Anna. Prince Myshkin, its hero, is an epileptic. Dostoevsky's conscious intention was to create a "positively good man," a "Prince Christ." He was, in terms of the present interpretation, attempting a fictional realization of the loving boy of his merger fantasy. The prince who appears in the pages of *The Idiot*, however, shows the impossibility of this idealization, for Myshkin is possessed of a bizarre sort of goodness. He is sweet-natured and seemingly without the rage, jealousy, and greed of the characters who surround him. Indeed, hate in the novel is mainly portrayed through these others. Myshkin continually turns the other cheek when insulted or abused. At the same time, he is a sort of walking disaster of well-meaning naiveté who creates chaos in his wake. And, he is an epileptic whose seizures ultimately reduce him to a state of idiocy and infantile helplessness. In these ways, Dostoevsky reveals the not-so-ideal impulses beneath the loving exterior.

We know from *The Notebooks for "The Idiot"* that, in the early versions of the novel, the central figure was both epileptic and overtly violent. Dostoevsky had a great deal of difficulty with this book and it was only after seven or eight revisions that he finally evolved a solution: the central figure was split into two characters, Myshkin—the erstwhile Christ—and the violent, impulsive, and wordly Rogozhin. The interplay between these two, like that between Raskolnikov and Svidrigailov, is an encounter between two sides of a single self. They are both drawn to the same woman, the sensual Nastasya, and, in a crucial passage, Myshkin's first seizure occurs. They have been verbally passing Nastasya back and forth and then Myshkin wanders about the city with the sense, real or imagined, that he is being followed by Rogozhin's burning gaze. He is ascending a shadowy staircase when he encounters Rogozhin who raises a knife to stab him. Myshkin falls to the ground in an epileptic seizure. We see here the "good" man's encounter with the split-off, murderous side of himself. This side of Myshkin, like the related side of his epileptic creator, is filled with rage, represented both by Rogozhin's attack and the seizure—also an "attack"—that is, at once, murder and punishment played out on Myshkin's body.

The Idiot ends, significantly, with Rogozhin's murder of Nastasya. Myshkin finds him in a state of madness by her body and, in comforting him, lies so close that his tears run down Rogozhin's cheeks. He, too, is regressed to a helpless state. So much is captured in this scene: the coming together of the two selves, mourning the loss of the loved woman, guilt and sadness over the damage wrought by the violent self, and, most important, the deep wish for acceptance of the whole person. Myshkin gives the love and comfort to the representation of his rageful self that the divided individual longs for.

In working out his conception of a "positively good man" in The Idiot, Dostoevsky uncovers the complexity beneath this idealized goodness. He explores this in many ways, including the different sides of the epileptic drama. As Myshkin himself puts it,

Thinking about this moment afterward, when he was again in health, he often told himself that all these gleams and flashes of superior self-awareness and, hence, of "a higher state of being" were nothing other than sickness, the upsetting of the normal condition and, if so, were not the highest state of being at all but on the contrary had to be reckoned as the lowest. And yet he came finally to an extremely paradoxical conclusion. "What if it is sickness?" he asked himself.

"What does it matter if it is abnormal intensity, if the result, if the moment of awareness, remembered and analyzed afterward in health, turns out to be the height of harmony and beauty.

In the end, Myshkin is regressed to a state of infantile helplessness, revealing the fate of one who is completely overtaken by the merger fantasy.

Dostoevsky continued to struggle with the meaning of epilepsy, both as a disease in his life, and as a complex psychological drama in his fiction. In his last novel, *The Brothers Karamazov,* epilepsy is not given to Alyosha—the Myshkinlike good man—but to Smerdyakov, the least appealing of the brothers. There is nothing blissful or harmonious about Smerdyakov's seizures. The murder of the father—the crime at the heart of the novel—is committed by Smerdyakov, who then uses fake seizures to cover his tracks. Not only has the rage and murder moved from the maternal to the paternal level in this final work, but the epilepsy is purged of its idealized quality, is more realistically confronted. By showing how Smerdyakov uses his disease for manipulative and selfish ends, Dostoevsky confronts the same tendency in himself.

Note on
Sources and Evidence

The present interpretation of Dostoevsky and his work rests on two kinds of evidence, one psychoanalytic and the other biographical and literary. A few words must be said about my approach to each of these.

Psychoanalytic Sources

I have reviewed all of the extant psychoanalytic studies of Dostoevsky's literature in English as well as those few—and there are surprisingly few —essays that bear on him as a person; I cite only the better ones where appropriate. More important than these studies, however, has been my own experience practicing psychoanalysis and psychoanalytic psychotherapy for more than twenty-five years. In the course of this practice I, like most analysts, have absorbed, modified, and worked out my own understanding of the major psychoanalytic techniques and ideas (My 1981 book, *Freud's Unfinished Journey*, presents my approach to theory). All of this is exemplified in the text itself and, with the exception of a few technical ideas, is not referenced with citations to Freud or the vast psychoanalytic literature.

In the course of writing this book, analytic work with several patients has proven extremely valuable. My understanding of them has facilitated my understanding of Dostoevsky, on the one side, and the working out of ideas in writing about him has, in return, sharpened my work with them. I think of three, in particular. A brilliant writer demonstrated the way personal conflicts are made conscious and mastered as they are transformed into fiction. Progressive movement across developmental levels occurred in his analysis and writing, in a way similar to that described for Dostoevsky. A young woman began an analysis some years ago, shortly after the death of her mother. Her protracted struggle to free herself from the inner legacy of the very ambivalent mother-daughter relationship taught me a great deal about the power of the negative introject; it is a conflict with which Dostoevsky also struggled over many years.

Most central was my work with a man—I will call him Cleavland Stone or "Cleave"—who had a very strong and direct connection with Raskolnikov; he identified with the hero of *Crime and Punishment* in several ways: as a guilt-ridden criminal, as a prideful isolate, as someone who existed more in fantasy than in reality; and as a person whose conflicting emotions sometimes threatened to tear him apart.

Cleave originally sought analysis because he found himself caught up in a series of sexual affairs that he did not understand and could not control. He was married, with a young son, and was involved with three or four other women and would, additionally, cruise the streets for prostitutes. This was his "crime." He attempted to keep all these affairs secret, was concerned to placate the women involved, and felt terribly frightened and guilty. Yet he could not stop. Like a Dostoevsky character—and the novelist himself—his immoral acts were balanced by deeds of generosity and self-sacrifice; a physician on the staff of a public hospital, he specialized in the treatment of seriously ill children and was devoted to their care. As his psychoanalysis progressed, the affairs and cruising abated; he settled down into two relationships, what we came to call his "double life." He lived in the suburbs with his wife and son, a life identified with family, home, and stability. Yet the wife was felt to be cold and unresponsive, an isolated and suspicious woman with few friends, his rage at her was often near the surface, though almost never openly expressed. The dominant emotion in the marriage was guilt. And he maintained a long-standing love affair with a nurse whom he experienced as warm, loving, infinitely patient, and understanding. She was his Sonia.

Each "life" was kept secret from the other. Despite a persistent fear of being caught, strong feelings of guilt and worthlessness, and energy-draining efforts to keep the whole complicated apparatus in motion—the lying, excuses, secret phone calls, and frantic running around—he remained terrified at the possibility of losing his two separate lives.

Over the course of his analysis we learned a great deal about the meaning of his complex relations with women, the origins of these in his childhood, and the reason the double life was maintained with such ferocity. He was living a version of splitting; he kept alive, in these two relationships, versions of the cold, ungiving, hated female, and the idealized, warm, all-loving one. What was most threatening to Cleave was the possibility of relating to one whole, real woman, without the protection of the split-off other.

Behind this pattern, we discovered the rage at his disturbed and sickly mother, a rage that was so easily turned on himself. Throughout his childhood his mother, an older, depressed, and frequently ill woman, could provide him with little of the love he needed. What he did receive from her was almost always given in a compromising way. She needed more care than she could give; some of his earliest memories were of her vomiting into the toilet because of her stomach problems. And, it was also clear that no matter how frustrated he felt over deprivation, attempts to express his longing for affection or his anger openly were met with mother's tears and physical complaints, reactions that turned the feelings back on himself. As a boy, he would retreat to his room, bang his head on the wall, and bite his arms. And he would fantasize, retreat to the comfort of a world of his own invention.

The double life was the eventual outcome of the complicated course taken by the conflicts of his childhood: his need for maternal love and understanding and the rage at deprivation; the impossibility of finding an acceptable outlet for either need or anger; and the variety of self-protective measures he had been forced to develop to keep his hopes alive, on the one side, and depression and annihilating rage at bay, on the other. The double life provided him with women to hate, fear, and attack with lies and deceptions, and women from whom he obtained love, warmth, and understanding. Like Dostoevsky, he deeply identified with victims and the unjustly treated. In his dreams and fantasies he was often black, a slum dweller or a skid-row bum. The unjust treatment he had suffered was expressed in these identifications.

I have gone into some length about this patient to illustrate what I consider to be an extremely important source of psychoanalytic evidence for the kind of interpretations I have developed through the course of this book. Discovering a pattern—an interrelationship of childhood history, unconscious conflict, character style, and symptom—such as this does not "prove," in a rigorous scientific sense, the validity of a related pattern in Dostoevsky. But rigorous scientific proof is inappropriate to psychoanalysis—and to biography and literature, I would add —as many contemporary analysts have shown (Breger 1981; Gill 1982; G. Klein 1976; Schafer 1976; Stolorow, Brandchaft, and Atwood 1987.) Psychoanalytic truth is truth of meaning and coherence. In the course of this study I have attempted to demonstrate the cohering patterns in Dostoevsky's life and literature; the discovery of a closely related pattern in a patient gives a living validation to the picture constructed from biography and literature; I think interpretations become convincing when one can see them in this firsthand way.

Finally, I want to express a debt of gratitude to the three patients mentioned above—and to many others I have seen over the years. I have learned a great deal from them and hope I have, in return, made a difference in their lives.

Biographical and Literary Sources

I must begin by expressing my gratitude to all those Dostoevsky scholars, translators, and Slavists who have made the novels, and much related material, available in English.

The primary sources used in this study have included all of Dostoevsky's fiction, portions of his journalism (including *The Diary of a Writer*) the notebooks for the major novels, and private journals (see Dostoevsky 1973–76). A selection of Dostoevsky's extensive correspondence is available in translation: the volume edited by Mayne (Dostoevsky 1961), which also includes reminiscences by Grigorovich, Wrangel, and others;

that edited by Koteliansky and Murry (Dostoevsky 1923); the Hill and Mudie selection of letters to his (second) wife (Dostoevsky 1930); and Frank and Goldstein's recent volume of collected letters (Dostoevsky 1987). Coulson's book (Coulson 1962) combines selected letters, interspersed with biographical information; it includes material on the family not found elsewhere.

Dostoevsky has been the subject of a large number of biographies and biographical studies over the years; I have primarily relied on five, which I list here from earliest to most recent. Leonid Grossman, a Russian literary critic and scholar whose work on Dostoevsky goes back many years; he had the opportunity of speaking directly with Anna Dostoevsky before the Revolution. A revised and translated version of his 1962 biography was published in 1975. Grossman is especially good for a firsthand appreciation of historical-cultural setting; his occasional attempts to align Dostoevsky with Soviet ideology are easy to ignore. Konstantine Mochulsky was a Russian emigré, living in Paris, a translation of his biography was published in 1967. Avraham Yarmolinsky's is a readable narrative biography, published in 1971. Hingley's 1978 book is the most concise. Joseph Frank is currently bringing out the most detailed of these biographies; three of a projected five volumes have appeared to date (volume I in 1976, volume 2 in 1983, and the third volume in 1986; Professor Frank was good enough to let me read the chapters on Suslova and gambling from volume 3, prior to their publication). Frank is particularly good at placing Dostoevsky in the literary, political, and intellectual context of his times.

While I have used these biographies as sources, they each have their own interpretations of both Dostoevsky's life and the meaning of the novels. None of them develops a psychological view at all close to what I present here, and, with one exception. I do not attempt a discussion of our differences. The exception is in chapter 11, where I present a comparison of my psychoanalytic interpretation of *Notes from Underground* with the interpretations found in the biographies.

In addition to these biographies, several specialized works have proven valuable. Dostoevsky's daughter Liubov (Aimée) published a biography of her father (1921); while generally considered unreliable— he was close to forty-eight when she was born—it contains interesting glimpses of the family's life in the later years. Of greater value are the

Note on Sources and Evidence

Reminiscences (published in translation in 1975) of Dostoevsky's second wife, Anna, compiled from a diary she kept in shorthand throughout the years of their marriage. Polina Suslova's diary, along with some correspondence, is contained in an edition of *The Gambler* (Dostoevsky 1972). Rice's 1985 *Dostoevsky and the Healing Art* gives an extremely detailed account of Dostoevsky's epilepsy and other illnesses in the context of nineteenth-century medical history (I have reviewed it in another place; see Breger 1986).

There exists a very large critical literature dealing with all aspects of Dostoevsky's fiction. Useful general works include Peace 1971; Simmons 1950; Wellek 1962; and Wasiolek 1964. The last, in addition to balanced essays on the major novels, contains much useful historical and bibliographical information. More specialized works include André Gide's *Dostoevsky* (originally published in 1923, English version reissued in 1961) and Bakhtin's *Problems of Dostoevsky's Poetics* (originally published in 1929, revised in 1963; English translation available in 1984).

Notes and Sources
for Quotations

For each chapter I first give the numbered notes and then the sources for all quotations in the chapter.

Prologue

SOURCES FOR QUOTATIONS

p. 1 "My first personal," *The Notebooks for "Crime and Punishment,"* 64.

p. 2 "Here there was," *The Diary of a Writer,* 185–86.

Chapter 1

NOTES

1. There have been a number of important advances in psychoanalytic dream theory since Freud's time, though many of these have not penetrated to the wider public. Popular misconceptions are still prevalent: that all dreams are wish fulfillments and that they may be decoded with a fixed set of Freudian symbols. It would take far too much space to discuss all the recent developments in dream theory, the interested reader is referred to the following sources: Breger 1980; Breger, Hunter and Lane 1971; Erikson 1954; French and Fromm 1964; Greenberg 1975, 1978; Jones 1970; and Rycroft 1979.

Here, I will simply outline the main features of a contemporary psychoanalytic approach to dreams.

Dreaming is a special form of psychological activity, a kind of "thinking" with its own "language." It belongs to the broader class of imaginative activities that includes play, daydreaming, and fantasy. Unlike spoken and written language, dreams consist of visual images; they can be nonlinear, illogical, idiosyncratic, and, since no one sees them but the dreamer, they are relatively free from the social rules that control language. Their private, unsocialized nature is the main reason they are uniquely suited to the expression of personal conflicts about which the dreamer feels anxious or guilty.

Freud called dream thought "primary process" as distinguished from "secondary process," or reality-oriented thinking. He saw dreams as analogous to neurotic symptoms; both were ways in which repressed impulses found compromised expression. In line with this, he mainly viewed the symbolism of dreams as disguise, as a way of keeping the dreamer ignorant of aspects of himself. Modern theorists recognize the way dreams participate in neurosis and unconscious conflict but do not see this as intrinsic to dream symbolism itself. Dreams, with their special images and symbols, are creative-imaginative activities, present in everyone from early childhood, and are not pathological in themselves.

One of the major developments in dream theory since Freud is the recognition of the nonpathological, potentially adaptive character of dreams. During dreaming, the person assimilates the emotionally aroused events and conflicts of the day into the "solutions" contained in his imagination. This corresponds to what I earlier termed dreams dreamt: it is a form of emotional release or fantasy gratification that allows the dreamer to awake feeling more in control of himself. A more complete adaptation involves access to the dream material and some active effort at integrating it into waking thought and life, as in psychotherapy or the construction of a work of art. This corresponds to dreams analyzed.

I will not attempt to describe the features of dream symbolism; that has been done by many authors, perhaps none better than Freud in *The Interpretation of Dreams*. There is both commonality and uniqueness in every person's dreams. We all begin life as infants, dependent on our parents, and focused on the sensations of our own bodies. There is a core of dream theme and symbolism that derives from this and related forms of primary human experience: the body and its functions (eating, defecating, pleasure, pain, injury, parents, birth, babies, siblings, sexuality, aggression, anxiety, and death). Dreams dealing with these issues have a generally similar shape though they cannot be decoded from a stock set of symbols. In addition, we each have individual versions of these issues as well as unique experiences —such as Dostoevsky's witnessing the horse and courier scene—that stand out in our lives and find their way into our dreams.

Notes and Sources for Quotations

Over the course of his life, everyone develops a set of themes and symbols that comprises the unique style and stamp of his own dream "language." These can be mapped out in those special situations—a patient in psychoanalysis, for example—where the observer has access to a sufficient amount of material. Freud presents a number of his own dreams in *The Interpretation of Dreams,* and, if you examine these, apart from the rest of the book, you get a feeling for his preoccupations, conflicts, the pattern of his relationships, as well as the recurring symbols in which all these are expressed. The same is true of Dostoevsky's novels: viewing them as a series of dreams analyzed reveals recurring themes and particular symbols. Abused children, Bronze Men, Christlike heroes, holy fools, horses being beaten, are just a few of these. An analysis in terms of repeated themes and symbols—in *Crime and Punishment* and the other novels—will be a major source of data for the understanding of Dostoevsky's life.

2. Examples that combine sensitive literary criticism and a firsthand knowledge of psychoanalysis can be found in the work of Skura (1981), whose book has already been cited, and my colleagues Victoria Hamilton (1986), Albert Hutter, and Jay Martin. See Hutter's 1975 paper on dreams and literature and his 1982 paper on the poets Hopkins and Rossetti. Martin has done a very sensitive essay on the poet Robert Lowell (1983) see, also, *Who Am I This Time?* (1988.) One should also mention Norman Holland, an earlier entrant in the field (see his *Psychoanalysis and Shakespeare* [1964] and *Dynamics of Literary Response* [1968]) These references are meant to be illustrative rather than exhaustive.

3. The concept of what I term internal selves or self-other scenarios is central to psychoanalytic thought. In Freud's own work it appears most clearly as the super-ego; his conception of conscience as an inner "agency" of the mind—a sort of person within the person—that judges the ego in a manner modeled on the child-father relationship. The concept has been much broadened, first by Melanie Klein and by those British analysts who have come to be labeled the object-relations school (Fairbairn, Guntrip, and Winnicott). See Ogden (1983) and Greenberg and Mitchell (1983) for general reviews.

People experience their self-other scenarios in very different ways; most of us probably not much like Dostoevsky. To give a more direct feel for the phenomena, let me again turn to an analytic patient, this time to the young woman whom I mentioned earlier. At a point well into her analysis she suffered a severe writer's block in the midst of an important graduate school examination. She later had occasion to describe the experience in writing; I quote from her account:

> For some time now I have been struggling to overcome a psychological block, a problem which might be called a fear of success, which plagues me in the form of self-punishing and self-defeating behavior. I am attempting with the help of my psychoanalyst to free myself from the grips of a sort of "internalized mother" which has been holding me back in the achievement of my aspirations.

Twelve years ago, during my sophomore year, my mother was diagnosed as suffering from acute leukemia, and she died the following year. As often happens when a parent dies, I must have decided, although not consciously, to keep my mother alive within myself, both to assuage the pain of losing her and to punish myself. My punishment was a consequence of the undeserved but unfathomable guilt which I felt over her sickness and death, and took the form of my denying to myself in certain ways the right to a life of my own. After all this time I am beginning, figuratively speaking, to lay my mother's soul to rest and to advance with my own life.

The relationship which exists between this biographical material and my performance on the exams is clear. I discovered that I had essentially reenacted my mother's behavior, that I had essentially allowed my "internalized mother," my mother within, to write the exams for me. I had done this in order to experience the perverse satisfaction of managing things so that my "internalized mother," which is modeled after my actual mother, would be rejected categorically by my readers. I had done this in order to confirm two false but strongly held convictions, for the rejection served to affirm my own guilt ridden childhood assessment of my mother as a person who had let me down with her vague and unsystematic behavior, and, paradoxically, to bring about the sacrifice of my own achievements to this massive guilt.

My mother, while she was living, both competed with me in my academic life and lived through me. An intelligent and intuitive woman of unfulfilled promise, she had been considered a prodigy in her early life. As the third of her four children and the one most like her and the one who had the stormiest relationship I, too, managed to win highest honors and awards as a child. In this environment it was necessary to compete, although the competition carried within it grave penalties. In the case of my exams, I managed to engineer a serious rejection in order to prevent any surpassing of my mother's achievements, even though I know and have been told that I possess the necessary intellectual equipment and the intelligence to produce good work.

4. Late in his life Dostoevsky described his duality in a letter to a woman artist who had written him about her own related experience:

But now to what you *have* told me of your inward duality. That trait is indeed common to all . . . that is, all who are not wholly commonplace. Nay, it is common to human nature, though it does not evince itself so strongly in all as it does in you. It is precisely on this ground that I cannot but regard you as a twin soul, for your inward duality corresponds most exactly to my own. It causes at once great torment, and great delight. Such duality simply means that you have a strong sense of yourself, much aptness for self-criticism, and an innate feeling for your moral duty to yourself and all mankind. If your intelligence were less developed, if you were more limited, you would be less sensitive, and would not possess that duality. Rather the reverse: in its stead would have appeared great arrogance. Yet such duality is a great torment. . . . There is but one cure, one refuge, for that woe: art, creative activity. (Dostoevsky, *Letters* [1961, 249])

SOURCES FOR QUOTATIONS

p. 4 "The true artist," Gide (1961, 50–51).

p. 5 "Therapy which resists," Iris Murdoch quoted in Skura (1981, 65).

p. 5 "It is not," Skura (1981, 4).

p. 9 "Dostoevsky . . . creates not," Bakhtin (1984, 6).

p. 11 "My nervous irritability," *Letters* (1961, 50).

Chapter 2

NOTES

1. Like a number of psychoanalytic concepts, unconscious reenactment occurs at various points in Freud, though there is no specific work given over to it. It is what transference, the heart of clinical psychoanalysis, is, after all, and thus underlies the clinical work of many later analysts. Some specific discussions of concept can be found in George Klein (1976); Schafer (1976); and Stolorow, Brandchaft, and Atwood (1987).

SOURCES FOR QUOTATIONS

p. 17 "There is an urge," *The Diary of a Writer*, 35.

Chapter 3

NOTES

1. Critical interpretations of *Crime and Punishment* from a variety of perspectives can be found in the collections edited by Gibian (1964); Jackson (1974); Wasiolek (1961); and Wellek (1962). For additional readings, see the biographies and the books by Peace (1971) and Wasiolek (1964).

Freud's 1928 (1961a) essay is the starting place for psychoanalytic interpretations of Dostoevsky though it does not deal with this novel. Kanzer (1948), was apparently the first to stress the role of matricidal impulses, thus breaking the hold of Freud's essay, with its focus on parracide. Snodgrass (1960), a literary critic without an acknowledged psychoanalytic orientation, describes the patterning of relations between Raskolnikov, his mother, and other mother figures in the novel, all revolving around indirect aggression and guilt. However, when he attempts to explain the motivation for this pattern, he returns to moral-philosophical concepts.

Wasiolek (1974) reviews and criticizes Snodgrass's article and presents his own, openly psychoanalytic, interpretation of Raskolnikov's motives. The essay contains many keen insights. He describes the interrelated patterns of hidden aggression and guilt, of sadistic attack and masochistic suffering that characterize the relations of Raskolnikov, his mother and sister, and the various related characters. Unfortunately, when Wasiolek tries to account for why Raskolnikov hates his mother and attacks her and himself, he postulates forbidden sexual wishes.

Just as Wasiolek corrects and expands Snodgrass, so Kiremidjian (1976) —again from an explicitly psychoanalytic point of view—does to Wasiolek. Kiremidjian's is by far the most complete and sensitive psychoanalytic interpretation of the novel. He locates Raskolnikov's rage at the mother in the preoedipal phase and relates it to maternal deprivation. He picks up the hostile interactions around debt and indebtedness, and accurately delineates the various subplots and characters. His account wavers toward the end; he is stuck with certain outmoded aspects of the psychoanalytic theory of sexual identity and the role of the father. And he mistakenly takes Freud's position with regard to Dostoevsky the person, expecting the great creative writer to manage a "normal" middle-class life. Kiremidjian shows how far one can go, working from psychoanalytic theory alone, without reference to clinical observations.

Rosenthal (1981) presents an interpretation of *Crime and Punishment* that coincides at a number of points with mine, at the level of description. We differ when it comes to theory; he relies heavily on the views of Melanie Klein and Bion.

2. No one has improved on Freud's original description of masochistic aggression in "Mourning and Melancholia":

> The self tormenting in melancholia, which is without doubt enjoyable, signifies . . . a satisfaction of trends of sadism and hate which relate to an object, and which have been turned round upon the subject's own self. . . . The patients usually succeed, by the circuitous path of self-punishment, in taking revenge on the original object and in tormenting their loved one through their illness, having resorted to it in order to avoid the need to express their hostility to him openly. After all, the person who has occasioned the patient's emotional disorder, and on whom his illness is centered, is usually to be found in his immediate environment. (Freud 1957, 251)

3. Raskolnikov's reaction to his mother is a version of narcissistic rage (see Kohut 1972; 1977, especially 90–92 and 120–25). The rage displayed by persons like this is aroused when a current event evokes an early experience of empathic failure by the mother. In analysis we see this in the transference when we misinterpret or are not in tune with the patient and he reacts to us "as a nonempathic attacker on the integrity of the self" (Kohut, 1977, 91).

Narcissistic rage is primitive and frightening; it easily flips over into guilt, and its expression in analysis—in contrast to the venting of anger by less-disturbed patients—gives no relief. Quite the contrary, it can threaten

the whole analysis. Why is this so? The basic integrity of the self develops in an understanding and empathic relationship with the mother, and serious failures of empathy constitute a threat to the person's very sense of existence. Narcissistic rage is like the anger of a cornered animal who is fighting for its life. In the novel, we see the repeated empathic failures of Raskolnikov's mother; she is unable to confirm his experience of himself. This is the stimulus, in their relationship as adults, for rage and guilt that are too dangerous to direct at the mother herself. We also see flareups of Raskolnikov's rage at Porfiry and others who challenge his grandiosity or prick his image of himself.

4. I am using the term *perversion* in its technical or clinical sense, where it refers to an acted- or lived-out version of a specific unconscious conflict. The best account of this sort of unconscious pattern is Robert Stoller's *Perversion: The Erotic Form of Hatred* (1975). See, also, his *Sexual Excitement: Dynamics of Erotic Life* (1979).

SOURCES FOR QUOTATIONS

p. 21 "As he came," *Crime and Punishment*, 13–14.

p. 22 "Outside the heat," *Crime and Punishment*, 14.

p. 22 "Somehow, and even," *Crime and Punishment*, 15.

p. 24 "She was quite," *Crime and Punishment*, 229–30.

p. 26 "When I am," *Crime and Punishment*, 24.

p. 26 "Well, then, so," *Crime and Punishment*, 24–25.

p. 27 "Suddenly she seized," *Crime and Punishment*, 36.

p. 29 "My dear Rodia," *Crime and Punishment*, 40.

p. 30 "In general quite," *Crime and Punishment*, 44.

p. 30 "An honorable girl," *Crime and Punishment*, 45.

p. 30 "Love her as," *Crime and Punishment*, 47.

p. 30 "She's a proud," *Crime and Punishment*, 231.

p. 30 "He felt it," *Crime and Punishment*, 48.

p. 31 " 'God,' he exclaimed," *Crime and Punishment*, 67.

p. 33 "Damn it all," *Crime and Punishment*, 114–15.

p. 33 "What are you," *Crime and Punishment*, 156.

p. 35 "He did not," *Crime and Punishment*, 195.

p. 35 "Yet he stood," *Crime and Punishment*, 196.

p. 35 "Don't torment me," *Crime and Punishment*, 197.

p. 36 "And how well" *Crime and Punishment*, 224.

p. 36 "Enough, Rodia," *Crime and Punishment*, 226.

p. 37 "I have a," *Crime and Punishment*, 239.

p. 37 "Enough! It's time!" *Crime and Punishment*, 421.

p. 38 "I may be," *Crime and Punishment*, 494.

p. 38 "No matter what," *Crime and Punishment*, 494.

p. 38 "Rodia, what's wrong," *Crime and Punishment*, 495.

p. 38 "Enough, Mama dear," *Crime and Punishment,* 497.

p. 38 "After an alarming," *Crime and Punishment,* 518.

p. 39 "You thought yourself," *Crime and Punishment,* 262.

p. 40 "No, such people," *Crime and Punishment,* 271–72.

p. 41 "Not just that," *Crime and Punishment,* 332.

p 42 "He suddenly felt," *Crime and Punishment,* 325.

p. 42 "Strange, though," *Crime and Punishment,* 275.

p. 43 "Why was it," *Crime and Punishment,* 282–83.

p. 43 "When I said," *Crime and Punishment,* 285.

p. 43 "Svidrigailov knows mysterious," *The Notebooks for "Crime and Punishment,"* 198.

p. 44 "It was either," *Crime and Punishment,* 447.

p. 45 "Terribly chaste," *Crime and Punishment,* 458.

p. 45 "An unopened bud," *Crime and Punishment,* 462.

p. 47 "I love you," *Crime and Punishment,* 475.

p. 47 "Let me go," *Crime and Punishment,* 478–9.

p. 48 "Only fourteen, but," *Crime and Punishment,* 488.

p. 48 "She was laughing," *Crime and Punishment,* 491.

p. 49 "His clothes were," *Crime and Punishment,* 493.

p. 50 "He saw a," *Crime and Punishment,* 234–35.

p. 50 "Although she was," *Crime and Punishment,* 237.

p. 51 "A kind of," *Crime and Punishment,* 311.

p. 51 "Haven't you done," *Crime and Punishment,* 322.

p. 52 "Have to tell," *Crime and Punishment,* 394.

p. 52 "Why do you," *Crime and Punishment,* 396.

p. 52 "I must be," *Crime and Punishment,* 398.

p. 53 "Enough, Sonia!" *Crime and Punishment,* 339–40.

p. 53 "You're in pain," *Crime and Punishment,* 402.

p. 54 "Do I love," *Crime and Punishment,* 504.

p. 55 "Tears came," *Crime and Punishment,* 527–28.

Chapter 4

NOTES

1. For a discussion of the meaning of names in *Crime and Punishment* see Monas's introduction to the novel. Passage (1982) presents a thorough survey of the meaning of the names in all of Dostoevsky's fiction.

Notes and Sources for Quotations

SOURCES FOR QUOTATIONS

p. 58 "Often recalled his,"
Grossman (1975, 10).

p. 58 "I am so," Dostoevsky in a
letter to his mother quoted in
Coulson (1962, 4).

p. 59 "Mysterious illness," Andrey
Dostoevsky's *Reminiscences*
quoted in Frank (1976, 69).

p. 62 *"First Part: Beginning," The
Notebooks for "Crime and
Punishment,"* 64–65.

Chapter 5

NOTES

1. Andrey Dostoevsky wrote down his *Reminiscences* in 1875. He put them in their final form in 1895–96, though they were not published until 1930. They have not been published in English. I have had a translation prepared by Karen Makoff; quotations are taken from this translation, supplemented by passages from the biographies.

2. For some specific cases in which fantasies of killing the baby and the mother are present, and then lead to guilt and masochism, see Kolansky (1960) and Breger (1980). Stolorow and Atwood (1979) present an interesting discussion of a pattern such as this in Freud's own life. They describe the jealousy and death wishes stimulated by the birth of his brother Julius and how this turned to guilt when the brother died some eight months later. As they note: "In addition to stimulating jealousy and resentment at the intruder, the arrival of a younger sibling would also be experienced as a betrayal by the mother and therefore as an infuriating disappointment in her (Stolorow and Atwood 1979, 50). They go on to show how this threatening infantile rage is split: much as in Dostoevsky's case, the mother was idealized and an alternate mother figure—an old nurse—became the recipient of the hatred.

3. As is often the case, Dostoevsky's intentions are more starkly revealed in his earlier drafts. In his notebooks, Lizeveta's pregnancy is emphasized; in fact, she is depicted as pregnant at the time Raskolnikov kills her, so that the unborn child also falls victim to his rage:

> Every mischief-maker has fun with her. But the infant they found was his. . . .
> What baby?
> But don't you know? They performed a Caesarean on her. She was six month's pregnant. A boy, born dead. (*The Notebooks for "Crime and Punishment,"* 96)

In a later section, crossed out, we find: "The old woman beat her when she was pregnant. I saw it myself. Pregnant, pregnant, sixth" (*The Notebooks for "Crime and Punishment,"* 165). These images capture the young Fedya's rage at his pregnant mother *and* at the baby who will once again replace him in her affections.

4. The English philosopher John Stuart Mill—a true genius who mastered Latin and Greek before he was five—always felt himself to be intellectually inferior due to the criticism levied at him by his teacher/father. The elder Mill, like Dr. Dostoevsky, a self-made man of great drive and insecurity, conscripted his child to his own ambitions in a similar manner (see Mazlish 1974).

5. Frank (1976, 85–91), citing recently uncovered evidence, argues that Dr. Dostoevsky was probably not murdered, though, in his view, Feodor and the other relatives believed that he was. In the most recent and extensive development of this position, Kjetsaa (1987, 29–34), reviews court and medical reports and argues that the father was not murdered *and* that Feodor believed he died of natural causes. (The story of the murder rests on the reports of Dostoevsky's brother Andrey, his daughter Liubov, and later tales told by the village peasants.) Kjetsaa's account seems driven by his need to descredit Freud's theory and to present a normalized picture of the novelist and his father—"Far from hating his father, Doestoyevsky clearly admired him greatly. There is no reason to believe he did not mourn deeply upon hearing of his father's death" (36). This argument rests on a number of assumptions about what people "must have" believed or could or couldn't have done in a Russian village almost 150 years ago. My own reading of the evidence leads me to think that it is impossible to establish what actually happened to the father; no one cites any first-hand witnesses. On the other hand, it seems likely that Feodor and his siblings believed that their father was murdered. And, what seems to me beyond question, is Dostoevsky's own intense ambivalence. When Ivan Karamazov exclaims, "Who has not wished for his father's death?" he is speaking for the author, despite Kejtsaa's attempt to prove otherwise.

6. John Gedo (1983) notes the need of certain creative artists for a "secret sharer"—a close friend or brother figure—who serves as another part of the artist's self. The novelist Joseph Conrad, who coined the term, used Ford Maddox Ford in this way; for the painter Vincent Van Gogh it was his brother Theo. Mikhail served in this capacity for Feodor, but he seems to have been relatively easily replaced by other brother figures after his death.

SOURCES FOR QUOTATIONS

p. 73 "I used to," *Winter Notes*, 36.

p. 77 "Dear Mama," Dostoevsky in a letter to his mother, Coulson (1962, 3).

p. 83 "The despised priestly," Frank (1976, 9).

p. 85 "Self-righteous and," Frank (1976, 17).

p. 86 "My Dear Good," Dostoevsky to his father at age seventeen, *Letters* (1961, 1).

p. 89 "Our poor father's," Dostoevsky to his brother Mikhail, *Letters* (1961, 6).

Chapter 6

SOURCES FOR QUOTATIONS

p. 96 "We were taken," Dostoevsky quoted in Frank (1976, 76).

p. 96 "Children of thirteen," quoted in Frank (1976, 76).

p. 97 "His uniform hung," quoted in Frank (1976, 77).

p. 97 "Already then," quoted in Frank (1976), 77.

p. 97 "I don't know," Dostoevsky to his brother Mikhail, *Letters* (1961, 3).

p. 99 "The failure would," Dostoevsky to his brother Mikhail, *Letters* (1961, 6).

p. 99 "I shed many," Dostoevsky to his brother Mikhail, quoted in Grossman (1975, 41).

p. 100 "Like the heart," Dostoevsky quoted in Frank (1976, 90–91; and Yarmolinsky 1971, 33).

p. 102 "The Minnas, Claras," Dostoevsky to his brother Mikhail, *Letters* (1961, 32).

p. 103 "Everywhere and in," Dostoevsky quoted in Grossman (1975, 49).

p. 104 "In some dark," Dostoevsky quoted in Grossman (1975, 51).

p. 105 "That I alone," *Poor Folk*, 25.

Chapter 7

NOTES

1. The "splitting" of the personality in *The Double* does not resemble the more popularly known cases of "split" or multiple personality; nor is it schizophrenia. The specific experience in which there is an encounter with a visual hallucination of oneself is found in the relatively rare autoscopic phenomenon. It is frequently, though not always, associated with brain injury or temporal-lobe epilepsy—the condition from which Dostoevsky himself suffered later in his life—making it likely that the novelist had a firsthand acquaintance with the phenomenon. See Lukianowicz (1958) for a discussion of the autoscopic phenomenon. Kohlberg (1963) and Meissner (1977) both discuss it in relation to Dostoevsky's novel. It should be clear that,

whatever the complex origins of the phenomenon are, they do not explain its specific meaning—a point on which Kohlberg is clear.

Otto Rank's 1914 *The Double: A Psychoanalytic Study* (Rank 1971). while outmoded in several ways, is still worth reading.

2. The reader, especially if he is familiar with psychoanalytic literary studies, may wonder if the "identity" conflict I have just described is a severe enough matter to explain the anxiety, paranoia, and near-psychotic experience that Dostoevsky gave to Golyadkin and, in another form, that made up his own "nervous crisis." Shouldn't there be something deeper? Guilt over murder of the father? Unconscious homosexual impulses? Castration anxiety, at least? I think not, and the reasons why may again clarify the difference between the present approach with its attempt to stay close to the data—both literary and clinical—and the approaches of some others in applied psychoanalysis. First, these other sorts of explanations rest more on theory than direct observation. For example, theory has it that conflict over latent homosexual impulses underlies paranoia or that the death of the father—especially his murder—arouses powerful guilt over parricidal impulses. And different psychoanalytic readers have posited these as central to Dostoevsky: Dalton in her 1979 book on *The Idiot* and Freud himself in his well-known essay. One can find support for these interpretations in the fiction; it is so vast and multifaceted that it can support a great variety of interpretations. The test must be in terms of central and persistent (repetitive) themes and symbols. And when this test is applied, to both the novels and the life, conflicts with the father of the oedipal variety, along with castration anxiety, are seen to play only a very small part, and homosexual anxiety almost none at all.

The second source of support for an identity explanation comes from contemporary clinical experience. Psychoanalysts from a variety of backgrounds increasingly recognize the centrality of the self, its integrity (cohesiveness), the anxiety aroused by threats to the self, and the defensive efforts and symptoms that are marshaled in response to such threats. It would take far too much space to review all this work here, let me just state that it amounts to a major shift in psychoanalytic theory, from the older, orthodox "id psychology," which placed the Oedipus complex at the center of unconscious conflict, to an "ego," "self," or "identity" psychology. The major names associated with the new view are Erikson, Fairbairn, Winnicott, and others of the British object-relations school and Kohut and his followers. What these various analysts show is that one's central sense of security comes from a stable and viable self and that threats to this self are, indeed, a matter of life and death. Dostoevsky as psychoanalyst is, once again, a forerunner of these theories.

Notes and Sources for Quotations

SOURCES FOR QUOTATIONS

p. 108 "Well, brother, I," Dostoevsky to his brother Mikhail, *Letters* (1961, 30).

p. 108 "It opened the," Frank (1976, 160).

p. 108 "A whole crowd," Dostoevsky to his brother Mikhail, *Letters* (1961, 37–38).

p. 109 "Sometimes a nameless" Dostoevsky to his brother Mikhail, *Letters* (1961, 44).

p. 109 "It was evident" Madame Panaeva quoted in Frank (1976, 162–63).

p. 110 "White as a," Madame Panaeva quoted in Frank (1976, 164).

p. 110 "Goldyadkin is a," Dostoevsky to his brother Mikhail, *Letters* (1961, 26–27).

p. 111 "The power, depth," Belinsky quoted in Frank (1976, 177).

p. 112 "Two years before," Dostoevsky to his friend Solovyev, quoted in Frank (1976, 167).

p. 116 "Brother, I am," Dostoevsky to his brother Mikhail, Frank (1976, 199).

p. 116 "I was for," Dostoevsky to his brother Mikhail, *Letters* (1961, 37).

p. 116 "It is indeed true," Dostoevsky to his brother Mikhail, *Letters. (1961, 43).*

p. 117 "When a man," Dostoevsky quoted in Frank (1976, 232).

p. 119 "Extremely withdrawn, cautious," Grossman (1975, 73).

p. 120 "Mr. Golyadkin, seeing," *The Double*, 132.

p. 120 "I was saying," *The Double*, 136–37.

p. 121 "Everything was stillness," *The Double*, 160.

p. 121 "If some casual," *The Double*, 166.

p. 121 "He began to," *The Double*, 167.

p. 122 "Anton Antonovich, I," *The Double*, 179.

p. 123 "Noble, frank and," *The Double*, 254.

p. 123 "It's like this," *The Double*, 269.

Chapter 8

NOTES

1. Some time after completing my analysis of Stavrogin I came upon an article (Pope and Turner, in press) that presents a perceptive psychoanalytic interpretation of his character that is consistent, in almost every respect, with mine. I draw on this source here, particularly for the material on Madame Stavrogin.

p. 127 *"Just exactly the,"* Dr. Yanovsky quoted in Rice (1985, 36).

p. 128 "I have taken," Dostoevsky to
Dr. Yanovsky, quoted in
Frank (1976, 269–70) and
Grossman (1975, 123).

p. 130 "Dostoevsky's testimony is,"
Grossman (1975, 142).

p. 135 "The way a," *The Possessed,*
419–21.

p. 136 "I neither," *The Possessed,*
426.

p. 136 "The boy knew," *The Possessed,* 41.

p. 136 "Her great love," *The Possessed,* 45.

p. 137 "Had become," *The Possessed,* 17.

Chapter 9

NOTES

1. This is the place for a consideration of Joseph Frank's argument that
   Dostoevsky underwent a far-reaching "conversion" experience in prison
   (see Frank 1983, 113–27.) There was a popular view that Dostoevsky was
   a radical or revolutionary before his arrest and that the years in prison
   changed him into a believing Christian. Frank presents convincing evidence
   to oppose this idea. Dostoevsky was neither an atheist nor a revolutionary
   before his arrest and his religious beliefs remained ambivalent and idiosyncratic to the end of his life. Yet, while his book contains much material to
   support this picture, Frank, paradoxically, attempts to make his own case
   for Dostoevsky's "conversion" in prison. Let us look at the way his argument both overlaps and contrasts with the interpretation developed here.
   Frank's argument may be summarized as follows: Dostoevsky underwent
   a "conversion experience" at a specific point during his imprisonment. He
   was under great stress, particularly a heavy burden of guilt, and had an
   illumination in which his beliefs underwent a transformation. It was not,
   significantly, a shift from atheism to Christianity but centered on his feelings
   toward the Russian people. He was, initially, filled with hatred for his fellow
   convicts—this, according to Frank, is the prime source of his guilt—and, in
   the *Peasant Marey* episode, shifted over to view them and the Russian
   people more broadly, as the embodiments of Christian virtue. Frank supports this theory of conversion by appeal to William James and Pavlov—a
   strange pair of bedfellows!—his only contemporary reference is to Sargeant
   (1971). He is apparently unfamiliar with the large recent literature in this
   area; see Bromley and Richardson (1983), Galanter (1982), Levine (1984),
   and Lifton (1961) for overviews.
   Frank's argument has several of the elements of a convincing interpreta-

tion yet it falls short due to a persistent tendency to normalize Dostoevsky, to see him as motivated primarily by intellectual and ideological concerns, to downplay his emotional, unconsciously driven nature. Dostoevsky's central conflict in prison did arise from exposure to his own hatred; he dealt with this both by attempts to project it into the other convicts and, at other times, by trying to idealize them as loving Mareys. The evidence is not convincing that the shift from hatred to idealization occurred in a single conversion experience. Dostoevsky himself—as Frank notes—does not mention such a conversion, either in *The House of the Dead,* or elsewhere. He does, in a letter of Mikhail, speak of "a regeneration of my convictions" (*Letters,* 1961, 62), but this is the sort of thing he was always experiencing throughout his life. Indeed, as the examination of his life and novels in the years after imprisonment amply demonstrates, he continued to struggle with this conflict. Seeing the prison years and *The Peasant Marey* as part of this continuing pattern obviates the need for the cumbersome structure that Frank erects to support his conversion theory: "brainwashing"; though there was no brainwasher; epileptic seizures as self-induced electric-shock therapy, and so on.

Frank is correct in seeing Dostoevsky's guilt as arising from rage and hatred; he is also correct in refuting Freud's view that the guilt was based on parricidal impulses. But he is wrong in asserting that Freud's is "the only serious alternative explanation" (Frank 1983, 125). He has all the ingredients for an alternative explanation in his own account but is stuck at the surface. What he does is akin to tracing day residues into the manifest content of a dream; it is not wrong, just incomplete. Bringing in the additional sources of Dostoevsky's hatred, guilt, and attempts to idealize the motherly Marey fills out the latent content by relating these feelings to the central elements in the novelist's life. It is significant that Frank makes no mention of the role of mother or women in his account of the conversion.

A person who has undergone a conversion, whether religious or political, becomes a true believer; he embraces, wholeheartedly, a new set of beliefs. It is the certainty with which such beliefs are grasped that settles doubts, alleviates guilt, and provides security. Dostoevsky never became a dogmatic believer, as his correspondence and notebooks and, even more, his novels show, he *wished* to believe, he *tried* to idealize—Christ, the Russian people, and women—but his awareness of himself and others always made this a goal beyond reach. His life is a *process,* a struggle between belief and skepticism, love and rage, idealism and cynicism.

SOURCES FOR QUOTATIONS

p. 144 "To be alone," Dostoevsky to Madame Fonvizina, *Letters* (1961, 72).

p. 144 "Believe me, there," Dostoevsky to his brother Mikhail, *Letters* (1961, 65).

p. 144 "They are rough," Dostoevsky to his brother Mikhail, *Letters* (1961, 59–60).

p. 145 "The character of," report of naval cadets imprisoned with Dostoevsky, *Letters* (1961, 283, 285).

p. 146 "Shut in my," Dostoevsky quoted in Hingley (1978, 81).

p. 146 "Still the eternal," Dostoevsky to his brother Mikhail, *Letters* (1961, 62).

p. 147 "The most unbearable," Dostoevsky to Madame Fonvizina, *Letters* (1961, 70).

p. 147 "I want to," Dostoevsky to Madame Fonvizina, *Letters*. (1961, 70–71).

p. 149 "All this had," *The Diary of a Writer*, 206.

p. 149 "In passing I," *The Diary of a Writer*, 207–10.

p. 153 "I can heartily," Freud quoted in E. Jones (1953–57, 226).

p. 154 "Even then one," Wrangel quoted in *Letters* (1961, 300).

p. 155 "If you only," Dostoevsky to Maria Isaeva, *Letters* (1961, 74–75).

p. 156 "On my knees," Dostoevsky quoted in Grossman (1975, 204).

p. 156 "What if he," Dostoevsky quoted in Grossman (1975, 207).

p. 156 "My relations with," Dostoevsky quoted in Hingley (1978, 85).

p. 157 "He [Dostoevsky] told," Wrangel quoted in *Letters* (1961, 299–300).

p. 157 "Resembled epilepsy and," Dostoevsky quoted in Yarmolinsky (1971, 125).

p. 158 "Either she had," Yarmolinsky (1971, 141).

Chapter 10

NOTES

1. Polina Suslova left a diary recounting her time with Dostoevsky and also wrote a short story based directly on their affair ("The Stranger and Her Lover"). This detailed record is invaluable though we must remember that it only presents her side of things. All of this material, along with related letters and the novel, are collected in the volume of *The Gambler* edited by Wasiolek.

2. Freud's 1928 essay (Freud 1961a) contains valuable insights about gambling in general though he is mistaken in crucial ways about Dostoevsky, in particular. The compulsive gambler does not play to win but for other, unconscious, motives. Prominent among these is psychic masochism: the need to lose as punishment for a sense of guilt. Freud situates this guilt in the Oedipus complex: Dostoevsky's parricidal wish, fulfilled in reality with the murder of his father. Freud also interprets the gambling itself—the "play" or "action"—as a disguised form of masturbation, a further source

of guilt. While later studies give support to oedipal-sexual motives in some compulsive gamblers, these are by no means the only nor the main sources of guilt. Symbolic masturbation finds little support as an explanation in the contemporary literature.

Freud's essay was the point of origin for psychoanalytic interpretations, which have grown in complexity; contemporary views also rest on a wider observational base. Rosenthal (1987) presents an excellent review of the psychoanalytic literature on gambling from Freud to the present. As he notes:

> Gambling is a complex activity. The gambling ritual—including the stages of anticipation, playing, and outcome, followed by either triumph or remorse—is an acting out of a meaningful fantasy, in which someone is doing something to someone else. There are rewards and punishments, with specific meanings, both conscious and unconscious, assigned to winning and losing. (41).

A range of different meanings can be expressed through gambling enactments. In addition to psychic masochism and self-punishment Rosenthal states,

> Gambling serves multiple defensive functions. There is an illusion of power and control as a way of defending against depression and loss;; uncertainty, helplessness and fragmentation; the inevitability of death; being overwhelmed by the uncontrollable. It may be utilized as a method of self-cure in the struggle to maintain a precarious sense of identity. (67).

Rosenthal presents a careful critical reading of Freud's essay and an analysis of Dostoevsky's gambling that is closely aligned with the present interpretation. He argues, as I do, that Dostoevsky's guilt and need to punish himself were aroused, primarily, by the death of his first wife which echoed the death of his mother. He notes that murderous impulses in the novels are directed, for the most part, at women, particularly mother figures.

Additional general accounts of pathological gambling can be found in Bergler's 1957 book; Bergler is good at description though his work is somewhat popularized. Other general reviews include Bolen and Boyd 1968 and Rabow el al. 1984.

SOURCES FOR QUOTATIONS

p. 160 "He suggested that," Suslova diary, in *The Gambler*, 207.

p. 166 "The Parisian absolutely," *Winter Notes*, 104–5.

p. 166 "I was annoyed," *Winter Notes*, 38.

p. 166 "The smug and," *Winter Notes*, 76.

p. 168 "Our love affairs," Wrangel quoted in *Letters*. (1961, 318).

p. 168 "She took care," Wrangel quoted in Grossman (1975, 187).

p. 168 "All kinds of," Strakhov quoted in Yarmolinsky (1971, 162).

p. 169 "I tell you," Dostoevsky to A. I. Schubert, Coulson (1962, 105).

p. 170 "Your love descended," Suslova's paraphrase of Dostoevsky, quoted in Grossman (1975, 277).

p. 170 "I gave myself," Suslova quoted in Grossman (1975, 277).

p. 170 "Beautiful, even grandiose," Suslova diary in The Gambler, 364.

p. 171 "You behaved like," Suslova diary, in The Gambler, 364–65.

p. 171 "Because he did," Suslova quoted in Frank (1986, 257–58).

p. 171 "People talk to," Suslova quoted in Grossman (1975, 278–79).

p. 172 "I thought you," Suslova diary, in The Gambler, 205–6.

p. 172 "He fell at," Suslova diary, in The Gambler, 206.

p. 173 "I would not," Suslova diary, in The Gambler, 211.

p. 173 "While we were," Suslova diary, in The Gambler, 215.

p. 173 "I don't understand," Mikhail Dostoevsky quoted in Mochulsky (1967, 237).

p. 174 "He said, looking," Suslova diary, in The Gambler, 217.

p. 175 "Apollinaria is a," Dostoevsky to N. Suslova, in The Gambler, 342–44.

p. 176 "To seek happiness," Dostoevsky to his brother Mikhail, Frank (1986, 261).

p. 177 "The fact is," Dostoevsky to his sister-in-law V. D. Constant, Coulson (1962, 113–14).

p. 177 "Dear friend and," Dostoevsky to his sister-in-law V. D. Constant, Coulson (1962, 116).

p. 178 "Forgive me, my," Dostoevsky to Anna, in The Gambler, 360–61.

p. 179 "Ania dear," Dostoevsky to Anna, in The Gambler, 362.

Chapter 11

NOTES

1. The concepts of manifest content (the dream as dreamt), day residue, and latent meaning remain central to psychoanalytic dream interpretation. Freud's elaboration of these ideas in The Interpretation of Dreams is the essential text, but I should clarify my usage of these terms, a usage consistent with a contemporary psychoanalytic approach to dreams (see chap. 1, n. 1).

Day residues are all those bits and pieces from the preceding day—people, scenes, feelings, and memories—that go into the construction of the night's dreams. Contemporary psychoanalysts assign a wider significance to day residues than did Freud, seeing them as the emotionally significant events from the preceding day that both set unconscious currents in motion and participate in the representation of these currents. That is, material is selected from the day's experience because of its connection with persisting unconscious patterns and it is these patterns that comprise the unconscious or latent meaning of a person's life. It is the task of interpretation—of dreams, transference, and literature—to illuminate such patterns.

A dream is dreamt in a single night, a novel written over a period of months or years. So, clearly, the concept of day residue must be broadened when applied to literature. Here, I will use the concept to refer to the emotionally significant events from the period of Dostoevsky's life concurrent with the writing of a novel. Memories from earlier periods in his life, connected with these current concerns, can also be considered a part of the residue material. Branching out from these residues are memories that reach back into childhood. The latent meaning consists of the themes and organizing principles that are common to all this material, themes that are brought forth in the novels themselves.

2. Almost all the biographers and critics agree that *Notes from Underground* is the prelude to the great novels of Dostoevsky's mature years. The following is typical:

> *Notes from the Underground* is the great prologue to the major novels that follow. ... In it Dostoevsky first touches on the great themes of free will, the rational organization of human happiness, and the value of suffering. It is great because Dostoevsky's psychology, metaphysic, and craft first take mature form in it. The psychology which he uncertainly discerns in *The Double,* which he pursues erratically in the forties, which life confirms in prison, and which the threat of the radical critics raises to a philosophical level, finds its mature metaphysic in *Notes from Underground.* (Wasiolek 1964, 53)

These critics also see the novel in political and social terms. Frank's is probably the most extreme argument that the novel be seen exclusively in this way:

> Critics are ready to expatiate at the drop of a hat—amid an increasingly suffocating smokescreen of erudite irrelevancies and melodramatic psycho-profundities—on the vast "cultural significance" of *Notes from Underground.* Meanwhile the real point of Dostoevsky's fascinating little work has gotten completely lost in the shuffle. (1961, 2)

"The real point," according to him, is the novel as a satire of *What Is to Be Done?* "Only if we approach *Notes from Underground* in this way can we understand Dostoevsky's choice of subject-matter and method of organization" (1961, 5).

While based on more data, Frank's interpretation (1986, 310–47) is essentially the same. A similar view is found in Steiner's *Tolstoy or Dostoevsky* (1959). Somewhat more balanced interpretations can be found in Peace (1971, 5–6); Simmons (1950, 105); and Wasiolek (1964, 42–56) and in the biographies by Grossman (1975, 310–17); Hingley (1978, 101–

3); and Mochulsky (1967, 242–61). None of these authors offer a psychological interpretation, nor do they connect the themes of the novel to parallel unconscious patterns in Dostoevsky's life.

3. A more precise translation of the Russian word, typically rendered as *underground*, is *beneath the floor* or *under the floorboards*. It refers to the space in traditional Russian houses where food was stored and, sometimes, fugitives hidden. It is the space where mice breed. These associations converge both on the Underground Man's antisocial stance and his sense of himself as a mouse.

SOURCES FOR QUOTATIONS

p. 181 "In my impatience," *Notes from Underground*, 84.

p. 184 "To prove," Dostoevsky's private journal (1973–76, 96).

p. 187 "She loved me," Dostoevsky quoted in Grossman (1975, 318).

p. 187 "Maria Dmitriyevna has," Dostoevsky quoted in Mochulsky (1967, 242).

p. 187 "My wife is," Dostoevsky quoted in Mochulsky (1967, 243).

p. 188 "April 16." Dostoevsky's private journal (1973–76, 39).

p. 188 "Meanwhile, after," Dostoevsky's private journal (1973–76, 40).

p. 189 "And so, on," Dostoevsky quoted in Grossman (1975, 318).

p. 193 "I am a sick," *Notes from Underground*, 15.

p. 194 "I was lying," *Notes from Underground*, 16.

p. 195 "Not only couldn't," *Notes from Underground*, 16.

p. 195 "Why is it," *Notes from Underground*, 17–18.

p. 196 "Despair can hold," *Notes from Underground*, 19.

p. 196 "A highly conscious," *Notes from Underground*, 21.

p. 197 "These gentlemen, although," *Notes from Underground*, 23.

p. 198 "In every man's," *Notes from Underground*, 45–46.

p. 199 "I did a lot," *Notes from Underground*, 51.

p. 199 "I would suddenly," *Notes from Underground*, 51–2.

p. 200 "Suddenly, three paces," *Notes from Underground*, 58.

p. 201 "But I had," *Notes from Underground*, 58–60.

p. 201 "When my dreams," *Notes from Underground*, 61.

p. 202 "Smiling scornfully, I," *Notes from Underground*, 78–79.

p. 202 "So here it," *Notes from Underground*, 81.

p. 203 "Anger and misery," *Notes from Underground*, 86.

p. 203 "They were carrying," *Notes from Underground*, 87–88.

p. 204 "It is heavenly," *Notes from Underground*, 94–95.

p. 204 "Pictures, you have," *Notes from Underground*, 95.

p. 204 "Somehow you," *Notes from Underground*, 95.

p. 204 "Die soon of," *Notes from Underground*, 99–100.

p. 205 "Never, never had," *Notes from Underground*, 100–101.

p. 205 "The thought that," *Notes from Underground*, 105.

p. 206 "One moment out," *Notes from Underground*, 106.

p. 206 "A lot of," *Notes from Underground*, 107.

p. 206 "Enter now then," *Notes from Underground*, 112.

p. 206 "She went white," *Notes from Underground*, 115–17.

p. 208 "A different feeling," *Notes from Underground*, 118.

p. 208 "Even now, after," *Notes from Underground*, 122.

p. 208 "We have all," *Notes from Underground*, 122–23.

p. 208 "This is not," *Notes from Underground*, 123.

Chapter 12

NOTES

1. An account of Dostoevsky's courtship of Anna Korvin-Krukovskaya is provided by her younger sister Sofya in her book *A Russian Childhood* (Kovalevskaya 1978). Her account gives a vivid picture of Dostoevsky's character. She herself went on to become a brilliant mathematician while the older sister married a radical Frenchman and later returned to Russia where the couple became friends of the Dostoevskys' in their later years.

2. Almost all Dostoevsky's letters to Anna in the later years make reference to his physical desire for her. In 1879, "I think of my queen and mistress here not only at night, but also during the day—beyond measure, till it drives me crazy. . . . I am burning with desire" (Dostoevsky *Letters*, 1987, 475).

And, in a later letter that same year:

"My rapture and delight are inexhaustible. You may say that this is only the crudest aspect of it. No, it is not crude and, as a matter of fact, all the rest is determined by it. . . . So good-bye, my angel, my golden treasure, my bright and beautiful wife . . . and if I weren't restrained by what you say about censorship of the mail, God knows what I'd write you." (Dostoevsky, *Letters*, 1987, 484)

SOURCES FOR QUOTATIONS

p. 210 "In spite of," Dostoevsky quoted in Grossman (1975, 49).

p. 212 "My father's illness," Anna Dostoevsky (1975, 12).

p. 212 "My father died," Anna Dostoevsky (1975, 12).

p. 212 "Was quick to," Anna Dostoevsky (1975, 14).

p. 213 "My love was," Anna Dostoevsky (1975, 90).

p. 215 "Fyodor Mikhailovich spoke," Anna Dostoevsky (1975, 165–66).

p. 216 "For hours on," Anna Dostoevsky (1975, 55).

p. 217 "I kiss you," Dostoevsky letter to Anna, *Letters* (1930, 270–71).

p. 218 "Despite numberless cares," Anna Dostoevsky (1975, 169).

p. 218 "He would constantly,"

Strakhov, in Anna Dostoevsky (1975, 170).

p. 228 "Stop indulging in." *The Brothers Karamazov*, 50–51.

p. 230 "Ivan Fedorovich is," Dostoevsky quoted in Simmons (1950, 293–94).

Appendix

NOTES

1. Freud revealed his dislike of Dostoevsky in correspondence with his disciple Theodor Reik (see Reik 1975), who raised questions about his interpretation of the novelist. A further critical discussion of Freud's essay is presented by the psychoanalyst Schmidl (1965). See also, Mindess (1967).

2. Several neurologists have examined the evidence bearing on Dostoevsky's epilepsy (Alajouanine, 1963; Gastaut, 1978, 1984; Geschwind, 1984; Voskuil, 1983. See, also, Rice, 1985, for an overview.) There remains some doubt as to the precise nature of the disease; Gastaut concludes that both temporal-lobe and primary generalized epilepsy were present, a distinction without consequence for the present level of discussion. The findings of these scientists, and their general approach to Dostoevsky's epilepsy, supports the present view. Alajouanine, for example, coordinates Dostoevsky's epileptic experiences with aspects of his literature, philosophical, and religious beliefs and speaks of the "good use" that the author made of his disease.

3. Two recent studies document the coincidence of pleasurable auras with the EEG patterns of temporal-lobe epilepsy: Cirignotta, Todesco, and Lugaresi 1980; Naito and Matsui 1988.

4. In her study *Unconscious Structure in "The Idiot"* (1979), Dalton presents a very perceptive analysis of the underlying "epileptic" structure of that novel. She notes how the action moves through phases of diffuse confusion and unclear tension, to scenes where emotion errupts with great intensity. This sequence corresponds to the prodroma-aura-seizure of Myshkin's— and the author's—epilepsy. While she explicitly confines her analysis to the literary text—an unfortunate restriction, in my view—she does note how Dostoevsky's own epilepsy was intensified during work on the novel. She quotes from his correspondence: "I wrote this finale in a state of inspiration, and it cost me two fits in a row" (Dalton 1979, 125).

    Dalton shows a fine appreciation for the novel and her ideas about its epileptic structure are extremely insightful. Unfortunately when she comes to applying psychoanalytic theory she lapses into formulaic reductionism. There is much talk of the primal scene, and all is explained in terms of oedipal dynamics and the castration complex

5. While I have not discussed them here, Dostoevsky suffered from a number of other symptoms and diseases throughout his life, some of which expressed personal meanings and were used in his emotional transactions with others in ways related to his epilepsy. His correspondence with his father during the years at the engineering academy show a virtual duel of guilt-inducing symptoms. His incorporation of his dying mother's tuberculosis has been noted earlier.

Rice presents the most thorough review of Dostoevsky's medical history, including other illnesses along with the epilepsy. His view of the way Dostoevsky mastered symptoms through writing is aligned with mine:

> In every regard Dostevsky's greatness lies not in the denial of illness but in its acceptance and mastery, and in the discovery (and invention, to be sure) of polymorphous and polyphonic values precisely within his pathological condition, which he consciously and ingeniously negotiated through art. (1985, 234)

SOURCES FOR QUOTATIONS

p. 237 "The height of," *The Idiot*, 245–46.

p. 237 "For a few," Dostoevsky quoted in Yarmolinsky (1971, 160).

p. 237 "I was an," Dostoevsky quoted in Yarmolinsky (1971, 161).

p. 239 "You wanted to," Freud (1961a, 232).

p. 239 "It is therefore," Freud (1961a, 227).

p. 242 "In most patients," Glaser (1975, 347).

p. 244 "Severe emotional problems," Glaser (1975, 329).

p. 248 "He [Dostoevsky] was," Strakhov quoted in Yarmolinsky (1971, 160).

p. 249 "That heaven had," Kovalevskaya (1978, 178).

p. 250 "Thinking about this," *The Idiot*, 145.

Bibliography

Alajouanine, T. 1963. Dostoiewski's Epilepsy. *Brain* 86:209–18.

Bakhtin, M. M. 1984. *Problems of Dostoevsky's Poetics.* Ithaca: Cornell University Press. (Originally published in 1929.)

Bear, D., R. Freeman, and M. Greenberg. 1984. Behavioral Alterations in Patients with Temporal Lobe Epilepsy. In: D. Blumer, ed. *Psychiatric Aspects of Epilepsy,* 197–227. Washington, D. C.: American Psychiatric Press.

Bergler, E. 1957. *The Psychology of Gambling.* New York: International Universities Press.

Bolen, D. W., and W. H. Boyd. 1968. Gambling and the Gambler: A Review and Preliminary Findings. *Archives of General Psychiatry* 18:617–30.

Breger, L. 1980. The Manifest Dream and Its Latent Meaning. In J. M. Natterson, ed. *The Dream in Clinical Practice,* 3–27. New York: Aronson.

———. 1981. *Freud's Unfinished Journey: Convential and Critical Perspectives in Psychoanalytic Theory.* London: Routledge and Kegan Paul.

———. 1986. Dostoeyvskii and Medicine. *Slavic Review* 45:735–37.

Breger, L., I. Hunter, and R. W. Lane. 1971. The Effect of Stress on Dreams. *Psychological Issues.* Mono 27. New York: International Universities Press.

Brod, M. 1960. *Franz Kafka.* New York: Schocken.

Bromley, D., and J. Richardson eds. 1983. *The Brainwashing Deprogramming Controversy: Sociological, Psychological, Legal and Historical Perspectives.* New York: Edwin Mellon Press.

Cirignotta, F., C. V. Todesco, and E. Lugaresi. 1980. Temporal Lobe Epilepsy with Ecstatic Seizures (So-Called Dostoevsky Epilepsy). *Epilepsia* 21:705–10.

Chernyshevsky, N. G. 1961. *What Is to Be Done?* New York: Vintage. (Originally published in 1863.)

Coulson, J. 1962. *Dostoevsky: A Self-Portrait.* London: Oxford University Press.

Bibliography

Dalton, E. 1979. *Unconscious Structure in "The Idiot."* Princeton: Princeton University Press.

Dostoevsky, Aimée (Liubov). 1921. *Fyodor Dostoevsky: A Study.* London: Heineman.

Dostoevsky, Andrey M. 1930. *Reminiscences* (published in Russian; unpublished translation prepared by K. Makoff).

Dostoevsky, Anna. 1975. *Dostoevsky: Reminiscences.* New York: Liveright. (Originally published in 1925.)

DOSTOEVSKY, FEODOR.

Fiction

1962. *Poor Folk.* London: Dent. (Originally published in 1846.)

1972. *The Double.* Baltimore: Penguin. (Originally published in 1846.)

1985. *Netochka Nezvanova.* Baltimore: Penguin. (Originally published in 1849.)

1923. *Uncle's Dream.* (Originally published in 1859.) In: *An Honest Thief and Other Stories.* New York: Macmillan, 18–144.

1983. *The Village of Stepanchikovo and Its Inhabitants.* London: Angel Classics. (Originally published in 1859.)

1983. *Memoirs from the House of the Dead.* New York: Oxford University Press. (Originally published in 1860.)

1955. *The Insulted and Injured.* New York: Grove Press. (Originally published in 1861.)

1968. *A Disgraceful Affair.* (Originally published in 1862.) In: *Great Short Works of Dostoevsky.* New York: Harper and Row, 203–60.

1955. *Winter Notes on Summer Impressions.* New York: Criterion Books. (Originally published in 1863.)

1972. *Notes from Underground.* Baltimore: Penguin. (Originally published in 1864.)

1968. *Crime and Punishment.* New York: New American Library. (Originally published in 1866.)

1972. *The Gambler (with Polina Suslova's Diary).* Chicago: University of Chicago Press. (*The Gambler* originally published in 1866.)

1969. *The Idiot.* New York: New American Library. (Originally published in 1868.)

1968. *The Eternal Husband.* (Originally published in 1870.) In: *Great Short Works of Dostoevsky.* New York: Harper and Row.

1962. *The Possessed.* New York: New American Library. (Originally published in 1871.)

1985. *The Diary of a Writer.* Salt Lake City: Peregine Smith Books. (Originally published in 1873–81.)

Bibliography

1971. *The Adolescent.* New York: Norton. (Originally published in 1875.)
1970. *The Brothers Karamazov.* New York: Bantam Books. (Originally published in 1880.)

Letters

1923. *Dostoevsky: Letters and Reminiscences.* S. S. Koteliansky, and J. M. Murry, eds. London: Chatto and Windus.
1930. *The Letters of Dostoevsky to His Wife.* E. Hill and D. Mudie, eds. London: Constable.
1961. *Letters of Fyodor Michailovitch Dostoevsky to His Family and Friends.* E. C. Mayne, ed. New York: Horizon Press.
1987. *Selected Letters of Fyodor Dostoevsky.* J. Frank and D. I. Goldstein, eds. New Brunswick, N. J.: Rutgers University Press.

Notebooks and Journals

1973–76. *The Unpublished Dostoevsky: Diaries and Notebooks (1860–81).* 3 vols. C. R. Proffer, ed. Ann Arbor, Mich.: Ardis.
1967. *The Notebooks for "Crime and Punishment."* E. Wasiolek, ed. Chicago: University of Chicago Press.
1967. *The Notebooks for "The Idiot."* E. Wasiolek, ed. Chicago: University of Chicago Press.
1969. *The Notebooks for "The Possessed."* E. Wasiolek, ed. Chicago: University of Chicago Press.
1971. *The Notebooks for "The Brothers Karamazov."* E. Wasiolek, ed. Chicago: University of Chicago Press.

Dowler, W. 1982. *Dostoevsky, Grigoŕev, and Native Soil Conservatism.* Toronto: University of Toronto Press.
Erikson, E. H. 1954. The Dream Specimen of Psychoanalysis. *Journal of the American Psychoanalytic Association,* 2:5–56.
Frank, J. 1961. Nihilism and Notes from the Underground. *Sewanee Review* 69:1–33.
———. 1976. *Dostoevsky.* Vol. 1, *The Seeds of Revolt, 1821–1849.* Princeton: Princeton University Press.
———. 1983. *Dostoevsky.* Vol. 2, *The Years of Ordeal, 1850–1859.* Princeton: Princeton University Press.
———. 1986. *Dostoevsky.* Vol. 3, *The Stir of Liberaton, 1860–1865.* Princeton: Princeton University Press.
French, T. M., and E. Fromm. 1964. *Dream Interpretation: A New Approach.* New York: Basic Books.
Freud, S. 1953. The Interpretation of Dreams. *Standard Edition* 4 and 5: xxiii–627. London: Hogarth Press. (Originally published in 1900.)

Bibliography

———. 1957. Mourning and Melancholia. *Standard Edition* 14:237–58. London: Hogarth Press. (Originally published in 1917.)

———. 1961a. Dostoevsky and Parricide. *Standard Edition* 21:175–96. London: Hogarth Press. (Originally published in 1928.)

———. 1961b. Civilization and Its Discontents. *Standard Edition* 21:57–145. London: Hogarth Press. (Originally published in 1930.)

Galanter, M. 1982. Charismatic Religious Sects and Psychiatry: An Overview. *American Journal of Psychiatry* 139:1539–48.

Gastaut, H. 1978. Fyodor Mikhailovitch Dostoevsky's Involuntary Contribution to the Symptomatology and Prognosis of Epilepsy. *Epilepsia* 19:186–201.

Gastaut, H. 1984. New Comments on the Epilepsy of Fyodor Dostoevsky. *Epilpesia* 25:408–11.

Gedo, J. 1983. *Portraits of the Artist: Psychoanalysis of Creativity and Its Vicissitudes.* New York: Guilford Press.

Geschwind, N. 1984. Dostoevsky's Epilepsy. In: D. Blumer, ed. *Psychiatric Aspects of Epilepsy,* 325–34. Washington, D. C.: American Psychiatric Press.

Gibian, G., ed. 1964. *Crime and Punishment: Background and Sources. Essays in Criticism.* New York: Norton.

Gide, A. 1961. *Dostoevsky.* New York: New Directions. (Originally published in 1923.)

Gill, M. M. 1982. *Analysis of Transference:* Vol. 1. New York: International Universities Press.

Glaser, G. H. 1975. Epilepsy: Neuropsychological Aspects. *American Handbook of Psychiatry* 4:314–55. S. Arieti, ed. New York: Basic Books.

Greenberg, J., and S. Mitchell. 1983. *Object Relations in Psychoanalytic Theory.* Cambridge: Harvard University Press.

Greenberg, R. 1975. A Psychoanalytic-Dream Continuum: The Source and Function of Dreams. *International Review of Psychoanalysis* 2:441–48.

———. 1978. If Freud Only Knew: A Reconsideration of Psychoanalytic Dream Theory. *International Review of Psychoanalysis* 5:71–75.

Grossman, L. 1975. *Dostoevsky: A Biography.* New York: Bobbs-Merrill. (Originally published in 1962.)

Hamilton, V. 1986. Grief and Mourning in Tennyson's "In Memoriam." *Free Associations* 7:87–110.

Hingley, R. 1978. *Dostoevsky: His Life and Work.* New York: Scribner's.

Holland, N. 1964. *Psychoanalysis and Shakespeare.* New York: McGraw-Hill.

———. 1968. *The Dynamics of Literary Response.* New York: Oxford-University Press.

Hutter, A. D. 1975. Dreams, Transformations, and Literature: The Implications of Detective Fiction. *Victorian Studies.* 19:181–209.

———. 1982. Poetry in Psychoanalysis: Hopkins, Rossetti, Winnicott. *International Review of Psychoanalysis* 9:303–316.

Jackson, R. L., ed. 1974. *Twentieth Century Interpretations of "Crime and Punishment."* Englewood Cliffs, N.J.: Prentice-Hall.

Bibliography

Jones, E. 1953–57. *The Life and Work of Sigmund Freud.* New York: Basic Books.

Jones, R. 1970. *The New Psychology of Dreaming.* New York: Grune and Stratton.

Kanzer, M. 1948. Dostoevsky's Matricidal Impulses. *The Psychoanalytic Review* 35:115–25.

Kiremidjian, D. 1976. "Crime and Punishment": Matricide and the Woman Question. *American Imago* 33:403–33.

Kjetsaa, G. 1987. *Fyodor Dostoyevsky: A Writer's Life.* New York: Fawcett Columbine.

Klein, G. S. 1976. *Psychoanalytic Theory: An Exploration of Essentials.* New York: International Universities Press.

Kohlberg, L. 1963. Psychological Analysis and Literary Form: A Study of the Doubles in Dostoevsky. *Daedalus* 92:345–62.

Kohut, H. 1972. Thoughts on Narcissism and Narcissistic Rage. *The Psychoanalytic Study of the Child* 27:360–400.

———. 1977. *The Restoration of the Self.* New York: International Universities Press.

Kolansky, H. 1960. Treatment of a Three-Year-Old Girl's Severe Infantile Neurosis: Stammering and Insect Phobia. *Psychoanalytic Study of the Child* 15:261–85.

Kovalevskaya, S. 1978. *A Russian Childhood.* New York: Springer-Verlag. (Originally published in 1889.)

Laing, R. D. 1960. *The Divided Self.* Baltimore: Penguin.

Levine, S. 1984. *Radical Departures.* New York: Harcourt Brace Jovanovich.

Lifton, R. J. 1961. *Thought Reform and the Psychology of Totalism.* New York: Norton.

Lukianowicz, N. 1958. Autoscopic Phenomena. *Archives of Neurology and Psychiatry* 80:199–220.

Martin, J. 1983. Grief and Nothingness: Loss and Mourning in Robert Lowell's Poetry. *Psychoanalytic Inquiry* 3:451–84.

———. 1988. *Who Am I This Time?: Uncovering the Fictive Personality.* New York: Norton.

Mathewson, R. W. 1975. *The Positive Hero in Russian Literature.* Stanford: Stanford University Press.

Mazlish, B. 1974. The Mills: Father and Son. In: *Explorations in Psychohistory: The Wellfleet Papers,* 136–48. R. J. Lifton and E. Olson, eds. New York: Simon and Schuster.

Meissner, W. W. 1977. A Case in Point. *The Annual of Psychoanalysis* 5:405–36.

Mindess, H. 1967. Freud on Dostoevsky. *The American Scholar* 36:446–52.

Mochulsky, K. 1967. *Dostoevsky: His Life and Work.* Princeton: Princeton University Press. (Originally published in 1947.)

Naito, H., and N. Matsui. 1988. Temporal Lobe Epilepsy with Ictal Ecstatic

State and Interictal Behavior of Hypergraphia. *The Journal of Nervous and Mental Disease* 176:123–24.

Ogden, T. H. 1983. The Concept of Internal Object Relations. *International Journal of Psychoanalysis* 64:227–41.

Passage, C. E. 1982. *Character Names in Dostoevsky's Fiction*. Ann Arbor, Mich.: Ardis.

Pawel, E. 1984. *The Nightmare of Reason: A Life of Franz Kafka*. New York: Farrar Straus and Giroux.

Peace, R. 1971. *Dostoevsky: An Examination of the Major Novels*. Cambridge: Cambridge University Press.

Pope, R., and J. Turner. In press. Towards Understanding Stavrogin. *Slavic Review*.

Rabow, J., L. Comess, B. A. Donovan, and C. Hollos. 1984. Compulsive Gambling: Psychoanalytic and Sociological Perspectives. *Israeli Journal of Psychiatry and Related Sciences* 21:189–207.

Rank, O. 1971. *The Double: A Psychoanalytic Study*. Chapel Hill: University of North Carolina Press. (Originally published in 1914.)

Reik, T. 1975. *From Thirty Years with Freud*. Westport, Conn.: Greenwood Press.

Rice, J. L. 1985. *Dostoevsky and the Healing Art*. Ann Arbor, Mich.: Ardis.

Rosenthal, R. J. 1981. Raskolnikov's Transgression and the Confusion Between Destructiveness and Creativity. In: *Do I Dare Disturb the Universe?: A Memorial to Wilfred R. Bion*, 197–235. J. Grotstein, ed. Beverly Hills: Caesura Press.

———. 1987. The Psychodynamics of Pathological Gambling: A Review of the Literature. In: *The Handbook of Pathological Gambling*, 41–70. T. Galski, ed. Springfield, Ill.: Charles C. Thomas.

Rycroft, C. 1979. *The Innocence of Dreams*. New York: Pantheon.

Sargeant, W. 1971. *Battle for the Mind*. New York: Doubleday.

Schafer, R. 1976. *A New Language for Psychoanalysis*. New Haven: Yale University Press.

Schmidl, F. 1965. Freud and Dostoevsky. *Journal of the American Psychoanalytic Association* 13:518–32.

Simmons, E. J. 1950. *Dostoevsky: The Making of a Novelist*. London: Lehmann.

Skura, M. 1981. *Literary Uses of the Psychoanalytic Process*. New Haven: Yale University Press.

Snodgrass, W. D. 1960. Crime for Punishment: The Tenor of Part One. *Hudson Review* 13: 202–53.

Steiner, G. 1959. *Tolstoy or Dostoevsky*. New York: Knopf.

Stoller, R. J. 1975. *Perversion: The Erotic Form of Hatred*. New York: Pantheon.

———. 1979. *Sexual Excitement: Dynamics of Erotic Life*. New York: Pantheon.

Bibliography

Stolorow, R. D., and G. E. Atwood 1979. *Faces in a Cloud: Subjectivity in Personality Theory*. New York: Aronson.

Stolorow, R. D., B. Brandchaft, and G. E. Atwood. 1987. *Psychoanalytic Treatment: An Intersubjective Approach*. Hillsdale, N.J.: Analytic Press.

Suslova, P. 1972. Polina Suslova's Diary. In: Dostoevsky, F. *The Gambler*, 199–333. E. Wasiolek, ed. Chicago: University of Chicago Press.

Terras, V. 1981. *A Karamazov Companion*. Madison: University of Wisconsin Press.

Voskuil, P. H. A. 1983. The Epilepsy of Fyodor Mikhailovitch Dostoevsky (1821–1881). *Epilepsia* 24:658–67.

Wasiolek, E., ed. 1961. *"Crime and Punishment" and the Critics*. San Francisco: Wadsworth.

———. 1964. *Dostoevsky: The Major Fiction*. Cambridge: MIT Press.

———. 1974. Raskolnikov's Motives: Love and Murder. *American Imago* 31:267–85.

Wellek, R. 1962. *Dostoevsky: A Collection of Critical Essays*. Englewood Cliffs, N.J.: Prentice-Hall.

Winnicott, D. W. 1965. *The Motivational Process and the Facilitating Environment*. New York: International Universities Press.

Wrangel, A. 1961. From the Reminiscences of Baron Alexander Wrangel, 1854–1865. In: *Letters of Fyodor Michailovich Dostoevsky to His Family and Friends*, 289–320. E. C. Mayne, ed. New York: Horizon Press.

Yarmolinsky, A. 1971. *Dostoevsky: Works and Days*. New York: Funk and Wagnalls.

Index

Index

self-analysis, 125–26; split of the self, 121–22, 269–70n

Dream interpretation, 5, 19–20, 25, 31–32, 47–49, 54, 56, 182–83, 259–61n, 276–77n

Durov, Sergey F., 128, 130, 132, 142, 145

Empathy, 36, 50–51, 95, 136–37

Epilepsy (D's), 100, 102, 220, 269n; current views of, 241–44, 280n; Freud's interpretation of, 238–40, 246, 280n; developmental course of, 156–57, 244–46; "hysterical" nature of, 239–41; in *The Idiot*, 220, 249–51, 280n; and marriages, 156–58, 214, 247–48; and "nervous crisis," 112–13; personal meaning, 243, 246–51

Epoch, The, 15, 64, 183, 211

Eternal Husband, The, 79–80, 217, 219, 221

False self, 113–14

Fonvizina, Natalya, 142, 144, 147–48

Freud, Sigmund, 3, 33, 153, 189, 231; analysis of D, 99, 238–40, 246, 263n, 270n, 273n, 274–75n, 280n; and D compared, 100–101; on D's epilepsy, 237, 246; on dream interpretation, 259–61n, 276–77n; on literature, 5–6, 246; on masochism, 264n; on unconscious reenactment, 263n; works: *Civilization and Its Discontents,* 189, 246; *Dostoevsky and Parricide,* 238–39, 274–75n; *The Interpretation of Dreams,* 100, 260n, 261n, 276n

Frolovna, Aliona (D's family nurse), 13, 57–59, 74–75

Gambler, The, 17, 160, 171, 176, 178, 212, 214, 258, 274n

Gambling, 15, 172, 175–80, 187, 214–16, 239, 274–75n

Gide, André, 4, 10–12; works: *Dostoevsky,* 258

Goethe, J. W. V., 97

Gogol, Nikolay V., 60, 103–5, 129, 153; works: *Dead Souls,* 103, 153; *The Diary of a Madman,* 118; *The Nose,* 118;

The Overcoat, 103, 105, 153; *Selected Passages from My Correspondence with Friends,* 129, 153

Goncherov, Ivan A., 108, 226

"Great Sinner" type, 9–10, 18–19, 132–41, 221, 227, 228

Grigorovich, Dimitri V., 106, 116, 256

Grigoryev, Apollon A., 162–64

Guilt, 10, 16–17, 29–31, 33–35, 40–42, 61, 65, 82–83, 86, 133–38, 175–80, 182, 196–99, 210, 222, 237, 239, 267n, 273n

Herzen, Alexander I., 17, 73, 108

Hoffmann, E. T. A., 97, 118

Hugo, Victor, 97

Idealization, 36–38, 50, 59, 65–68, 77–78, 80, 89, 103, 148, 157–58, 167, 170, 212–13, 229, 273n

Identification, 3, 8, 24, 50, 62, 63, 82, 87, 89, 97, 100–101, 146, 191–92, 232

Idiot, The, 8, 10, 101, 140, 146, 156, 174, 192, 217, 219–21, 224, 227, 237, 249–51, 270n, 280–81n

Insulted and Injured, The, 161, 185

Introjects, 9, 11, 13, 59–61, 87, 93, 96, 261–62n

Kafka, Franz, 7–8

Katkov, Mikhail N., 135, 211

Kohut, Heinz, 113

Korvin-Krukovskaya, Anna, 93, 211, 279n

Kovalevskya, Sophia, 93, 248, 279n

Laing, Ronald D., 113

Landlady, The, 131–32, 147, 191

Lawrence, D. H., 231

Lermontov, Mikhail Y., 226

Little Hero, A, 132

Maikov, Apollon N., 91, 116

Maikov, Valerian N., 116

Maria Stuart (D), 103, 191

Masochism, 26–28, 34, 44, 57, 132, 178–80, 194–98, 264n, 267n, 274–75n

Index